SR-71 BLACKBIRD

Stories, Tales, and Legends

SR-71 BLACKBIRD

Stories, Tales, and Legends

Richard H. Graham
Colonel USAF (Ret)

ZENITH PRESS

Dedication

To the men and women of the Blackbird community.

First published in 2002 by MBI Publishing Company and Zenith Press, an imprint of MBI Publishing Company, 400 1st Avenue North, Suite 300, Minneapolis, MN 55401 USA

© Richard H. Graham , 2002

All rights reserved. With the exception of quoting brief passages for the purposes of review, no part of this publication may be reproduced without prior written permission from the Publisher.

Zenith Press titles are also available at discounts in bulk quantity for industrial or sales-promotional use. For details write to Special Sales Manager at MBI Publishing Company, 400 1st Avenue North, Suite 300, Minneapolis, MN 55401 USA.

To find out more about our books, join us online at www.zenithpress.com.

Library of Congress Cataloging-in-Publication Data Available

ISBN-13: 978-0-7603-1142-4
ISBN-10: 0-7603-1142-0

Edited by Kris Palmer
Designed by LeAnn Kuhlmann

On the front cover: Lieutenant Colonels J. T. Vida (left) and Ed Yeilding suited up in front of Blackbird #972 prior to their record-breaking flight across the United States. On 6 March 1990, they set a coast-to-coast record, covering 2,089 nautical miles in 67 minutes, 54 seconds, before turning the aircraft over to the National Air and Space Museum in Washington, D.C.

Printed in the United States of America

Contents

Foreword

SR-71 Blackbird: Stories, Tales, and Legends takes you back to those thrilling days of yesteryear when the Blackbird was the hottest plane in the cold war. So revolutionary were this aircraft's capabilities that it would still be the hottest plane in the air, both literally and figuratively, if it were operational today. The Blackbird is one of the most asked-about aircraft in the National Air and Space Museum (NASM) collection, and we constantly get requests for permission to view it in its temporary hangar at Dulles International Airport. When the new Hazy Center opens at Dulles in December 2003, the SR-71 will be one of the first things the visitor will see.

This book answers all of the questions you might have about this legendary plane, and many that you would never think to ask. You will learn the meaning of such Blackbird-related terms as Habu, unstart, Bat Caver, and hook. Habu, for example, is a sacred word given to those SR-71 crews who have flown operational missions. Only they are entitled to wear the Habu patch on their flight clothing.

Rather than covering the many aspects of Blackbird operations himself, which he is well qualified to do, Rich Graham has wisely chosen to let the pilots, reconnaissance systems officers (RSOs), engineers, and maintenance personnel tell their stories in their own words. Colonel Graham introduces each chapter with a brief description of the author's background and inserts clarifying paragraphs where required. The chapters run chronologically from the first A-12 flights to the record-breaking transcontinental delivery flight of the SR-71 now in the NASM collection. I was privileged to be at Dulles Airport in March 1990 when it arrived and it was quite a thrill because I had never seen one before, even on the ground. Even though it has been around since the 1960s it still looks like something out of *Star Wars* and still outperforms all other aircraft.

One thing that impressed me about the program was the bonding of the Habus. After going through the rigorous selection process and joining that elite fraternity, they truly became a band of brothers. Within that band each crew, pilot and RSO, flew virtually all of their missions together, forming a symbiotic relationship in which the whole was greater that the sum of its parts. They spent so much time away from their home base in California that the detachment became their family. This devotion is exemplified by Colonel Graham's generous donation of royalties from this book and his earlier book, *SR-71 Revealed*, to the J. T. Vida Memorial Fund.

The late Lieutenant Colonel J. T. Vida was the RSO on the record-breaking delivery flight of the SR-71, #972, to Dulles, and his love for the airplane is indicated by the remarks he entered in the AF Form 781 following the flight. "*For the NASM—Please take good care of our Flight Test Blackbird. Find her a place of honor, keep her safe, and may all of America respect her for her many accomplishments.*" He can be assured that his wishes will be honored. That responsibility goes to Colonel Tom Alison, who, before becoming head of NASM's Collections Division, flew many operational missions with Lieutenant Colonel Vida in #972.

I found the book very readable and informative, and I recommend it highly to anyone interested in this marvelous airplane. I have found no fliers and very few nonfliers who are not interested in the SR-71 Blackbird. I am sorry that it is no longer flying.

—Mr. Don Lopez
Deputy Director
National Air and Space Museum
Smithsonian Institution

Preface

After 28 years of association with the Blackbird program, I thought I'd heard all of the stories and tales that could possibly be told. However, I soon found I had only scratched the surface. Whenever Blackbird crewmembers gather, new stories come to light. Some stories have a new slant to them from a previous version, while others vary, depending on who is telling the story. Some stories correct what was once thought to be true . . . others expand on previously held truths. Over the years we have lost many people closely associated with the Blackbird program, and unfortunately, that number will continue to rise. I felt it was time to write a book of their stories and in their own words.

After writing my first book, *SR-71 Revealed, The Inside Story,* I learned from reader comments just how much aviation enthusiasts enjoy hearing stories from other aviators, especially firsthand accounts of the Blackbird program, from its early beginning to its fateful end. My goal was to find a crossection of aircrews, maintenance personnel, and people from other disciplines eager to relate their experiences. I asked crews who flew the original A-12s as CIA pilots, to those who flew the final SR-71 missions. The response was overwhelming.

The book is written through the eyes and perspective of many Habus who were willing to share their thoughts, emotions, and stories. From small details, personal accounts, legends, traditions, and behind-the-scene activities, the reader gains a greater appreciation of just how unique the Blackbird program really was. The participants tell their stories in their own words, and the stories are organized chronologically. Throughout the book I've added sidebars where it seemed appropriate to amplify and expand on certain aspects.

As with my first book, royalties from this book will go to the J. T. Vida Memorial Fund. I set up the fund in 1996 with the National Air and Space Museum in Washington, D.C., to be used exclusively for the restoration and display of its SR-71 (#972) at the new Udvar-Hazy Center at Dulles International Airport in 2003.

Lieutenant Colonel (Ret) Joseph "J. T." Vida was the first of my SR-71 contemporaries to pass away. He was one of our most highly admired and respected crewmembers, always a pleasure to have around. Because of his love and passion for the SR-71, J. T. set several records no one will ever match. He flew the SR-71 for 16 *continuous* years, ending up with 1,392.7 hours—a milestone. He also made the record-setting coast-to-coast flight you will read about in chapter 16, when the SR-71 was turned over to the Smithsonian National Air and Space Museum, landing at Dulles airport in Washington, D.C.

— Richard H. Graham,
Colonel USAF (Ret)

Acknowledgments

I would like to acknowledge the efforts of the primary contributors to this book. Their stories, tales, and legends give this book life and make it unique. They are Gil Bertelson, Tony Bevacqua, Donn Byrnes, Ken Collins, Al Cirino, Jerry Crew, David Dempster, Don Emmons, Pat Halloran, Jim Kogler, Steve Koren, Curt Osterheld, Geno Quist, Lee Shelton, Jim Shelton, Frank Stampf, Jack Veth, Ed Yeilding, and Mike Zimmerman. Without their first-hand stories, this book would be dull and lifeless.

I am indebted to Don Lopez for taking the time and effort to write the foreword to this book, sharing his thoughts with the reader. A special thanks to Paul Crickmore for letting me use his well-researched and documented data from his book, *Lockheed SR-71: The Secret Missions Exposed.* John Stone, one of the SR-71 Web site managers (www.Blackbirds.net) has graciously allowed me to include an abbreviated portion of his Blackbird Time Line in Appendix B. My deepest appreciation goes to Mike Haenggi, former editor for MBI Publishing Company, for all his guidance, and more important, his confidence in my ability to put this book together. Thank you, Mike! A big thanks goes to Sara Perfetti, who took over from Mike and put the final touches on the book.

Last, but by no means least, I would like to thank my wife, Pat, for her patience during my many hours spent in front of the computer, compiling and writing this book. She's been my chief editor, making suggestions and smoothing over the rough edges. As a former "Brit," her understanding of the Queen's English helped me immensely. I could not have done it without her. Love you, Pat!

Introduction

Before the A-12 there was the U-2, a reconnaissance aircraft built for a specific purpose—to gather intelligence on foreign countries. The chief architect and designer of the U-2 was Clarence L. "Kelly" Johnson, head of Lockheed's Advanced Development Projects (ADP, or better known as the Skunk Works) in Burbank, California. On 4 August 1955 the first U-2 took to the skies.

Kelly knew that someday the U-2 would become vulnerable to enemy defenses, and even as early as 1958 he began to conceptualize a reconnaissance aircraft that would fly higher and over three times faster than the U-2. In competition with General Dynamics, Lockheed received approval on 28 August 1959 to proceed with the development of five A-12 aircraft, under the Central Intelligence Agency (CIA) code name of "OXCART," for a price of $96.6 million. The program called for Lockheed to develop a single-seat reconnaissance aircraft capable of Mach 3 speeds, to be flown by civilian CIA pilots.

On 26 April 1962, just 22 months after Kelly started building the first A-12 Blackbird, he had the plane flying. Lockheed test pilot Lou Schalk was at the controls. This short construction period was an unbelievable feat, even by today's standards, especially when you realize that the planes were built completely with slide-rule technology. Kelly was writing the book on high-temperature effects of Mach 3 flight. All of the aircraft's systems—fuel, hydraulic, oil, engines, electrical, cameras, and others—had to withstand the searing temperatures generated at Mach 3 cruising speeds and still function properly.

Lockheed produced a total of 15 A-12 aircraft for the highly classified OXCART program. Two of the aircraft were converted to a two-seat configuration to carry the D-21 drone, at which point they were renamed M-21 aircraft. The Museum of Flight in Seattle, Washington, proudly displays the sole surviving M-21/D-21 combination. Another A-12 was also converted into a two-seat aircraft for crew training.

Of the 15 OXCART aircraft produced in total, five A-12s and one M-21 were lost through crashes. Two CIA pilots, Walter L. Ray and Jack Weeks, were killed. Walter Ray successfully ejected, but was killed after he failed to separate from his ejection seat. Jack Weeks was flying an A-12 on a Functional Check Flight (FCF) when it was lost off the Philippine Islands and never recovered. Lockheed launch control engineer Ray Torick successfully ejected from an M-21 over the Pacific Ocean, but tragically drowned.

Another Blackbird variant, called the YF-12, was designed to be a high-altitude, high-speed interceptor aircraft. The YF-12s proved the technology and capability, but were soon canceled. Of the three YF-12s that were built, one crashed in June 1971.

The best-known of the Blackbirds was the SR-71. Lockheed built 29 SR-71A models, 2 SR-71B models, and 1 SR-71C. The B and C models had dual controls and a raised rear cockpit for the instructor pilot (IP) to supervise and teach pilots in training. The first SR-71 flight took place on 22 December 1964, flown by Lockheed test pilot Bob Gilliland.

The C model is unique. Following the loss of B model #957 on 11 January 1968, project leaders decided to make another trainer aircraft. The only problem was that all of the Skunk Works' tooling to build more Blackbirds had previously been ordered destroyed by Secretary of Defense Robert McNamara. The innovative and resourceful solution the Skunk Works engineers devised was truly unbelievable. They grafted together the front fuselage section of a static test specimen that had been at Lockheed, with the aft section of a YF-12 in storage. This created the second two-seat trainer, which was called the C model and given the Tail Number 981. Since the plane did not follow standard maintenance procedures like the rest of the fleet, maintenance personnel affectionately nicknamed it "the Bastard."

As told by Donn Byrnes in his book, *Blackbird Rising,* the tragic story of Jim Zwayer's death went like this.

"Bill Weaver released the brakes and lit the afterburners; 68,000 pounds of thrust pushed the crew and a fully fueled SR-71 into the air and on their way. They climbed and accelerated to Mach 3 and cruise-climbed to about 80,000 feet. Approaching a planned turning point over New Mexico, they entered a right turn with a programmed bank angle of 40 degrees. They experienced a violent unstart causing the aircraft to roll uncontrollably to the right, but at the same time pitch up.

"The aircraft turned plan-view against the oncoming airflow. There was no time for thought or action. It was beyond human control. Everything happened at once. From the unstart on, what followed was driven by aerodynamics, relative wind, dynamic pressure, inertial coupling, structural mechanics, and the laws of physics. The fuselage broke apart at station 720, the point where the forward fuselage was joined to the delta portion of the wing. The forces in command caused this forward section of the fuselage to turn backward with the pilot and RSO compartments now at the rear of the tumbling structure. The airflow stripped all the skin off this forward piece of the aircraft. Both crewmembers and their seats were ripped from the structure by the incredible forces of this disintegration. Jim died at that moment."

Over the years, a total of 11 SR-71A models and 1 SR-71B were lost due to crashes. Lockheed flight test employee Jim Zwayer was tragically killed in January 1966 when he and his pilot, Bill Weaver, were literally thrown out of an SR-71 that broke apart and disintegrated at Mach 3 speeds.

If you add up the total Blackbird family of aircraft it comes to 50 planes, with 19 losses (none due to unfriendly fire). Between the 10-year period from 1962 to 1972, a total of 18 Blackbirds were lost. As the learning curve leveled off, however, we flew for the next 21 years (including the plane's return in 1995) with only a *single* loss. The last Blackbird crashed on 21 April 1989 just off the northern coast of the Philippines.

Many brave and determined individuals gave their hearts, their minds, and in some cases their lives, to put the remarkable Blackbird aircraft in the sky. Their stories could fill a book. And they deserve to. This is that book, and those stories follow. At the beginning of each chapter, I introduce the authors with a brief biographical sketch, along with my own personal experiences and thoughts concerning the writers.

Only 11 pilots were chosen to be in the highly classified Central Intelligence Agency OXCART project. Eight of them flew the A-12, and only 7 flew it operationally. Ken Collins was one of them. In chapter 1 Ken talks of the difficulties qualifying to fly the single-seat A-12—the extensive physical examination, the interviews, his cover story, and what his wife was allowed to know. Ken was the first person to eject from a Blackbird, which makes for exciting reading.

In chapter 2, Donn Byrnes, author of *Blackbird Rising*, gives you his perspective of all the major hurdles that had to be overcome for the Blackbird's sensors to work in the harsh environment of 85,000 feet, at Mach 3 speeds, and searing temperatures of more than 500 degrees F. In layman's terms, Donn describes what is required of a camera to gather photographic intelligence at the SR-71's altitude and speed.

David Dempster was one of the first eight SR-71 crewmembers. In chapter 3, David describes some of the humorous events that took place in the early days of the program. There was plenty of danger, too. On the first two SR-71 operational sorties ever flown out of Okinawa in 1968, both experienced double engine flameouts while beginning their descents. It happened again on the third sortie to David and his pilot, Jim Watkins. However, they figured out why it happened and how to prevent its recurrence.

Pat Halloran entered the SR-71 program after flying the U-2. He became the 9th Strategic Reconnaissance Wing (9th SRW) commander at Beale AFB, California, and directly oversaw nine of the longest operational missions ever flown by the SR-71. In chapter 4, Pat tells about the trials and tribulations of flying sensitive reconnaissance missions over Israel and Egypt in 1973. These sorties were directed by National Command Authority (NCA) and the president of the United States. The SR-71 had never before been in this part of the world or flown such long operational missions. There were plenty of unknowns facing them.

Another former U-2 pilot, Tony Bevacqua, tells in chapter 5 what it was like coming into the SR-71 program. Tony and his Reconnaissance Systems Officer (RSO), Jerry Crew, had several SA-2 Surface-to-Air (SAM) missiles launched at their plane during a reconnaissance pass over North Vietnam. Jerry relives the emotional few seconds during the firings. Taking an SR-71 to and from Okinawa was always a treat—except when Tony and his RSO, Jim Kogler, had some bad luck and had to spend a few days on the remote island of Midway.

In chapter 6, we hear firsthand what it was like to fly the first long-distance operational sortie over Israel and Egypt during the Yom Kippur War. Jim Shelton details all the obstacles he had to overcome during that mission, inside the cockpit as well as outside. Only a handful of Habus ever overflew North Korea, and Jim tells his story. He also talks about his unplanned barrier engagement with the SR-71—one of the few successful engagements on record!

On 21 April 1989, after flying for 17 years without a loss, an SR-71 crashed off the coast of the Philippines. In chapter 7, Al Cirino recounts the circumstances leading up to the crash, and recovery of the plane from the ocean floor. Al was the on-site commander during the salvage operation and president of the Accident Investigation Board.

I flew with the same RSO for over six years: his name was Don Emmons. Normally, we only operated the SR-71 out of three worldwide locations—Beale AFB, California; Kadena AB, Okinawa, Japan; and RAF Mildenhall, England. In chapter 8, Don tells about flying the SR-71 into, and out of, the SR-71's most unusual location: the coral atoll of Diego Garcia. Wait until you read how Don navigated the Blackbird, over thousands of miles of open ocean, with only a whiskey compass! When an Air Force plane crashes, there are written procedures on how to dispose of the remains. In the case of an SR-71 wreckage, Don soon discovered those procedures don't always work.

For well over five years, the SR-71s never flew night operational sorties. The Blackbird was not well suited for night flying—its first (and best) sensors were optical cameras, requiring daylight photography. Suddenly, times changed. Radar imaging of targets improved dramatically and became a new way of life. Jack Veth flew the very first night sortie out of Okinawa after a five-year layoff and tells his story in chapter 9. Christmas is a special time of the year for everyone, and Jack tried to make it even more special for those on Okinawa, but was tripped up by U.S. customs officers.

In chapter 10, Lee Shelton eloquently tells some outstanding Habu stories. On one flight, Lee was literally seconds away from having to eject from the SR-71. You can read just how lucky he was! Lee flew some unique missions in the Blackbird. One of the most challenging was being able to meet another

SR-71 head-on, at 75,000 feet, with a closing velocity of Mach 6, passing each other at a specific time, and abeam a specified location. Even Steve Canyon would find that difficult!

The number of maintenance man-hours preparing an SR-71 for a Mach 3 sortie was staggering. No other plane in the Air Force went through as many checks and rechecks to ensure it was 100 percent ready for flight. In chapter 11, SR-71 maintenance supervisor Steve Koren tells what it took to prepare a Blackbird for a mission, from start to finish.

Many Air Force crewmembers wanted to be part of the elite fraternity who flew the Blackbirds. In chapter 12, Frank Stampf tells what prompted him to hand-carry his SR-71 application all the way from England to California. He explains why aviators wanted to join the SR-71 program and lets you know just how demanding the "dreaded" simulator training was. The SR-71 missions at RAF Mildenhall were considerably different from those flown out of Okinawa. Frank explains those differences.

Like many Air Force flying units of the past, the motto was to "work hard and play hard." The SR-71 squadron was no different. In fact, I often felt that motto was designed just for our squadron. We were notorious for playing jokes on one another, some more elaborate than others. Picking up on a Vietnam term, we called our pranks "frags." In chapter 13, Gil Bertelson tells one of the best "frags" ever pulled on another unit. Everyone wants to know how fast the SR-71 would really go. Gil answers that burning question.

In chapter 14, Curt Osterheld describes one of the strangest in-flight emergencies with the SR-71. Their mystery is not solved until after they land! Curt's second story draws on his firsthand experience in the Pentagon to shed light on the insurmountable, uphill battle he and others fought to try to keep the SR-71 program alive.

When I left the Pentagon and returned to Beale in 1986, rumors were beginning to circulate about the possible retirement of the SR-71 fleet. During the final years before its retirement, there were not many friends of the Blackbird program running around the halls of the Pentagon. Every weapon system in the Air Force had one individual in the Pentagon who was the spokesperson and advocate for that program, called the Program Element Monitor (PEM). Geno Quist was the PEM for the SR-71 program in 1987. In chapter 15, Geno talks about the hostile environment he had to face daily throughout the Pentagon, while trying to promote and save the SR-71 program.

Few Habus were fortunate enough to set world speed records. In chapter 16, Ed Yeilding reveals the details that went into his record-setting coast-to-coast speed record in 1990. The flight came very close to being aborted, but Ed and RSO Joe "J. T." Vida worked out the true nature of a fuel problem and fixed it in-flight. Ed explains how it is possible to see three sunsets, and three sunrises, all within one hour!

SR-71 Blackbird

When the decision was made by Congress to bring back SR-71s in 1995, everyone knew it would be a challenging task. The Air Force Reactivation program manager assigned to make it all happen was Mike "Zman" Zimmerman. In chapter 17, Zman tells what the major hurdles were, the politics involved, and the successes he experienced in bringing the Blackbirds back from retirement.

In the Epilogue, I summarize the Blackbird's first and second retirements and explain why I believe the SR-71s are needed even *more today* than they were 20 years ago.

CHAPTER ONE

Colonel (Ret) Kenneth S. Collins Sr.

Ken was born 5 February 1929, in Leavenworth, Kansas, the home of Fort Leavenworth, one of the oldest Army posts of the new western frontiers. It was from here that his grandfather, Sergeant Edward E. Collins of the 10th U.S. Cavalry, was sent out with the troopers to fight in the Battle of Wounded Knee.

Across the Missouri River from Fort Leavenworth is Park University, which Ken attended for two years. There he joined the Naval Air Reserves. During the summer of 1950 he applied for pilot training and went to Goodfellow AFB, Texas, for basic flight training in January 1951. Ken completed advanced pilot training and was commissioned at Vance AFB, Oklahoma, on 9 February 1952. In late May 1952, Ken finished F-80 jet transition at Moody AFB, Georgia, and volunteered for Korea. He was assigned to Shaw AFB, South Carolina, for combat crew training in the RF-80 with the 18th Tactical Reconnaissance Squadron (TRS).

Ken arrived at K-14 (Kimpo Air Base, Korea) in mid-August 1952. By March 1953, he had checked out in the RF-80A, the F-80C, the RF-86A, and had flown 113 combat missions in the 15th TRS. Ken's next assignment was back to the 18th TRS at Shaw AFB as an instructor pilot (IP) in the RF-80 and the RF-84F. In October 1955, Ken went overseas and had several IP assignments in Germany with those aircraft, instructing U.S. and German Air Force pilots. In 1959, Ken returned to Shaw AFB as a flight commander and operations officer.

In 1960, the USAF Office of NASA requested that he volunteer for testing for a classified space program. He didn't know it at the time, but he was volunteering for the highly classified A-12 OXCART Program. Ken's first flight in the A-12 was on 6 February 1963. The A-12 experimental test phase lasted through the early months of 1967, followed by the operational deployment to Okinawa. Ken flew 13 operational A-12 combat

Ken Collins in his white pressure suit with liquid oxygen cooler, standing beside an A-12 at Area 51 in March 1968. The stirrups affixed to Ken's boots attached to a ball-joint under the ejection seat. During ejection, a cable attached to the ball-joint retracted aft, locking your feet firmly in place—particularly useful if you had to eject at 2,000 miles per hour! *Ken Collins*

missions, for which he was awarded the Distinguished Flying Cross and the Intelligence Star from the Central Intelligence Agency.

The A-12 program was canceled and Ken took an assignment to the 9th Strategic Reconnaissance Wing at Beale AFB to fly the SR-71. He became the 99th SRS operations officer, an instructor pilot, and test pilot in the SR-71 program. When Ken was promoted to lieutenant colonel in 1970, he was selected to be squadron commander of the 1st SRS, and when promoted to colonel was chosen to be the 9th SRW deputy commander for operations (DCO) in 1972. Two years later Ken was reassigned to Headquarters, 15th

Air Force; when he retired in 1980, he was deputy chief of intelligence. Ken's many distinguished military awards include the highly coveted Silver Star.

After Air Force retirement, Ken took a managerial position with California Microwave, Inc., Government Electronics Division, in Woodland Hills, California. Over the next 19 years he served as a program manager of the classified RIVET KIT program (RC-130 aircraft), and as Business development director for the RC-135, Combat Sent (electronics reconnaissance) system, and other reconnaissance systems. He retired in 1998 as vice president and general manager.

Ken was one of only 11 pilots selected and recruited by the CIA to fly the A-12 aircraft as part of Project OXCART. I first met Ken shortly after I arrived at Beale AFB, California, in 1974. Our initial meeting took place when I was slated to fly a T-38 out-and-back sortie with the 9th wing commander, Colonel John Storrie. Colonel Storrie wanted to fly to March AFB, California, to visit his Habu friend, Ken Collins, who was working at 15th Air Force Headquarters.

Ken met us at March Base Operations, and after a brief introduction, he drove us to his base quarters, where I met his wife, Jane. By the way, I remember thinking at the time how lovely she was. It was obvious they were all close friends. This was my first glimpse of the Habu kinship that lay ahead for me, and gave tremendous insight into the Habu world that I was entering.

I have come to admire and look up to many Habus over the years, but Ken has a special way about him that I liked from the first time I met him. During one of my early tours of duty, flying the SR-71 out of Kadena, I discovered Ken really did have the right stuff.

Small Air Force units that are located away from their main home base, but still assigned to one, are called Detachments. Beale's SR-71 unit on Kadena at the time was called Detachment 1, shortened to just Det 1. A typical SR-71 Detachment comprised about 150 personnel, including maintenance, supply, intelligence, mission planners, operations, Lockheed technical representatives (tech reps), and other civilians who maintained the specialized and unique sensors on the Blackbirds. The Det 1 Commander was typically a former SR-71 crewmember with the rank of colonel. On Okinawa, just to exist among all the rank running around the base, eagles on the shoulder really helped to get things done.

The Det 1 commander at the time had just issued an edict that crewmembers could no longer wear their "sacred" orange flight suits around base. The crews protested this ban, but to no avail. These orange flight suits were our trademark. We wore them proudly, displaying the patches of our unit and mission. When I was flying F-4s on Kadena, I was envious (OK, I'll admit it, I was jealous) of the guys strutting around in their orange flight suits.

Ken was still working at 15th Air Force and made a trip to Kadena, along with others, on what was called a "Staff Assistance Visit." The idea behind their visit was to delve deeply into Det 1's operations for a week and then write a formal report of their findings. The theory being that "they were there to help you." (Sure!)

This reminds me of the two biggest lies ever told in the Air Force. When General Curtis E. LeMay commanded the Strategic Air Command (SAC), he developed an inspection system called the Operational Readiness Inspection (ORI). The ORI inspection team at SAC headquarters was under the inspector general's (IG) office and was thus called the SAC/IG team. It was a no-notice evaluation of each flying unit's ability to accomplish its wartime mission. For better or for worse (mostly worse), the SR-71s, U-2s, T-38s, and KC-135Q tankers at Beale AFB were under the command of SAC, which made us a target for one of their no-notice ORIs.

Unannounced, the team arrived day or night in a KC-135. The most notice you might have was when the plane was 30 minutes out from landing. The team consisted of about 70 personnel, who were "experts" in every facet of the wing's business. During their week-long evaluation they examined everything from shoeshines to how many seconds your planes took to get airborne. At the end of a week of torture, the ORI team chief held a briefing to go over their findings and give an overall rating to the inspection. The ratings ranged from Unsatisfactory (not good, because it meant that they would be back soon!) to Excellent. Beale had one ORI during my time as wing commander and received the prized Excellent rating. We had a true team spirit with our reconnaissance mission and excellent personnel.

In September 1988, the Beale Command Post called me on my portable two-way radio (called the "brick," having the shape and weight of a brick) to inform me of an inbound KC-135 with no flight plan. Once I pushed the button on the brick, informing key personnel that the SAC/IG team was inbound, the response was tremendous. Everyone on base was immediately energized. Battle stations! Key personnel rushed to Base Operations to be on hand to greet their counterparts on the ORI inspection team. The plane came to a stop, thr engine's shut down, the large cargo door opens, stairs are put in place, and down walks the first team member, the SAC inspector general . . . in my case, Brigadier General Brett Dula.

After exchanging salutes, the two biggest lies in the Air Force are about to take place: The smiling inspector general reaches out to shake hands with the wing commander saying, "We're here to help you." While still firmly gripping his hand and smiling back, the wing commander replies, "We're glad to have you."

—Rich Graham

Ken, being a former Habu, knew precisely where to go for after-hour socializing—Bachelor Officer Quarters (BOQ) 318—the dormitory structure that housed all of the SR-71 and KC-135Q aircrews. Ken arrived for one of our informal debriefing parties in 318, and after a few drinks, we all went out to dinner, returning later that night. Eventually, the new rule about wearing our orange flight suits surfaced. When Ken heard this he was flabbergasted, and none too pleased!

Sometime after midnight, Ken phoned the Det commander at his home on base. He simply stated, "I would like to see you over at 318 as soon as you can get here." Within a few minutes, the tired and weary Det commander arrived, knowing he was facing a hostile audience. Ken calmly took up our cause, and logically explained to him why he thought the crews should be allowed to wear their prized orange flight suits. Guess what? Reason prevailed, and once again we were all strutting around in our signature orange flight suits!

Later, when I was assigned to the Pentagon in 1982, Ken was retired and working for California Microwave. During his frequent business trips to Washington, D.C., Ken always made a point to phone a group of Habus to get together for drinks and dinner. Ken certainly knew how to combine business with pleasure. He looked for any excuse for a party, the drinks and memories being the important part of the evenings.

I asked Ken to write stories about the early days of the CIA OXCART program, giving readers an inside look from a pilot's perspective. Here are his stories.

Project OXCART

The primary professional selection criterion for the OXCART program was flying time in Century Series fighter-type aircraft. The pilot needed more than 1,000 operational flight hours in the aircraft and a total of 2,000 flight hours. He had to be currently qualified and proficient. At that time I was an experienced IP in the RF-101, having had over 50 air-to-air refueling sorties and about 10 transatlantic deployments, each with multiple air refuelings. This was the easy part for the Pentagon selection group. Either you had it or you didn't. The requirements that you were highly qualified as an officer and a pilot were basic . . . an absolute minimum. All of your flight, professional, and medical records were meticulously scrutinized at all levels before your name was released for further evaluation.

> At the time, the F-100, F-101, F-102, F-104, F-105, and F-106 were called the Century Series aircraft.

The initial personal requirement was that you had to be married and preferably that you had children. They were adamant about this after some problems they experienced with the previous U-2 program. Their explanation was that the family unit is more socially established, dedicated, and dependable. Our wives were also interviewed separately, and psychological evaluations were conducted. Expanded background investigations were run on each wife.

At this phase (April 1961) of the overall evaluation, we still did not know for what we were being evaluated. The following events and schedules were generally the same for all of the pilots being considered. Each was individually and separately tasked for the respective events. Initially I didn't know that there was another pilot (Captain Walter Ray) from Shaw AFB. We started running into each other about a year later, when the field of consideration was narrowed by elimination. From the beginning, we were given the option of withdrawing from the selection at any time without prejudice. This option continued throughout the program.

Our medical records were acceptable for the initial evaluation, because we were all on flying status. However, Air Force physicals were not extensive enough for the final evaluation and we were about to find out what that really meant. I was scheduled for my "astronaut" physical at the Lovelace Clinic in Albuquerque, New Mexico. This is the same facility where the original astronauts received their medical evaluations, and it was the medical facility for the original U-2 pilots. I discovered this later during a return visit to the clinic, where I met Francis Gary Powers. The late Dr. Lovelace, who was one of the pioneers of aviation medicine, founded the Lovelace Clinic. His son, Dr. Randy Lovelace, continued the work, until he, his wife, and their pilot were killed flying into a mountain west of Colorado Springs.

I had a government contact (an Air Force flight surgeon) whom I met at the clinic. He established all of my schedules and appointments and observed all of the tests. He and I would have dinner together more as a part of the evaluation than just being social. The first medical phase lasted for five days. I arrived there on Sunday and departed the following Saturday. During those five days they checked out every bodily orifice, X-rayed every part of you from head to toe, flushed you out totally, took samples, and measured everything. (I carried a large brown bottle around for 48 hours to collect every drop of urine.) They conducted extensive EKGs and EEGs. I was hydrostatically weighed in a large water tank, ran the bicycle pulmonary functions, and passed

Talk about lead time for pilots! Ken was being evaluated a full year before the first flight of the A-12 even took place—26 April 1962, flown by Lockheed test pilot Lou Schalk.

other physical stress exercises. I was then flown to the Los Alamos Laboratory in New Mexico to be inserted into the "body counter," which mapped the fat versus muscle tissue of my body. When correlated with the data from the hydrostatic weighing, theoretically, they could determine the total body capacity, regardless of size. After all of that I was ready for the hospital!

From that date forward, I was subjected to many different kinds of personal and professional evaluations. There was the soundproof black box where you had to remain for 12 hours—total darkness, sleepless in Philadelphia—and then the polygraph. Various dinners and lunches with a whole variety of "professional" people—medical and intelligence people, ranging from senior managers to the basic company employee. All were there to get an opinion, except the lesser guy. He was there to keep me out of trouble.

After the sorting was near completion, I learned that eight would be selected for the initial program. This sounded reasonable, since that was the average-size group for the astronaut program, or so we thought!

I finally received my orders assigning me to the Headquarters, USAF, Washington, D.C., with a reporting date of 28 October 1962. In fact, the day the movers finished packing me—and we were leaving the next day—I received a call from Lieutenant Colonel Clyde East, who was my squadron commander (20th Tactical Reconnaissance Squadron, Shaw AFB). He said that I was to report to the base, because the RF-101s were on alert for immediate deployment (to MacDill AFB, Florida, for the Cuban Crisis). Obviously, I was not available for the deployment, although I would have liked to have gone with the squadron. The week before I departed Shaw AFB, I was again called to Washington, D.C., for a final meeting, at which time I still had the option of withdrawing from the program. For the first time, I was told it was not the astronaut program, but a project to fly and test an exotic new airplane for the Central Intelligence Agency. There were no pictures or any other details. I then met Bill Skliar and Lon Walter. I already knew Walt Ray from Shaw. (Note: Lon Walter resigned after a couple of flights in March 1963; Bill Skliar was killed in his racer in Reno, Nevada, after he retired; and Walt Ray was killed during an A-12 ejection in 1966).

I arrived in Washington, D.C., with my wife, Jane, and our four children. The next day I was taken to headquarters to sign on the dotted line. We headed west the following day. Jane had been interviewed and evaluated separately during this entire process. She was *not* told what I would be doing, and was told not to talk about it to anyone. She could say that I decided to resign from the Air Force and go to work for Hughes Aircraft. (For all who thought we received a great salary, we all made about $4,000 per year more than our Air Force pay; however, the job was well worth it.)

The first time I saw the A-12 or even heard the name was in December 1962 after I arrived at Area 51. Colonel Doug Nelson, project operations officer, took me to the hangar and let me walk in by myself. What an amazing sight! There were no hangar lights. The sun's rays entered the upper hangar windows, illuminating only the nose and the spikes. As my eyes adjusted to the restricted light, I began to take in its sleek length, the massive twin rudders, and its total blackness. A vision I'll never forget.

A-12 Pilot Training

Most people are familiar with the military term "R&R" (Rest and Recreation). For the family it has a totally different connotation. For them it's "reassignment and relocation" and a lot of work. Air Force life has many positive aspects, usually benefiting both the Air Force and the military member and his family. Assigning you a sponsor eased the transition of settling into a new Air Force unit and community. However, this job was as a civilian, working as a flight test pilot/consultant to Hughes Aircraft Company. They only helped with the job administration. For housing and the family, I was on my own.

Coming from the little country town of Sumter, South Carolina, to a megametropolitan area like Los Angeles was a culture shock. Jane and our four children and I departed Sumter, via Washington, D.C., making family pit stops in Memphis, Tennessee, and San Angelo, Texas, and from there on to Long Beach, California. This was the only city in California that I had ever visited. I had flown to Long Beach airport in 1951 in a B-25 trainer out of Vance AFB with my instructor, Captain Cook, and my flight classmate, Chuck Costantino. The family and I stayed there only two days. After talking to Walt Ray, another project pilot, we moved to the San Fernando Valley. This was at the suggestion of Clay Lacy, a pilot-training classmate and friend of Walt Ray. At that time, Clay Lacy was a pilot for United Airlines; he now owns Clay Lacy Charter, a very successful air charter company at Van Nuys Airport.

Getting the family settled and feeling secure was important to the program. They knew that the project pilots would generally be out of touch from Monday through Friday and some weekends. If there was a serious problem, my wife was given a telephone number to call any time and request that I call back. The return call could be immediate, or in one or two days, depending on my schedule and location. My wife knew that I was on a very special operational flying assignment, but not my location, what I was flying, my sponsor, or my associates, other than the project pilots. Once I had the family in place, I was ready to dedicate myself to the project.

I began the flying training by again checking out in the F-101. Since I already had over 1,000 hours in the RF-101A, C, and B (trainer) as a combat-qualified crewmember, and IP less than three months before, I completed the checkout in the F-101 and air refueling quickly. The flying was accomplished in accordance with Air Force standardization and evaluation regulations. All the staff and operations personnel were permanent party

Air Force. Colonel Doug Nelson was the operations officer, and Major Ray Haupt was the standardization and evaluation officer.

The standardization and evaluation office, abbreviated to "Stan/Eval" in Air Force jargon, was responsible for making sure flying rules, regulations, and procedures for each aircraft were as standardized as possible. The handful of select pilots in the Stan/Eval office also administered annual flight checks to the aircrews. They had the power to either pass or "bust" you on check rides.

The project pilots studied the existing A-12 procedures documents and reviewed the systems with aircraft systems engineers and Lockheed test pilots. We got as much cockpit time as possible. It's important to note that there was little established or tested data for procedures at this point of the program. The existing systems were new and untried. Changes were being made daily with the completion of each test flight; procedures were developed in-flight and during the debriefings. Each flight was critically reviewed. Kelly Johnson repeatedly said that this was a truly experimental test program—he was right!

The A-12 flight training began with three or four flights in the A-12 trainer, which had Pratt & Whitney J-75 engines with afterburners. The cockpit and flight systems were basically the same as the other A-12s, but the trainer could only reach Mach 2-plus.

Clarence "Kelly" Johnson was Lockheed's chief architect and designer of the SR-71. You will hear more about his outstanding work throughout the book.

The massive Pratt & Whitney J-58 engine produced 34,000 pounds of thrust. The engines were designed for continuous operation at compressor inlet temperatures (CIT) of 427 degrees C. Each engine had six bypass tubes (three shown), routing bleed air from the compressor to the front of the afterburner, where it was used for increased thrust and cooling. *Author collection*

There was no simulator, so the trainer was the best means of instruction available, and it was a good trainer. The takeoffs and landings in the trainer were very similar to the operational A-12, as was aerial refueling. I wanted to ensure that I got all the trainer flight time possible in preparation for my first flight in the A-12 (single cockpit with J-58 engines). Bill Skliar, the first project pilot to fly the trainer, flew on 4 February 1963, and my first A-12 trainer flight was two days later. Walt Ray followed me on 10 February, and Lon Walter some time after that. Lon opted out of the program shortly after he started flying the J-58–equipped A-12 aircraft.

Pratt & Whitney was behind on developing the J-58 engine, so a decision was made to equip A-12s coming off the production line with J-75 engines until J-58s became available. For nine months, Lockheed test pilots and CIA pilots flew the A-12s with J-75 engines only. It wasn't until January 1963 that the first flight of an A-12 equipped with (two) J-58s finally took to the air. The A-12 trainer aircraft, #927, was never modified with the J-58 engines. Affectionately, it was called the "titanium goose" by crewmembers.

The most critical event that the trainer could not prepare you for was the inlet unstarts, because it didn't have moveable spikes (variable geometry inlet) and could not accelerate to Mach 3. Many A-12 features evolved during testing. Initially, the A-12s did not have aft bypass doors: they came along later when engineers realized more air flow control was needed. We had no spike and door position indicators in the cockpit, until we complained that we needed some way to "see" their position. We only had manual spike/door restart switches—no automatic restart features. Both the fuel control units and inlet controls were unreliable. Everything was very dynamic, changing all the time, usually for the better.

As soon after the A-12 trainer checkout as possible, we were put on the A-12 flying schedule. Every flight was different, with the exception that *every* flight had multiple inlet unstarts. When you began the climb and acceleration out to 80,000 feet and Mach 3, you were certain that there would be a "popped shock" and an unstart between 2.5 Mach (40–50,000 feet) and 2.9 Mach (60–70,000 feet). You never knew the extent. All unstarts were severe and serious emergencies in the beginning. Since we only had a restart switch for each inlet (no inlet position indicators until much later) we were reacting, usually too late, to an unstart in progress. An unstart of an inlet "popped" the supersonic shock wave out of the throat of the inlet, immediately stopping the air flow through that inlet—the compressor then stalling the engine, and causing

It seems like every time you talk to someone who never flew the Blackbird they want to know what an "unstart" is. Unstarts only occur after you're supersonic. Once supersonic air is positioned inside the inlet, it becomes "started." Our unstarts were most commonly caused by incoming air pressure *inside* the inlet becoming too great or the spike positioned too far aft. Problems with hydraulic pressure, electrical supply, and the air inlet computer (AIC) were other faults that could create unstarts.

A turbojet engine cannot take supersonic airflow through the engine. On jet aircraft such as the F-4 Phantom, a ramp at the entrance to the intake opened as your speed increased, stopping supersonic air from entering the intake. That was the purpose of the SR-71's spike, to slow down supersonic airflow, and, at the same time, accurately position the supersonic shock wave inside the inlet throat. The computer-controlled forward bypass doors surrounding the inlet dumped excess air piling up in front of the compressor into the airstream. When the spike's movement or the forward bypass doors go awry by the slightest amount, the supersonic shock wave inside the inlet is disrupted and immediately expelled outside the inlet, creating an unstart.

During an unstart, the engines and afterburners do not typically flame out, but either or both easily could because of the disrupted airflow. You just never knew what you lost until you scanned the engine instruments. The "BANG" grabbed your immediate attention, followed by roll and yaw in the direction of the offending inlet. The roll-and-yawing moment was created by two factors. Not only were you losing a tremendous amount of thrust on the bad inlet, but also, to make matters worse, there was a large amount of drag associated with an unstarted inlet and the automatic features that attempted to "restart" the inlet.

Most unstarts happened only once and cleared up as quickly as they arrived, allowing you to proceed. Sometimes unstarts would not "clear" themselves, but kept recurring, one after another. You could try to override the automatic features and fly with the inlets in a manual mode of operation. However, if the manual mode did not clear the inlet, you had to descend and slow to subsonic speeds. If I were to guess, crews of my generation experienced unstarts about every third flight.

an afterburner blowout. It was then impossible to continue accelerating and gaining altitude. At this phase of the test program we were only guessing which inlet unstarted, left or right.

For any hope of restarting the inlet and continuing acceleration, we hit both inlet restart switches immediately. We always had the option of making a quick guess which inlet was the culprit, activating only either the left or right inlet restart switch, hoping that you could catch it before the unstart stalled the engine and blew out the afterburner. Even guessing right, we were usually too late, because it all happened in a nanosecond. After an unsuccessful attempt to get an immediate restart, we were in for a head-knocking (your helmet was knocking rapidly against the side of the canopy), rapidly decelerating, shuddering dive toward the ground. We weren't concerned about the inlets at this point.

Our primary efforts were devoted toward getting the engines restarted. The severity of the initial inlet unstart (it's called an Aerodynamic Disturbance, or AD, by the engineers) put the aircraft in a hard yaw, causing the *other* inlet to unstart, the *other* engine to compressor stall, and the *other* afterburner to flame out, leaving us with more serious problems and very few options. We had to get one or more engines started. Reflecting back to those days, we always got at least one engine running again.

The most serious problems occurred when the triethylborane (TEB) probes started "coking"—acquiring a chemical residue buildup that restricted the flow of the TEB. This prevented the engine/afterburner from starting. We had a lot of other mechanical and electronic system problems throughout the program, but none as big as the inlet unstarts.

There isn't an A-12 pilot who hasn't experienced the severity of the inlet unstart and thought he would have to "punch" out. This was unthinkable for every A-12 pilot. Most of us needed a lot of luck and someone up there looking out for us.

TEB was the acronym for triethylborane, a liquid chemical used to ignite both the J-58 engine and afterburner fuel. When TEB is exposed to air above minus 5 degrees C, it spontaneously burns. As the pilot moved the throttles forward, a metered amount of liquid TEB was sprayed into the engine, or afterburner.

The First Blackbird Ejection

As we were having a lot of problems with engine fuel controls during acceleration and cruise, I was scheduled for a flight test mission to perform subsonic engine test runs. Jack Weeks was scheduled as my F-101 chase pilot. The date was 24 May 1963. Takeoff and initial cruise at 25,000 feet was routine. I made the planned right turn to a heading of 180 degrees and climbed to 27,000 feet to stay out of the building cloud formations. During these missions the chase plane was to stay close enough to observe the engine nacelles and the afterburner areas, but far enough away to maintain safe flight. The F-101 had a historical pitch-up problem if it got too slow in flight. As we continued south in the Wendover Danger Area (northwest of the Great Salt Lake) I entered an area of heavy cumulus cloud formations. My chase moved in to keep visual contact. Minutes later, Jack signaled that we were getting too slow for the F-101. All my A-12 instruments (airspeed, altitude) were giving normal indications. Jack signaled that he could not stay with me. I waved him off and he cleared to my right and disappeared into the clouds.

I dedicated my efforts to determining what the real problems were. I engaged the autopilot and reviewed all of the instruments and systems. There were no observable failures or abnormal indications. I then disengaged the autopilot, maintaining my planned airspeed and 30,000 feet altitude.

In a matter of seconds, all hell broke out. Without any noticeable change of aircraft attitude or speed, the altimeter was rapidly "unwinding," indicating a rapid loss of altitude. The airspeed indicator was also unwinding, displaying a rapid loss of speed. In heavy clouds, with no visual references, and with what felt like a solid platform under me, I advanced the throttles, attempting to stop the indicated loss of airspeed, but with no apparent results. At this point, I could not assume that any of my flight or engine instruments were providing correct data. And I was right! Without any warning the A-12 pitched up and went into a flat inverted spin.

The reader needs to understand that Blackbirds do not stall—they merely depart controlled flight! The wing has no flaps, slats, spoilers, or artificial stall warning device of any kind. Its pitch-up characteristics are graphically demonstrated to every crewmember during simulator training. As the SR-71 flight manual states, "There is no stall in the classic sense where an abrupt loss in lift would occur at a critical angle of attack. Instead, a nose-up pitching moment develops, as angle of attack increases, which becomes uncontrollable (even with full nose-down elevon). The uncontrollable pitch-up occurs at the critical angle of attack boundary. Recovery from this condition is extremely unlikely." Our maximum angle of attack at supersonic speeds was only 8 degrees.

Realizing that I had no effective controls, and that the aircraft was unrecoverable from the flat, inverted spin, and that I had no true indication of my actual altitude, it was time to eject. I could have been much lower and over higher mountains, which would put me dangerously close to the ground or hilltops. I closed my helmet visor, grabbed the ejection D-ring between my legs, firmly pushed my head back against the ejection seat headrest, and pulled. The aircraft canopy flew off instantly, the boot stirrups snapped back into the seat retainers, and the ejection seat rocket shot me downward (remember, I was inverted!) and away from the aircraft.

The man/seat separator worked great. Shortly after separating from the seat my 'chute opened. I looked up to confirm that I did indeed have a 'chute (this was my first ejection). I then looked down at the ground to get a general idea of the terrain where I would land. At that very moment, the 'chute broke away, separating from my parachute harness. I knew that my luck had just run out! There was a momentary, quieting sensation—a pause in my life.

When I ejected I didn't know what my altitude was. After the ejection I was just happy that I had a parachute and was out of the clouds. I had safely separated from the aircraft. While descending through 15,000 feet, the drogue 'chute is programmed to separate. At that moment, I truly thought that my parachute was gone. Just as suddenly, this beautiful 35-foot canopy blossomed, quickly slowing my descent.

(The A-12 parachute was actually two parachutes. A smaller drogue 'chute deploys shortly after ejection and seat separation. Its primary purpose is to slowly decelerate the pilot ejecting at high speeds and altitudes. Then the main parachute—35 feet in diameter to compensate for the extra weight of the pressure suit—opens. If only the main 'chute were deployed at high altitude and excessive speeds, the pilot would be killed by the instant deceleration.)

One of the improvements that took place from the A-12 to the SR-71 was the ejection sequence of events. We had a 6 1/2-foot-diameter drogue (stabilizing) 'chute stowed in the ejection seat headrest. It deployed 0.2 seconds after the seat catapult fired. The drogue 'chute was connected to the seat at four points, and allowed seat deceleration. After 10 seconds, the lower two lines are automatically severed to stabilize the seat in an upright position. The crewmember stayed connected to the seat and enjoyed the elevator ride down to 15,000 feet, at which time seat-man separation took place and the 35-foot parachute deployed.

For an ejection below 15,000 feet (down to the surface) the seat's drogue chute deployed precisely in the same manner. However, because time was now more critical, seat-man separation took place 1.4 seconds after drogue chute deployment, and the main parachute deployed 0.2 seconds after you separated from the seat.

During my descent I saw the A-12 spiraling toward the ground and then a large black column of smoke and flames behind a hill. I had time to look around. I saw a road miles to the right and a lot of rough terrain covered with rocks and sage. As I got closer to the ground, I assumed the parachute landing position with feet together and knees bent. I hit the ground and rolled on my right side into a standing position. I immediately released the riser safety clips and collapsed the 'chute. You keep the parachute canopy to sleep in. I was in the middle of a hilly desert with little prospect of being rescued any time soon. My chase plane (Jack Weeks) didn't know where I was, and because of the program's tight security, we didn't maintain radio contact with the base operations. I began collecting all of my flight checklist pages, which broke loose during the ejection, and any other aircraft items lying around. Much to my amazement, I saw a pickup truck bouncing across the rocks coming toward me with three men in the cab. When they stopped, I saw they had my aircraft cockpit canopy in the truck bed. They asked me if I wanted a ride. They said that they would take me over to my airplane. I told them that it was an F-105 fighter with a nuclear weapon on board. They got very nervous and said that if I was going with them to get in quick, because they were not staying around here.

Ken Collins after an SR-71 flight. Notice the American flag patch on his left shoulder. While flying the A-12, his pressure suit had no identification patches. Ken was one of two A-12 OXCART pilots who returned to the Air Force to fly the SR-71. After 11 years in the Blackbird program, he ended up with 365 hours in the A-12 and 340 hours in the SR-71. *Ken Collins*

There were four of us in that cab. I asked them to drop me off at the nearest highway patrol office, which was in Wendover, Utah. I thanked them and that was the last I saw of them. I made my "secret" phone call. A Lockheed Constellation loaded with security people and aircraft engineers arrived in less than two hours. Kelly Johnson's jet arrived after the "Connie" to pick me up. Our flight surgeon and I flew directly to Albuquerque, New Mexico, to the Lovelace Clinic for my physical checkup.

An intense accident investigation was conducted. I submitted to sodium pentothal ("truth serum") to confirm my statements relating to the flight and accident. The person who solved the true technical cause of the accident was Norm Nelson. Norm was a dedicated government engineer and a fine, caring man, who became vice president of the Skunk Works. As always, the initial belief is that there was pilot error. Fortunately the real causes of the accident were discovered and later corrected. It turned out to be an inadequate pitot tube (thus the Rosemont Probe we have now) and failed air data computer. Ten years after the accident, I received a package in the mail. Unwrapping it, I found a framed shadowbox with the D-ring mounted inside, with the inscription, "To Ken Collins, 'A Friend In Need.'" It was my ejection D-ring from the A-12. Keith Beswick, a Lockheed engineer on the OXCART program, sent it to me.

This personal rapport was typical of the relationships between the project pilots and all of the Lockheed personnel, from Kelly Johnson down. The Air Force personnel were no less professional and supportive. The OXCART program will remain in the hearts and minds of all those who participated. I would especially like to honor the names of Walt Ray and Jack Weeks. Both were killed while performing their duties as A-12 project pilots. I respectfully keep in my memory their wives, Diane Ray and Sharene Weeks, who lived through the worries, followed by their personal losses.

Of those who were in the OXCART program from the inception through to the last A-12 overflights, I want to commend all of you. They were Colonel Bill Skliar (killed after retirement racing his aircraft), Major General (Ret) Mel Vojvodich, Brigadier General (Ret) Denny Sullivan, Colonel (Ret) Jack Layton, and Lieutenant Colonel (Ret) Frank Murray. They all were "friends in deed."

I owe the most gratitude and appreciation to my wife, Jane Bingham Collins. Thank you for your perseverance in the face of the unknown, support of me and our children, understanding when I could tell you nothing, and your love.

CHAPTER TWO

Colonel (Ret) Donn A. Byrnes

I first met Donn during an SR-71 symposium at the Pima Air & Space Museum, Tucson, Arizona, in 1996. I knew Donn had worked on the SR-71 during the early design and testing days, but wasn't quite sure what part he played. After briefly talking with him it was clearly evident he, and a handful of others, were the individuals directly responsible for putting all of the bits and pieces of the SR-71 together and making it a viable reconnaissance platform.

Donn entered the Air Force in 1951 at the age of 19, and after a year as an aircraft mechanic and crew chief, decided to try the Aviation Cadet Program. During his flying career, spanning 28 years, he flew 17 different types of aircraft, accumulating over 3,200 hours of flying time. In his spare time (he sounds so busy, I'm surprised he had any) he acquired an electrical engineering degree. Donn served with the Blackbird program in

Without cameras and a variety of other sensors, the SR-71 would merely be another fast jet. Donn Byrnes, coauthor of *Blackbird Rising*, joined the SR-71 program in early 1964 and became instrumental in putting together all of the systems and sensors that made the aircraft the world's greatest intelligence collector. *Donn Byrnes*

various capacities from 1962 through 1968. He was responsible for sensor development, integration, and flight testing of the SR-71 at Wright-Patterson AFB, Dayton, Ohio, and Edwards AFB, California. In 1999 Donn coauthored a book with Lieutenant Colonel Ken Hurley, titled *Blackbird Rising, Birth of an Aviation Legend.* Their fascinating story chronicles the political and technical events that molded the SR-71.

My goal in asking Donn to write about the technological challenges he faced in integrating the SR-71's camera was to give the reader a perspective of what level of complexity this involved. Here are Donn's stories.

Russ Daniell—The Interface King

People look at the SR-71 in many ways. It projects a unique image to each of us. The casual observer sees a long, lean airframe, and to some it will appear sinister. The aircrews see an airplane that has carried them on many missions and brought them home safely. The maintenance and support people see an assembly of systems, parts, sheet metal, and engines—a remarkable ensemble of rivets, stringers, bulkheads, electrical wiring, hydraulic tubes, and hoses. All who operated and attended the Blackbirds on the flightline and elsewhere are aware of individual aircraft personalities and each machine's hardware soul. As an engineer, I saw this blended assembly of systems and subsystems as a mechanical symphony of carefully arranged interrelationships. Music written by a few, played by a small number of people, but heard throughout the world. A refrain that is sorely missed in the current times of hunger for timely and detailed reconnaissance data. Gone are the days when we could show the flag in some obscure country during troubled times. The Blackbird was a thoroughbred in every sense of the word. She reached her aerodynamic stature by taking both large and small technical steps. She achieved her international standing and fame by unflinchingly carrying her share of the load and our national pride everywhere she went.

Kelly Johnson and Ben Rich did a superlative job of designing an air-breathing aircraft, the likes of which the world had never seen before. Aerodynamics, inlets, and structures were their forte. In addition, they collected an amazing team of people around them—the unsung heroes of the Skunk Works. Each subcontractor had a similar organization, a mini-Skunk Works, also populated with stellar people. On the Lockheed side, one of the best was James Russell (Russ) Daniell.

A longtime Lockheed employee with years of "Kelly Johnson experience," Russ was among the upper structure of the Skunk Works organization. He did what many of us would view as "the dog work of systems design and development." One of his functions during the 1960s was to facilitate and consummate all of the intersystem relationships with internal Lockheed organizations, as well as outside subcontractors. Russ Daniell was the czar of

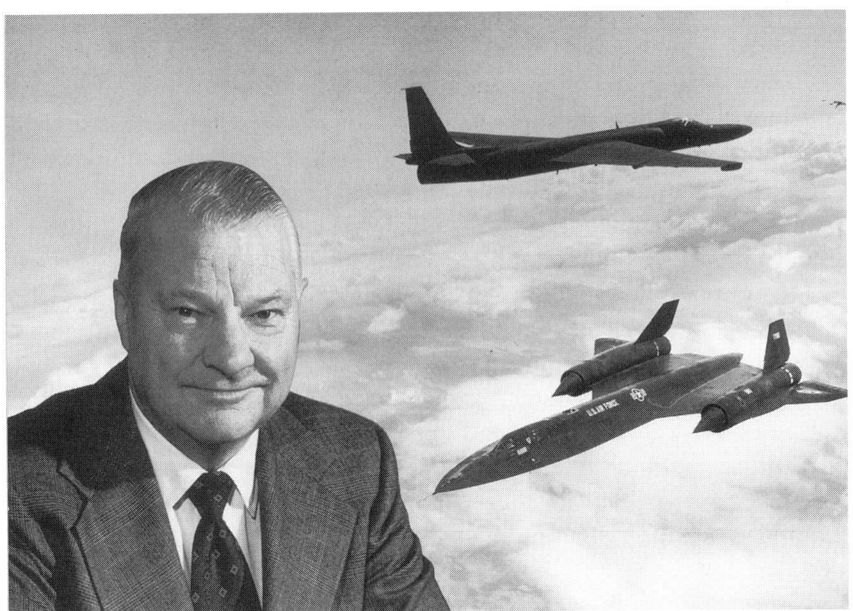

Clarence "Kelly" Johnson, former president of Lockheed's famed Skunk Works, with the two prized reconnaissance aircraft he designed and built—the U-2 and SR-71. The formal name for the Skunk Works was the Advanced Development Projects (ADP). Its forte was building a small number of very technologically advanced airplanes for highly secret missions. *Lockheed Martin Skunk Works*

one of the most exacting and frustrating disciplines in the entire development process—interface agreements.

Russ was a quiet guy who went about his business without a lot of flair or emotion. He viewed the world as a series of events and problems needing a logical and methodical solution. Always present and ready to deal with whatever came down the pipe, he turned the crank on a series of incredibly complex issues. Most of the external subcontractor engineers and designers dealt with Russ directly. Because this facet of the design business is, in some respects, a zero-sum game, having one individual in place who could keep a knowledgeable balance between all systems and subsystems was of paramount importance. There is a fixed amount of electrical power available, a limited amount of cooling air, and environmentally suitable space within any aircraft is always at a premium. If there is too much of any of the above, the aircraft is overdesigned, too big, too heavy, or inefficiently shaped. Russ was the ultimate high-tech muleskinner, driving all toward a common goal—each entity pulling its own load, sharing the pain, and contributing its unique capabilities to the overall solution. He drove a hard but technically sound and fair bargain. He cracked a mean whip.

What are interface agreements? They are simple-sounding things. Where do the mounting bolts for a camera go? How many? What size? Where is the power connector located on the camera? What wires do what, how many wires, how big, should they be shielded or not? What size connector, standard or nonstandard, male or female connector? Which wires are connected to which pins? In the final design, all of these questions must be answered. Every Blackbird camera and every Blackbird aircraft was required to be the same with regard to these connections.

If you put one of the SR-71's cameras in a plain box and wanted it to operate, just imagine all of the things that would be needed to penetrate the surface of that box to supply information, power, and cooling to the camera. Furthermore, the camera needs to tell the aircraft systems what it requires and what it is doing, and to confirm that it has done what it was told to do.

All details in such areas as commands, physical connections, power requirements, cooling air, heating coils, vibration isolators, and connectors must be defined, spelled out, and agreed to, between the aircraft manufacturer and every subcontractor who makes something to go in the aircraft. These are the questions and answers that appear in the volumes and pages of interface agreements. Not only are there detailed engineering agreements between the aircraft maker and the subsystem contractors, but between the subsystems themselves, as they speak to each other through the aircraft's wiring system or interact through other aircraft systems.

Russ had a group of dedicated Skunk Works engineers working for him and was able to translate this seemingly impossible and endless series of hardware and electronic questions and definitions into written documentation. He had one unique management style: two inboxes. Here's how his system worked. If you sent Russ something requiring his attention, he would put it in inbox number one. If you didn't call to follow up in about four or five days, he would take that item out of inbox number one, put it in the round file, and never give it another thought. If you called within the required time, he would put that action item into inbox number two. That was the inbox he worked from. Once your request or action item was in the second inbox, you were sure it would get instant and aggressive attention, and most likely a solution in very short order.

The Ultimate Dilemma

The parliamentary and diplomatic people skills, both interpersonal and intrasystem, are stretched to the limit when one attempts to balance power, range, engine output, fuel capacity, cooling air, and electrical power in a modern aircraft. While not new to these trade-offs, Russ found himself right in the middle of some extremely difficult issues.

Lockheed had guaranteed certain performance factors—speed, altitude, range, and payload capacities. A series of engine thrust profiles was developed and the Pratt & Whitney Company promised to provide a pair of engines with sufficient push to make all that come true. Kelly, Ben Rich, and lots of others worked on the solutions to these problems. But, and there is always a *but*, the engines needed to supply more than raw thrust. They had to furnish the aircraft's electrical power, its hydraulic power, cooling air for all of the electronics and the aircrew, and power for pressurizing the cockpits. The design had to be such that even with only one engine running, the aircraft would remain flyable and could return home.

Every drop of energy taken from an engine to perform these absolutely necessary support functions subtracts from the amount of thrust the engines can deliver. The lower the delivered thrust, the longer it takes to cover a fixed distance. That means the aircraft has to carry more fuel, which makes the aircraft heavier and larger, increasing drag; this means you need more thrust, and on and on. Russ was right in the middle of all of this. If you give away too much electrical power to the subsystems, the engine performance will suffer. Then the range, altitude, and speed will suffer. This problem was compounded by the fact that Russ worked for Lockheed, and Kelly was his boss. Kelly promised the speed, altitude, and range. The engine people agreed to deliver the thrust, and that is where it started.

There are many basic truths associated with the act of bringing aircraft from the drawing board to the end of the runway. The aircraft weight always increases, while the engines usually produce less thrust than originally promised and end up using more fuel per hour. Support and payload systems demand more electrical power, hydraulic power, and cooling air than first thought, and—the final insult—the center of gravity (CG) always moves aft as the design progresses, not good for aircraft stability! Each of the aircraft subsystems mirrors this general developmental path: They all take more of whatever they originally asked. Russ accepted these challenges, and knowing exactly how much thrust was available, all the range factors and fuel requirements, he deftly parceled out the valuable resources of power and cooling to each subcontractor.

Cooling air is probably the most precious commodity available in the modern jet-powered aircraft, because it directly robs the engine of power. The engine does all of the work to compress the incoming air. However, just before that air is fed into the burner section to produce valuable thrust, a portion of it is routed away to a turbine, to be turned into cold air. If that were not enough, more hot air (thrust) is taken from the engine to "adjust" the temperature of this newly created cold air, to make it just the right temperature.

It doesn't take a rocket scientist to see that the person trying to iron out working relationships between the engine manufacturer, the aircraft designer/builder, and the various subsystem companies is strapped into a serious lose-lose situation from the very beginning. Now put this person in the position of working for Lockheed in general, and Kelly Johnson in specific, and you can see the terrible problems that came across Russ Daniell's desk. Yet, when you visited his office he always appeared to be in complete control. Amazing!

Every contractor dealing with Russ had, and still has, only praise for the way he went about the job of getting the details on paper. Solutions were negotiated in a way that brought the pain of compromise in equal shares to the prime contractor and the subs. From the first test for fit, with cardboard or plywood mockup, to the final hardware compatibility testing, Russ was in the middle of every level of technical documentation.

Sometimes Cooling Air Is Hot!

There is a fixed hierarchy to the cooling-air food chain. The systems needed to keep the aircraft in the air get the first, the most, and the coolest air. Progressing down the priority list, some of the systems get cooled by the exhaust air from other systems. In the SR-71, one of the systems near the bottom of the cooling-air distribution system was the side-looking radar (SLR).

The SR-71 had a remove-and-replace nose as shown in the picture. Inside the nose was either the Optical Bar Camera (OBC), or the radar imaging system. The OBC took excellent photography at long distances from the flight path. The original radar imaging system was called the CAPRE (Capability Reconnaissance). By the 1980s, we were using the Advanced Synthetic Aperture Radar System (ASARS-1), giving us detailed imagery, day or night, rain or shine. *Rich Graham*

At the end of the radar cooling air pipe was the SLR transmitter. On occasion, in the flight test program, the cooling air to the SLR transmitter was 200 degrees F. On an early test flight, when the transmitter was opened, orange fuzz was all over the inside of the transmitter box. The fuzz came from elements of the various components and cards within the transmitter box—yet the radar did a fine job that day. It's all in the design.

The entire nose of the SR-71 was a remove-and-replace item. Depending on the target weather, the nose of the aircraft was equipped with either an optical camera or SLR imaging system. The first radar imaging system we had was called "CAPRE." The greatest asset of radar imaging is that you can use it day or night and "see" through weather. The CAPRE could map a swath from 10 to 20 miles wide, at any distance between 20 to 80 miles from the flight track of the aircraft, depending on the aircraft's bank angle. It could do this on either side of the aircraft, but not both sides at once. All of the imagery was recorded aboard the aircraft, for intelligence use after landing.

By 1986 we had a newer generation of radar nose called the Advanced Synthetic Aperture Radar System (ASARS-1), which covered a 10-mile swath, positioned 20 to 100 miles left or right of the ground track. When the SR-71s were brought out of retirement in 1995, a downlink antenna was installed to transmit the high-resolution radar images directly to a ground site, for immediate viewing. The radar imagery could be recorded onboard the plane for about one hour, or around 2,000 miles along the track. In the rear cockpit, the RSO had a real-time radar display of the current imagery.

Sometimes the Problem Is Not All That Clear

Everyone agreed that the astro-inertial navigation system (ANS) was important and rated a first-class cooling-air connection. Russ Daniell and George Fritzell of Nortronics (manufacturer of the ANS) hammered out a deal in which the ANS got all the cooling air it needed. This system was right at the top of the food chain, along with the crew and cockpits. Engineers designed the delivery piping and the mixing muffs to ensure that hot air was mixed with the cold, and a resulting air temperature of 65 to 70 degrees would be fed directly to the ANS.

When we first started flying with the "full up" system aircraft at Edwards AFB, there was a problem with keeping the ANS cool. These aircraft were flown in a configuration that the test force felt was identical to the way operational aircraft at Beale would use their sensor payloads. Initially, the ANS overheat light would come on about the time the aircraft reached the end of the runway. If not by then, it illuminated on takeoff, just about the time the gear came up. There were many test mission aborts, along with very frustrated crews.

The ANS worked basically as a star tracker to provide an extremely accurate means of navigation for the SR-71. It also supplied inputs to other sensors and systems that needed to know the plane's location. The heart of the ANS was the guidance group, which was affectionately referred to as "R2-D2," after the robot in *Star Wars*. It provided computations for navigation, guidance, and avionics control of the plane. A 3/4-inch-wide tape, with holes punched out by the mission planners, told the cameras when to look, where to look, and at what angle to look, as it passed through the computer.

The ANS utilized a telescope to search and lock onto stars, day and night. It looked through a highly polished quartz glass window, located directly behind the rear cockpit. The guidance group had a 61-star catalog stored in its computer, a clock accurate to one one-hundredth of a second, and knew the Julian date of the year. The theory was, if you knew the day of the year, the time of day, and were locked onto stars in the computer, the ANS would keep the SR-71 within 300 feet of the commanded course (except in turns) at Mach 3.

Some thought there was insufficient airflow, so the water separator was removed. The overheat light continued to illuminate, but now the circuit boards in the ANS got wet, and there was a great debate about coating them. Finally, a young test force engineer, Second Lieutenant Frank Doyle, was assigned to the job and told "get a grip on this problem or die." Frank was a young mechanical engineer, short on rank but long on brains. Back at the Nortronics plant, designers were working the problem as hard as they could. Skunk Works engineers were scratching their heads. After all, Lockheed's cooling air was not doing the job. Every simulation and mockup arrangement known to mankind was tried, and each test showed that the ANS was receiving plenty of cold air and should be working just fine.

The ANS had such a high priority for mission success that its cooling air came directly from the "mixing muff." This muff was not much more than a long, wide-diameter tube. Its only function was to provide a place to mix extremely cold air coming from the air conditioner turbine, with hot air coming directly from the engine compressor. The proportion of these two air supplies was varied, based on the output temperature and flow perceived by a sensor within the muff.

After several disappointing "adjustments" to the system, Frank decided to put thermocouples (thermometers) over the entire surface of the muff and all the tubes leading to and from the device. Large quantities of thermocouples were made up in one of the test force shops. Frank needed a way to calibrate these thermocouples before he could proceed with his test. The test force, following the true Skunk Works spirit, did the calibration. Not only was it done correctly, but it was fun. We decided the reference for the calibrations would be liquid Freon 12. To obtain this, we took a can of ordinary Freon 12 from my garage (the kind used to refill car air conditioners), hooked a pressure gauge to the top, and then proceeded to chill the can with a spray of liquid nitrogen until the internal pressure in the can was zero. Once that was done we turned the can upside down, took a can opener from my wife's kitchen, and removed the bottom. There, boiling at a constant temperature, was the Freon. The perfect reference junction for calibrations.

Once the thermocouples were in place and a recorder installed in the aircraft, a test flight was launched. The ANS performed as expected: The overheat light came on just as the gear came up. After the aircraft landed, Frank and others looked at the thermocouple data and discovered the problem. Imagine a large tube with air swirling around inside. The hot air and the cold air did not instantly mix in a homogeneous manner. Instead, they combined like the stripes on a barber pole, with the spirals of red, white, and blue turning, but not mixing. At high power settings and other engine rpm, this barber pole pattern was rather consistent. The outlet of the cooling air muff that fed the ANS happened to be right where there was a swirl of hot air before it had been cooled sufficiently. While the flow rate was just what the ANS needed, the temperature at that connection was not nearly cool enough. Lockheed made modifications to the mixing muff, killing the barber pole effect and the test program got under way again. Another month in cooling-air purgatory was history.

An Abbreviated View of a Camera's Interface Needs

Putting a camera aboard any aircraft is more than just bolting the device to the floor over a hole that faces the ground. Modern high-resolution cameras are fussy, cranky, and temperamental beasts requiring great care and patience to coax them to their best performance. When you marry a sophisticated camera to a state-of-the-art aircraft and its systems, things get tougher.

Installing a high-resolution camera in the SR-71 took the best of the best to obtain the desired performance. The technical objective camera (TEOC) serves as a perfect example to illustrate the difficulty in making a camera perform at its best. The TEOC had a 48-inch focal length lens and carried up to

2,000 feet of 9-inch-wide film. The camera was designed to image a 6-inch object on the ground from the SR-71's operational altitude of 85,000 feet. The TEOC sat horizontally in its bay and looked out at the ground through a highly polished, carefully plated beryllium mirror, and an optical-quality window made up of separate layers of two different kinds of glass. The camera contractor supplied the mirror and the rest of the camera, while Lockheed furnished the windows. Russ was in the middle again.

Cameras, especially large cameras, with massive lenses and long focal lengths, need to stay at a relatively constant temperature. This alone was a tough requirement to satisfy. The great variety of environmental conditions—from 100-degree F ground conditions, to aerial refueling, where the outside air temperature could be as low as minus 45 degrees F at 25,000 feet, to cruise conditions, where the outer skin around the camera bays was on the order of 450 degrees F, gave designers fits. The camera required cooling at cruise, but once the Blackbird descended to refueling altitude and began to cool off, the camera needed heating. Yes, there were significant layers of insulation, but insulation only delays heat transfer. It does not prevent it from happening.

But Wait, There's More

The thermal problems alone were significant and such wide swings in temperature had never been faced before. However, there were many other design issues impacting this camera. At cruising altitude and speed, the Blackbird clicked off about 3,000 feet every second. If the camera's shutter speed were set for one one-thousandth of a second, then the aircraft would travel about 3 feet during the exposure. But the problem was worse than that, because the TEOC used a focal plane shutter. Like a window shade with a slit in it, this curtain crossed just in front of the film. The slit traveled along at a rate that would expose every slit-width increment of the film for the selected exposure time. Depending upon the slit width, the exposure time for the entire negative could be considerably longer than one one-thousandth of a second.

Here are some rudimentary numbers to put this in perspective. The TEOC camera had two speeds for the focal plane shutter curtain. They were 40 and 80 inches per second. Regardless of the slit width, the total time required to expose one 9-inch film frame was 9 divided by 40, for the slow curtain speed (0.225 second), or 9 divided by 80, for the fast curtain speed (0.1125 second). During these brief times the SR-71 travels just over 742 feet along its flight path during the exposure when the camera was using the slow curtain speed, or about 371 feet while the camera made one exposure using the faster curtain speed.

Without some form of image motion compensation, the resulting photos would be terribly blurred along the direction of the aircraft's flight path.

During exposure, the image of the ground projected onto the negative must remain perfectly still. By moving the mirror in a very precise manner during this brief time, the camera was able to compensate for the SR-71's forward travel. The mirror's motion held the image at the back of the camera still while the window shade moved its slit across the entire negative. This motion of the mirror provided image motion compensations (IMC). The signal that told the mirror how fast to move was the velocity over height (V/H) signal. In the SR-71, the value of the V/H signal could be set in manually by the RSO or generated automatically by the ANS and fed to the camera during the period of picture taking. During the test program at Edwards, some flights were conducted using a V/H signal generated by a separate sensor carried on the head of the camera itself. However, the best high-resolution photos made during the test program were taken when the cameras used the V/H signal generated by the ANS. Proving, once again, that the painstaking detailed work of writing down and controlling each piece of information, or signal transfer between systems, was indeed worth the trouble.

Pretend You're the Camera

To appreciate how difficult it would be to have everything in sync and take the perfect picture, just imagine that *you* are this camera. A simple analogy of your task is to take a 9-inch by 9-inch piece of plywood (this represents the film at the back of the camera) and in the center of that square you insert a dowel perpendicular to the surface of the wood. The length of that dowel would be as long as the distance from the aircraft to the ground. On average, that dowel would be about 15 statute miles long if the aircraft were cruising at about 80,000 feet. Now during the time of exposure, you must hold the near-the-ground end of that dowel absolutely still. Fortunately for you, as a camera, the SR-71 was a very stable platform, so essentially all you have to compensate for is the speed of the aircraft and some vibrations here and there.

To be sure the target end of the dowel is at the proper location on the surface of the earth (the target you want to photograph), you, the camera, will have to take your instructions from the ANS to be sure you "point and click" at exactly the right time and in the right place. While the RSO had the capability of pointing the heads of the TEOCs and taking a photo manually, the complexity of the situation and the critical timing made this an almost impossible task. The job of operating the TEOCs was left to the navigation system and its computer. (Just another one of those pesky interfaces that needed to be ironed out.)

Suppose your desired target was as large as a square mile, although it was highly unlikely it would ever be that large. With the TEOC covering an area of about 2-1/2 square miles, that leaves a time frame of less than five seconds to take the photo, if the camera head is pointed at the correct place on the ground. (Remember, you are at least 15 miles away from your target.) This was a daunting, nearly impossible task without computer and navigational system help.

Woven Together Like a Fine Tapestry

Every sensor system in the aircraft depended extensively on inputs and support from the Blackbird's aircraft systems. The aircraft systems were likewise dependent upon each other for information and data needed to do the jobs they were assigned. The autopilot, air data computer, inlet systems, fuel system, and countless other systems were all tied together by mechanical, electrical, electronic, and hydraulic connections, making the SR-71 what she was and who she was. All of the details for each of these relationships were worked out in a very deliberate manner. This kind of engineering dog work is about as nonspectacular as is gets, but without such dedication to detail, the Blackbirds would not have accomplished what they did. Many of the relationships were less than straightforward, and quite a few seemed convoluted beyond comprehension. None of this came easy, yet without all the struggles over the nitpicky details, the SR-71 would never even have gotten its engines started. Because many people took the care and patience to deal with interfaces and a zillion details, the Blackbirds wrote page upon page of aviation history.

Russ Daniell and his band of Skunk Works system and sensor engineers worked long and tough hours, as did their subcontractor counterparts. Most worked the entire program unrecognized by anyone except the closest of fellow workers. The world has viewed the fruits of their individual and collective labors without a clue as to the monumental task they accomplished. The results are still around for us to see. The exploits of the Blackbird family and their systems populate this country's aviation historical legends, making us all proud.

CHAPTER THREE

Colonel (Ret) David P. Dempster

David retired from the Air Force in 1980 after a 27-year career. At age 19, David enlisted in the Air Force and qualified for the Aviation Cadet Program. He graduated from Harlingen AFB, Texas, in 1955 as a rated navigator and second lieutenant. David has observed that however you may feel about him today, you would not have liked him as a 20-year-old second lieutenant . . . he knew everything then, having not yet mellowed with humility.

During the next 14 years, David flew as a navigator/bombardier in SAC in the B-36, B-47, B-58 Mach 2 Hustler, and the SR-71. In the SR-71 program, David was one of eight B-58 crewmembers chosen to be the original cadre for the Blackbird program. He was also part of the first Air Force contingent to fly operational reconnaissance sorties from Okinawa into "denied areas." David has often said that even though they sometimes got lost at Mach 3-plus speeds, they would always remind themselves that at least they were making good time!

> The terms "denied" and "sensitive" areas were two labels used to define the airspace we flew into during operational missions. A "denied" area, over or around a foreign country, was thought of as airspace where you could encounter anything and everything . . . from MiGs to SAMs. A "sensitive" area was treated the same, but could become a very delicate issue between foreign countries politically if anything happened. I think an overflight of Cuba would be a prime example of a denied area. You expected to encounter possible threats, but the United States did not care what Cuba thought about reconnaissance flights over the island. The former USSR would qualify as a "sensitive" area.

In 1969 David joined the B-1 bomber program office at Wright-Patterson AFB, Ohio, and for the next five years worked on the development of the B-1 and its avionic subsystems. In 1971, David took a one-year "paid vacation" in Thailand, where he flew 159 combat sorties into Vietnam, Laos, and Cambodia as a navigator on an AC-130 gunship.

In 1975 David completed Air War College as a distinguished graduate and obtained an MBA degree from Auburn University. He then spent his last five years on active duty back at Wright-Patterson AFB as a program director for various organizations, responsible for the development of aircraft avionics and electronic warfare systems. David joined the aerospace industry after his USAF days and spent 13 years working on the B-2 stealth bomber, the Condor unmanned air vehicle (UAV), and other advanced development projects. He retired from Boeing in 1993.

At the time David joined the program, very little was known to the general public about Lockheed's Advanced Developmental Projects (ADP), more informally, and better known as, the Skunk Works. Inside the Skunk Works at Burbank, California, was a small, intensely cohesive group of about 50 engineers and designers, and about 100 expert machinists and shop workers. Their forte was building a small number of very technologically advanced airplanes for highly secret missions, to be used by the CIA and the Air Force. Years later, the head of the Skunk Works, Clarence L. "Kelly" Johnson, became famous among his aviation peers for his unique management style and ability to get the job done. He had a knack for doing the impossible. He designed more than 40 airplanes, the most noted being the P-38, P-80, F-104, U-2, and SR-71.

David and the other initial crews were tasked with figuring out how to employ the SR-71 aircraft in its reconnaissance and intelligence-gathering roles around the world. Flying at speeds and altitudes once only dreamed of created many unknowns and more questions. How do you even approach this task? David and the other crews began their learning curve at the very top—inside Lockheed's Skunk Works. He became instrumental in developing the initial SR-71 training programs at Beale for all the future crews. When I began my SR-71 training in 1974, David's legacy was still evident everywhere.

On 10 November 2000, around 30 former SR-71 crewmembers met in Branson, Missouri. This reunion was my first opportunity to meet David Dempster, a former RSO. I started chatting with David at the Branson Reunion, and soon knew he had some great stories up his sleeve. He agreed to share these.

Ink Blots

Much has been written about the space-pilot physical that we all had to take at Brooks AFB, San Antonio, Texas, as part of our entry into the program.

Mine was a seven-working day physical. Besides all of the medical interviews and testing, an interview with both a psychiatrist and then a psychologist were scheduled into the activities. I was apprehensive about all of the testing, since I wanted to pass so badly, but had completed six semester hours of college psychology in night school and knew about the Rorschach Ink Blot Test.

Brooks AFB is home to the USAF School of Aerospace Medicine. Its mission is focused on aerospace medicine and human physiology. Brooks medical personnel subjected many military aviators to the limits of aviation physiology, as well as giving astronaut physicals. Anyone on flying status *dreaded* the thought of having to go to Brooks to be evaluated for a medical problem.

During my hour with the psychologist, I was given the Ink Blot Test . . . OK, no sweat, I knew that. Boom! The first one up was a red smear! Blood! Blood! It had to be blood! But wait, I was smart, I had six hours of college psychology in night school. So I said, "Ah, that's a lipstick smear, like on a wine glass, you know, you're loading the dishwasher and it's on the edge of the glass your wife was drinking out of." Hmmm, the doc's taking notes. More ink blots. The Boom! This one was OBVIOUSLY two naked Africans, mating on a hollow log! But, wait, I was smart, I had six hours of college psychology in night school. So I said, "Ah, I see a hollow log, lots of ferns and plants, a jungle scene there." Hmmm, the doc's taking notes.

Finally, after more of this he finishes and clears me to leave. So, I say, "You know, I've never had a test like this. Can you give me a critique on how I did?" "Sure," he says, as he flips through his notes, "Like most of the other, normal crewmembers I've interviewed for this program, you've lied to me a lot. But you've shown imagination in your replies." Whoa! Did I get out of there in a hurry! No more questions for that guy. I just wanted to finish testing and go home.

James Bond and the Topless Bar Adventure

I was very fortunate to be handpicked by Colonel Doug Nelson to be one of the first eight crewmembers assigned to the SR-71 program. In May of 1965, all eight of us were to attend a 7-1/2-week-long course on the SR-71 at Lockheed's Skunk Works in Burbank, California. Guess who our instructors were going to be? Yes, none other than Kelly Johnson himself, and Ben Rich, the architect of the SR-71's inlet system. We were going to learn directly from the masters! During those weeks Kelly's chief engineers and designers were also to teach us the nuts and bolts. Since this was a "first," our goal was to

Early picture (1966–1967) of the SR-71 squadron briefing room. Front row (left to right) is John Storrie (the ultimate party animal!), Jim Watkins, and David Dempster. Looking directly at the camera is Phil Loignon, and on the right with his leg bent upward is Charlie Daubs. These were some of the initial cadre of SR-71 crews . . . best of the best! *David Dempster*

learn firsthand as much as we could about the Blackbird. After completing our training, we were to return to Beale and establish the SR-71 training program for the cadre of aircrews to follow.

The Beale wing commander, Colonel Nelson, called all eight of us into his office and briefed us on our trip to the Skunk Works. He instructed us to wear only civilian clothes, and to have cover stories ready, just in case someone asked what we did for a living. On the appointed day, we departed Beale and formed a miniconvoy down Highway 99 for Burbank. Can you imagine the thrill? Here we were, each of us feeling like James Bond, on a clandestine trip to Southern California, arriving at the Burbank Travel Lodge, and registering under assumed names.

Now you have to remember back in 1965, there was a phenomenon going on: the advent of topless bars. They were front-page news, and could only be found in Southern California. None of us had ever been to a topless bar. It just so happened that near our hotel was the Brew Mistress Beer Bar with a bright neon sign that said "Topless!" We all agreed to change into our jeans and head quickly in that direction. Just for a cold beer, of course!

The bar was arranged so that the girls served beers from an elevated platform behind the bar, directly in front of us, as we drank. Their topless attractions were swinging and swaying right before our eyes. There we were, feeling on top of the world—cover stories, aliases, secrets, cold beer, and topless girls—who could ask for more? Sierra Hotel! After a while the waitress delivered more beers and said to Tom Schmittou, "How long have you all been in the Air Force?" We were all caught totally off guard by her question. Tom thought for a second, and replied back, "What do you mean Air Force, I am not in the Air Force." The waitress came back immediately with, "Yes you are. You're all wearing those funny black Air Force watches that all the crews wear." She went on her way and we just looked at each other, dumbfounded, laughed loudly, and said, "What the hell, we're not James Bonds." All our cloak-and-dagger fantasies of becoming the next 007 faded instantly. From then on we relaxed and had a great time being just ordinary Air Force crewmembers.

Wagon Wheels and Hand Shakes

Years after I left the Blackbird Program, I would describe Kelly Johnson's Skunk Works to other military Research and Development (R&D) or aerospace industry personnel as an old-fashioned wagon wheel. Imagine a wagon wheel in your mind, with Kelly sitting in the hub and various disciplines of engineers located on the radiating spokes. All of them could walk around the outer diameter of the wheel and down the spokes. This was the organizational uniqueness of the Skunk Works in 1965. The management style proved extremely productive due to Kelly's technical genius and ability to solve problems.

We had access to some portions of the Skunk Works and other parts were off-limits; as an example, we knew nothing at that time about the D-21 drone program. In the areas where we had access, we observed rooms full of engineers working at their open desks and talking among themselves to solve design problems. Writing memos was discouraged. Instead, the hydraulic engineer with a fit problem would walk over to consult with an airframe engineer. If other disciplines were needed, they would be included. Solutions would evolve and the engineers would go back and do the design implementation.

When differing views would block a solution, engineers were free to walk down the spokes of this imaginary wheel to Kelly for discussion. He would listen, probe opinions with questions, and then if necessary, make decisions that would get everyone back to work and "on task."

What a system! What great results! His management system was years before the 1980s' total quality buzz words of Integrated Design Teams and the host of other "Dilbert-like" inventions.

Kelly Johnson just did it!

Our seven weeks in the Skunk Works during May and June 1965 was a great learning experience, leaving us feeling privileged to have witnessed this creativity. Not only did we have Kelly Johnson and Ben Rich themselves "at the chalkboard" teaching us about the "article," but also sharing stories of the development and challenges of getting this Mach 3-plus beast to fly. Of course, there were other Lockheed training instructors who gave us many hours of slides, lessons, and technical manual familiarity, but the "Kelly and Ben" show was the best of them all!

Later, at Beale, as I participated in the development of the ANS, I witnessed other efficiencies that were unique to the Skunk Works' ways in cutting red tape and delays. A test flight at Edwards would uncover some software glitch that would be duplicated on the simulator at Beale. Within hours, a conference call would be ongoing between such personnel as Denny White, the SPO (Systems Program Office) engineer in Dayton; Frank Dembroski, the Link software representative at Beale; Cecil Braeden in the Category II Test Force at Edwards AFB; Harvey Mitchell, a key ANS engineer at Nortronics; me, having just flown the problem in the simulator; and a Lockheed contact in Burbank. Solutions would be proposed and discussed; man-hours would be estimated; costs would be decided upon; and commitments would be made—and then authorization would be by verbal agreements only.

Imagine a $650,000 verbal handshake! Paper to follow!

Long after the problems had been solved and a software patch tested and put into use, an engineering change proposal (ECP) or contract change proposal (CCP) would make the necessary contract adjustments for the multitude of "fixes" that were done in real time. During my four-year involvement at Beale with this process, I witnessed commitments being met with honesty and integrity and no attempts at gouging Uncle Sam.

In my following 11 years in USAF acquisition management, and 13 in aerospace industry management, I participated in "hot button" quick reaction capability (QRC) modifications and other urgent "do-now" programs. But never again did I see the efficiency or speed of Kelly Johnson's amazing way of getting things done!

My First SR-71 Flight

My first flight in the Blackbird occurred on 19 April 1966 with John Storrie as my pilot. All of the pressure suits had not yet arrived at Beale, so until they did, we took turns wearing the few pressure suits we had. We made do by using other crewmember's pressure suits that approximated our body size. The wing commander, Colonel Nelson, and I were about the same size so I wore his suit for my first mission.

No one warned me about drinking too much liquid before the flight. I was so eager it probably wouldn't have mattered anyway. We launched and everything proceeded normal. Great, just like our practice missions in the simulator! About halfway through the mission, however, I began to get the urge to pee. Bad news! At this stage of the early Blackbird years, there was no relief method built into the pressure suits. A jug, fastened to the side of the cockpit, was there for use when flying at low altitudes. However, at 80,000 feet, we were not allowed to open our pressure suits. Opening up your suit at that altitude would be catastrophic if the cabin pressure failed, or you had to eject.

I told John about my growing need. He was unconcerned at this point and kept on humming and whistling. Now the urge was getting stronger and I mentioned it again. After a short while John calmly stated, "Well, Dave, it looks like you have two choices. Either hold it or pee in your suit . . . by the way, whose suit are you wearing today?" I laughed and told him it was Colonel Nelson's suit. That ended my problem—there was no way I was going to "let go" in Doug Nelson's suit!

The urine collection device (UCD) was basically a large condom made from hard rubber and held in position on your long underwear with Velcro. At the far end of the UCD, a plastic tube traveled inside the pressure suit, through a valve, to your lower leg pocket. The pocket contained a superabsorbent sponge to collect and hold urine. On the outside of the pressure suit, at about your left thigh level, was a zippered pocket. Inside the pocket was a valve device you lifted up and locked in the "open" position when you needed to urinate.

There was a definite technique to urinating *successfully* in the pressure suit . . . it's not as easy as you think. First, you had to inflate your suit to provide an outward pressure, then "open" up the valve. The most important step was next! As you opened the valve, it was *highly* recommended that you feel (sense) a flow of cool air rushing over your penis. This meant the air pressure was heading in the right direction and all connections were tightly sealed, otherwise potential disaster.

After that incident, I took the precaution of purposely dehydrating myself before every flight. It wasn't until several years later, after I had left the program, that all the pressure suits were finally modified with a urine collection device (UCD) that allowed crewmembers to relieve themselves without opening up the suit.

First SR-71 International Sortie

On 20 July 1967, Jim Watkins and I flew what we believe was the first international sortie flown in the SR-71. We were flying Blackbird #972 on a routine training mission called "Kitty 3." The route of flight took us east, with a loop back to our tanker for refueling; we would accelerate to Mach 3 heading toward the vicinity of Brownsville, Texas, then fly up along the Rio Grande border to San Diego, and up the Pacific Ocean coast until abeam an Oregon turn point, and then back into Beale.

A "loop" is a term Habus used to describe how many "hot" (supersonic) legs the mission included. After refueling to full tanks (80,000 pounds of gas) we could cruise at Mach 3 for around an hour or more, depending on what our fuel reserves (called "bingo" fuel) were to the next refueling track. That was considered one loop. If you topped off the tanks again, the next Mach 3 cruise leg would be a second loop.

While refueling, our primary navigation system, the ANS, stopped working. Normally, this malfunction would cause us to abort and fly back to Beale subsonic. However, at this time we were gearing up for the first overseas operational deployment with the SR-71 and flew every mission with this in mind—we were literally writing the rulebook. With that rationale, Jim and I thought, "What would we do if we were on an operational sortie in the middle of the South China Sea and found ourselves with the same problem?" So, with our backup attitude/heading system, magnetic compass, and TACAN, we decided to simulate reality and try flying the mission "as planned."

Tactical Air Navigation (TACAN), used exclusively by the military, is nothing more than VOR navigation with distance measuring included.

We finished refueling and began our climb on course with magnetic headings, my stopwatch timing between waypoints, and TACAN monitoring. The one thing we didn't fully compensate for was precession errors induced in our compasses by the acceleration to Mach 3. Thus, after cruising at Mach 3.2 for some time, we were puzzled by the strange radio call that we heard from Air Traffic Control (ATC) calling us, "Aspen 30, be advised you are leaving the State." What a strange radio call.

The explanation was that, somewhere over Arizona, we had strayed into Mexican airspace! We continued with our basic dead-reckoning navigational techniques and exited Mexico over Ensenada, about 75 miles south of San Diego. The rest of the flight was uneventful. Although we were mildly "chewed out" for our adventure, we proved that it was possible to use backup navigation in an emergency.

Tie-Cutting Ceremony

Throughout the history of the SR-71 program there has been a tie-cutting ceremony associated with each crewmember's first operational sortie. After successfully flying their first mission, taxiing into the hangar, and shutting down, the newly initiated crew would be met at the foot of the ladder by Chief Master Sergeant Bill Gornik, along with other detachment personnel. Crews knew to put a tie on before getting into the pressure suit, so it would be around their necks on landing, ready to be cut.

This is how the tradition began. It was 29 May 1968, and all the SR Detachment crews and officers were at the Kadena Officers' Club. First, we had dinner in the main dining room and were wearing coats and ties. After dinner we moved to the section of the club call the "stag bar." It was a place for men only. Here they could let their hair down, cuss and swear, drink as much as they liked, and swap flying stories. Be kids again! That night, besides the SR-71 crowd, the stag bar had its usual complement of other crewmembers—from B-52 and KC-135 tanker crews to fighter pilots based on Kadena. It was a big crowd and everyone was getting in the party spirit!

We were there to honor our wing commander, Colonel Bill Hayes, better known as the "White Tornado," who was finishing his first visit to the Detachment and about to return to Beale. As a going-away gift, we had all chipped in and bought Colonel Hayes a jacket and baseball cap. On the back of the jacket we had the words "HABU COMMANDER" embroidered along with his rank on the shoulders. The cap also read "HABU COMMANDER" and had the standard "scrambled eggs" embroidered on the bill. He gratefully received the gifts that evening.

We continued drinking and partying when suddenly, dressed in casual clothes, in walked three of our maintenance line chief master sergeants—Bill Gornik and two others. A great "Hurrah" went up from all of us and although our three new visitors had been drinking already, we wet them down with new ones immediately. The bond and camaraderie between Blackbird crewmembers and our maintenance personnel was so strong that this crashing of the Officers' Club was greeted with great enthusiasm!

Soon the booze was flowing freely, and everyone was feeling no pain. Chief Gornik found the jacket and hat we had given Colonel Hayes and decided to put them on. Well, once he put Colonel Hayes' jacket and hat on, he adopted the rank of colonel. You have to understand that outsiders in the stag bar had no idea who Bill Gornik was. In civilian clothes, you would assume he was an officer, unless you knew otherwise. Soon he had some young B-52 officers standing at attention and began chewing them out.

After having his fun impersonating an officer, and during the wee hours of the night, he took out his penknife and proceeded to cut our ties off right there and then! He collected the bottom half of the ties and the next day, andafter much sobering up, he attached a grommet in each of the tie pieces and mounted all of them on a long pole. From that day forward, every crewmember had his tie cut immediately upon landing from his first operational mission in the SR-71. A Habu tradition was born!

The tie-cutting ceremony that Bill Gornik started continued until the SR-71 was retired. In later years it was decided to display them prominently in our Habu tie board. You can see the crewmember's name, flight position, and date of his first operational mission. *Rich Graham*

The ties were later kept in a large-framed shadow box, with labels identifying the crewmember and the date of his first sortie. The shadow box, along with other squadron memorabilia, is currently on display in the SAC Museum in Omaha, Nebraska.

Nighttime in the Daytime

One 1967 afternoon, Jim and I took off from Beale, climbed and accelerated to Mach 3, and headed east on our mission profile. As we did, the approaching horizon was getting darker and darker, and Jim commented we were rapidly flying into nighttime.

Using the sun angle display from our ANS, I logged the time when the sun went below the horizon heading eastbound. It was dark. We flew on and then made a planned 180-degree turn back to the west. Unbelievably, we witnessed the sky getting lighter and so again, using the sun angle display, I logged the time when the sun came above the horizon heading westbound. We had outflown the setting sun as we headed westward at Mach 3.2 and after landing, we logged 20 minutes of nighttime!

During the next two weeks, however, we must have had three clarifying calls from the ladies running the Form 5 Flight Records section. How, they wanted to know, had we taken off in midafternoon, landed in late afternoon of the same day, and yet logged "night" time? We chuckled to ourselves, but patiently explained to them the surprise that had happened to us at Mach 3-plus. They understood, and our flight records stayed as submitted.

The Texas Cowboy and Standard Adiabatic Lapse Rates

Jim Watkins was a great pilot to be crewed with in the Blackbird. A Texas cowboy who raised horses in his off time, Jim loved, breathed, and lived for flying.

The tie-cutting ceremony was one of many traditions perpetuated by Blackbird crews. However, on a recent six-day goodwill visit to Moscow, a former SR-71 pilot, Lieutenant General Tom Keck, participated in a tradition that most U.S. aviators would find strange. The following appeared in the 27 August 2001 *Moscow Times.*

"Russian pilots swinging a senior U.S. Air Force official by the arms and legs might seem to be breaching international military etiquette, but Lieutenant General Thomas Keck took all this and more with good humor on his visits to Russian air force bases last week.

"On Wednesday, Keck became the first NATO serviceman to fly a Tu-22M3 Backfire strategic bomber, and dropped bombs on a test field, after which Russian pilots in Ryazan gave him a shot of vodka, then grabbed his arms and legs and swung him against the craft's landing gear in an initiation ritual they said is often inflicted on newcomers.

"'I was very impressed with everything from the beginning . . . from the ground crew preparing the aircraft, to the aviators in the sky, the ones who make it all happen,' the U.S. 8th Air Force commander told reporters after meeting Russian air force commander Anatoly Kornukov in Moscow last Friday.

"'When I landed I was introduced to your tradition of drinking vodka and the opportunity to touch my backside to the front tire of the nose gear of the bomber. It's an unusual tradition. It has been a very jam-packed five days but every minute has been worth it. The opportunity to see your units firsthand and fly your aircraft has been incredible, something I will never forget for the rest of my life,' Keck said.

"Commenting on his traditional initiation as a Russian strategic air force pilot, Keck said there were similar traditions back home in the U.S. 'Sometimes you get very wet being dumped in water, another tradition cuts your necktie off, occasionally, even a tail of your shirt is cut off and saved,' he said."

I can assure you, Habus would look forward to the shot of vodka, but being thrown against the landing gear after your first flight is not a tradition they would continue very long! I wonder if the Russians knew General Keck was a former SR-71 pilot, often flying reconnaissance sorties near their borders.

But, like his horses, he "felt" and handled them with cowboy common sense. Imagine checking out in the Blackbird, a World War II B-24 pilot who flew fighters, transports, KC-97 tankers, and KC-135 tankers at Beale. In the tanker, Jim was on the initial OXCART team and provided the air refueling support for the A-12s flying from the Ranch. Jim checked out in the SR-71 like a cowboy putting on an old familiar leather glove!

We were honored to be among the four SR-71 crews selected to deploy for the first time to Okinawa in March 1968. On 21 March, the first operational sortie flew and the crew encountered a double-engine flameout during descent to their tanker as they exited the target area. After refueling, they returned to Okinawa. A week later the second operational sortie flew, and again, with a different crew and different Blackbird, they encountered the same double-engine flameout at the start of their descent. They landed in Thailand due to the left generator not working. What was happening? Both planes checked out good on the ground after landing and we had lots of jawboning among ourselves and with Lockheed tech reps, with no conclusions.

Then, on 19 April 1968, Jim and I launched on the third operational sortie (the first for us and Crew Chief Technical Sergeant Bud Martin's #974). We zipped through the target area with no problems and began the start descent checklist. As Jim pulled the throttle back to the rpm setting called for in our procedures, we had a double-engine flameout. Excitement, adrenaline pumping, and we dropped like a rock into Northern Laos! Jim got both engines started around 30,000 feet, and we headed south. Our tanker, the real hero of this story, saw our rate of closure on him stop. He knew what had happened and headed north immediately, unprotected, into enemy territory and rendezvoused with us. Refueling with him, we headed back into Thailand and proceeded to our preplanned end refueling point.

Proud of #974's first Habu (operational) sortie are (left to right) Crew Chief Bud Martin, David Dempster, and Jim Watkins, pointing to the newly added Habu. Not only was it the plane's first Habu sortie, but Jim and David's as well. *David Dempster*

What to do now? We were scheduled to go back to the target area for another "hot loop." Over the intercom, I heard this commonsense cowboy say, "Dave, I think if when we start our descent, we hold a higher-than-normal rpm we can avoid the flameouts. Want to give it a try?" "Sure," I answered. We accelerated back to Mach 3-plus and on course into the target area. We eyeballed adding about 30 miles to the start descent range and when the time came, Jim's theory worked perfectly. No flameouts and a smooth descent.

What was the secret and why did this work? The answer turned out to be the way the engine's fuel controls were programmed. They used standard adiabatic lapse rates, which engineers all over the world assumed depicted the height of the tropopause and outside air temperatures at varying altitudes. WRONG! What we discovered was that in Southeast Asia, the tropopause (and magnificent thunderstorms we would look down on) could go as high as 65,000 feet, rather than the textbook 55,000 feet. Moreover, the air was much colder. Lockheed and Pratt & Whitney Co. eventually reprogrammed the fuel controls correctly and the problem went away. In the interim,

Jim Watkins congratulating David Dempster after their record-setting swearing-in ceremony at Mach 3. Each crewmember eventually had two pressure suits, one as the primary and the other as a backup suit in case excessive leakage was found during preflight. Each pressure suit and helmet cost around $125,000. *David Dempster*

however, all of the crews adopted the cowboy's technique and the flameout problems disappeared.

The day after this flight Jim, Technical Sergean. Bud Martin, and I proudly stenciled the first Habu on the side of #974, which went on to be so successful that it was dubbed "Ichiban," the "number one" Habu in the 1968 period on Okinawa.

A Never-Before-Published First in the Squadron

For many years I held a reserve commission in the Air Force, but was selected for a regular commission in 1969. Jim and I planned that my swearing in would take place during an SR-71 flight. We flew a training sortie from Beale, and in the last few quiet moments before our start descent point, we each took out a small American flag, plus copies of the Oath of Office, and Jim swore me in over the intercom.

On the ground we repeated the Oath of Office, but in my recording AF Form 133, which was part of my official military records, we typed in, "Sworn to and subscribed before me, at 2026 (GMT), in a Strategic Air Command SR-71, aircraft Number 61-7967, while flying more than three times the speed of sound (Mach 3+), this Fifth day of February 1969, over Caliente, Nevada. Signature: James L. Watkins."

Our 1st SRS thought this would make a great "First for the 1st" story in the Air Force Times newspaper. A base photographer met us on landing and took pictures of Jim and me shaking hands, wearing our pressure suits. The picture and story were sent to the *Air Force Times*. It was never published! Finally, I called them on the phone and found the editor who knew all about it and why. "Oh," he said, "You sent us a handshake picture and we get so many of those they're boring, so we didn't run the story." Geeeeze! We couldn't believe it!

CHAPTER FOUR

Major General (Ret) Pat Halloran

If there is ever a true Godfather of the SR-71 program, it's Pat Halloran. He's done it all and done it well—a highly respected individual, not only in the Blackbird program, but the entire Air Force. The mere mention of his name in conversation evokes comments ranging from "What a neat guy" to "Outstanding gentleman."

Pat Halloran (top row, second from left) is congratulated for his flight in the U-2 over Cuba. He had just taken the 1,000,000th foot of film over Cuba in the U-2 behind him. Colonel Desportes is to his right and technical representative Jim Combs to his left. In white uniforms are Chief Master Sergeants Burns and Hayes, with two assistants kneeling. The plane's crew chief is kneeling in the center. Picture taken at Del Rio, Texas, in 1963. *Pat Halloran*

When I arrived at Beale in the summer of 1974, Colonel Halloran was the 9th Wing Commander. To put his outstanding military leadership in perspective, he achieved the position of "bachelor" Wing Commander, an extremely rare event. As a bachelor, you would have to be held in high regard by your superiors to be chosen as an SAC Wing Commander.

I am sure the current philosophy has changed, but back in the1970s the Air Force selected married wing commanders. It was a prerequisite. The theory was that you got two for the price of one. It was never in print, but the wing commander's wife was "expected" to head up all the ladies' organizations on base and encourage other wives to participate. It was a demonstration of commitment . . . a subtle intimidation factor on an officer's promotion potential. As the "career woman" began to get her roots into American society, fewer demands were placed on wing commanders' wives to conform. My wife walked her own path, but still felt obligated to fill certain roles. She says I still owe her big-time for this!

—Rich Graham

Individuals chosen for the SR-71 program came from many backgrounds; however, in the early days, this was not the case. SAC was protective in keeping its own officers, so a large majority of the initial crewmembers came from B-47s, B-58s, and U-2 crews. SAC had a known product, trained, and, it was hoped, indoctrinated in SAC's operational methods. Once the initial crews began departing the SR-71 program, their replacements were being selected from other Air Force sources. When I entered the program, Blackbird crewmembers were being selected from practically every plane in the Air Force. General Halloran fit the role as a former U-2 pilot. He knew the reconnaissance operation backward and forward. The perfect candidate for 9th Wing Commander at Beale.

General Halloran was raised in Minnesota and received his Air Force wings and commission through the Aviation Cadet program in 1950. He spent his first seven years in the Air Force flying F-84 jet fighters, including 100 combat missions in Korea. He was selected in the first group of pilots to fly the U-2 aircraft. He flew it for almost nine years, accumulating over 1,600 hours in the plane. From there General Halloran moved to the SR-71 and flew it for over eight years, accumulating over 600 hours. He flew missions over Vietnam in both the U-2 and the SR-71, a distinction few pilots can claim.

His next eight years were spent in command and staff positions in various headquarters, ending in the Office of the Joint Chiefs of Staff, in the Pentagon. He retired in 1983 as Major General, with over 8,000 hours of flying time and 34 years of service. He considers his best job in the Air Force as that of being the commander of the SR-71s. He lives in Colorado Springs, where he is active in the Experimental Aircraft Association (EAA). He has owned several experimental airplanes and has flown a variety of replica vintage racing airplanes for air show displays.

I asked General Halloran to focus on the early days of the program and tell his stories.

Habu 101

I guess I should start by defining Habu for those new to the subject. Habu (ha'-boo) is the unofficial nickname of the SR-71 Blackbird, and is also applied to those who flew it. It was bestowed on the program by some unknowns on Okinawa when they first observed the Blackbird at Kadena back in the late 1960s. The real Habu is a deadly black snake, native to Okinawa. One story goes that the view of the extremely long black nose of the SR-71, slowly creeping out of our special hangars at Kadena, reminded them of the snake. The name stuck and has never changed. Being involved with the beginning of the SR-71 program at Beale AFB, I thought I might have some special insights and memories to relate.

Assemble the Troops

I was fortunate to have a very special relationship to the Blackbird. Not only was I one of a select few chosen to be in the initial cadre of pilots for the original Strategic Air Command (SAC) SR-71 crew force, but I had come from an equally select group who flew its predecessor, the original Lockheed U-2. It was the shooting down of Francis Gary Powers in a U-2, on 1 May 1960, over Sverdlovsk, USSR, that triggered the decision to develop and build the Blackbird family. My nine-year background as one of the original Air Force pilots in the U-2 put me in the unique position to understand firsthand its operational limitations, allowing me to appreciate the challenge involved in finding a replacement that could survive modern aircraft defenses. The dramatic solution was offered by the same gentleman who had developed the U-2—Mr. Kelly Johnson, from Lockheed's famous Skunk Works facility.

When it came time for initial crew selection into the SR-71 program, the man selected to be our new wing commander, Colonel (later Major General) Doug Nelson, initiated a screening process. Like the U-2s, it was going to be a SAC program, and he had carte blanche to pick from SAC's professional crew force. Most of his attention was focused on two groups of people. One group was the crew force of SAC's B-58 Hustler supersonic bomber, from which both pilots and navigators were selected. The other group was the U-2 crew force, all pilots, of which I was a part. Ten of us were chosen from the U-2 program in 1965 to transfer to Beale AFB, California, to become pilots in the initial cadre of crewmembers. I was the senior U-2 crewmember selected and was the first of that group to check out in the SR-71. These two primary crew sources proved an ideal combination. Those of us from the U-2 brought experience in high altitude, pressure suit flying, and a thorough knowledge of the reconnaissance mission. The B-58 crews brought experience in supersonic flight in a single-pilot, high-performance, complicated aircraft that demanded the very best in crew coordination and systems knowledge.

One notable exception to the route followed by those of us who came to the program from the U-2 was a superb pilot, Lieutenant Colonel (later Brigadier General) Ray Haupt. I first met Ray back in 1950 when I joined the 31st Fighter Wing at Turner AFB, Georgia, my first assignment upon graduation from pilot training. We later joined forces again as pilots in the initial U-2 program, where we worked together on several special projects. He had quietly disappeared from our U-2 base back in the early 1960s and wasn't heard from for years. It turns out that he had been selected by the Air Force to participate in the very early flight development of the Blackbird program for both the A-12 and SR-71 aircraft, at Area 51. In that capacity, he joined a small group of test pilots who did the scary work of helping Lockheed achieve the aircraft's design performance goals. A long and frustrating test endeavor. Ray was picked to be the first crew input to Beale directly from his work at Area 51. Because of his past experience in the Blackbird, he served as an initial instructor to start the training program.

The first SR-71 was delivered to the Air Force in January of 1966. It was a two-seat trainer, and was flown into Beale AFB by our new wing commander, Colonel Doug Nelson in the front seat, with Ray Haupt in the rear. Along with a large group of future crewmembers and interested onlookers, I had my first look at the most awesome airplane I had ever seen. I drew comfort that my good friend Ray was bringing with him a bucketful of experience that he would soon impart to us.

Pick a Number

Doug Nelson's initial crew sequence allocation had Ray projected as crew number 01, followed, by date of rank, with the four highly qualified B-58 pilots, Gray Sowers, Al Hichew, Pete Collins, and John Storrie (later major general). Soon after arrival at Beale, Ray was promoted to colonel and moved to be a squadron commander in the program. Doug Nelson replaced Ray with John Storrie as the pilot for crew 01. John, along with his original back-seater, Dave Dempster, had been assigned the additional duty of running our new simulators, and was the first of the B-58 group to actually arrive at Beale. John's old crew number, 05, was then assigned to Major (later Lieutenant General) Bill Campbell. Bill was a graduate from the Air Force Test Pilot School, and was probably the finest, smartest pilot I ever knew. I followed Bill with crew number 06, and was the first of the new U-2 inputs to check out in the plane.

Those of us who came from the U-2 program were delighted to find not only a simulator for the SR-71, but also a two-seat pilot trainer version of the aircraft. We had none of those luxuries in the U-2. We went through a very basic, squadron-level ground school and then got in the airplane (solo) and flew it. It was 15 years after the U-2 program started before the Air Force bought a two-seat trainer. We had paid dearly for that delay. Many aircraft were destroyed in early transition training, including one tragic fatality on a first flight.

Pat Halloran's retirement as major general in the Pentagon, January 1983. Congratulating him is General Jerry O'Mally (left), who presided over the ceremony. Jerry flew the very first SR-71 operational sortie out of Kadena. Destined to be the next chief of staff of the Air Force, Jerry was killed with his wife in a T-39 crash in April 1985 on the way to a speaking engagement. *Pat Halloran*

The initial block of four B-58 pilots, along with the first four B-58 navigator-bombardiers (Coz Mallozzi, Butch Sheffield, Tom Schmittou, and David Dempster), spent 7-1/2 weeks attending preliminary ground school at Burbank with Lockheed personnel. Doug Nelson and Ray Haupt also attended. After ground school, the crews were then sent on temporary duty (TDY) to Edwards AFB to get a checkout in the plane—a difficult objective since there were few airplanes available. A side trip to Area 51, to fly the A-12 two-pilot trainer, was provided to several of the B-58 pilots. At this time, Ray was the one and only IP in the system. John Storrie and David Dempster were assigned the job of setting up the Crew Training School's classroom and integrated simulator program, so they proceeded directly to Beale, while the others flew at Edwards.

Gray Sowers and Al Hichew were the first pilots from that group to fly the airplane. Upon arrival at Beale, Ray upgraded Sowers and Hichew to IP status, and they became our first assigned IPs in the new SR-71 crew force. Sowers gave me my first flight in the SR-71B model trainer aircraft on 6 May 1966.

Five flights later, I completed a standardization check flight with Hichew. I was then ready for my first crew sortie in the SR-71A model with my backseater, Mort Jarvis. Mort had been a B-52 radar navigator and made a very smooth, successful transition into the SR-71. After a very limited number of sorties we also became an instructor crew. I then frequently flew in the B-model trainer aircraft checking out follow-on pilots. When a program first starts, it's amazing how fast you can become an instructor in the system with very little experience! Mort and I flew together as Crew 06, and later as Chief Standardization Crew, until I moved from the crew force and took over as commander of the 1st SRS.

Kelly, Our Father, Who Art in Burbank . . .

While in the U-2 program in the 1950s and 1960s, I served as a standardization check pilot. I was therefore frequently involved in the development and writing of our pilot flight handbook procedures for operating the U-2 and its equipment. This necessitated my visiting selected parts of the Skunk Works, and it provided me an early opportunity to see and make the acquaintance of Kelly Johnson and many of his pilots and superb engineers. The chance to interact with Skunk Work personnel continued once I arrived in the SR-71 program, as I assumed many of the same duties in the Standardization Division for that program. That gave me a 17-year window of opportunity observing the Skunk Works operations close-up.

With that background, people would frequently ask me if I knew Kelly Johnson. When asked if I "know" someone I always turn the question around in my mind and ask myself, "Does he know me?" By that I mean if he saw me in public would he call me by name? With that caveat, I am proud and happy to say, "Yes, I knew Kelly Johnson." I have spent many hours in both a professional and social atmosphere with him. Both were equally rewarding for me. I have listened in awe, while seated in his office, as he briefed several of us on the special projects he envisioned, some of which never came to fruition. He spoke of the frustrations he endured in making the Blackbird "work," and of trying to get the Department of Defense (DoD) to get off the dime on some petty requirement that didn't make much sense to him, but was delaying efforts to "do it his way." Another problem that he fought in both the U-2 and SR-71 programs was trying to keep down the weight of the planes. There was a big penalty in altitude for every unnecessary pound of weight we carried. I'm surprised he never asked his pilots to diet!

I have seen him as a formal and an informal speaker at social functions at both Del Rio, in the early U-2 program, and at Beale during our difficult, early times there. On two occasions, one at each location, he was guest speaker at dining-in banquets when we had a major aircraft accident resulting in the loss of both aircraft and, in one case, one of the pilots. It was an interesting sight to see the local commander scurrying out of the door with Kelly close on his coattails. He could quickly transition from the successful executive genius he was, to a very concerned member of the investigation team. That concern was not just for his airplane, but primarily for its crewmembers.

He kindly accepted our invitation to be the guest speaker at one of our early Blackbird reunions at Reno, Nevada. Several times at Beale he joined us for special dinners at the Officers' Club, including farewell functions for some of our early commanders. Kelly's wife frequently accompanied him. His impromptu visits to Beale in the company's Lockheed Jetstar were always a thrill for the crew force. He would usually stop by the squadrons and offer words of encouragement to the crews, and answer our stupid questions with the patience of a good teacher. To be in the crew force of either airplane when Kelly was still running the programs made you feel you were participating in a very special segment of aviation history.

Speed record crews at Farnborough International Air Show, September 1974, New York to London in 1 hour, 55 minutes. Top row from left to right: William Reynolds, Noel Widdifield (RSO NY-London), Jim Sullivan (pilot NY-London), Pat Halloran, Jim Shelton, Buck Adams (pilot London-LA), Bill Machorek (RSO London-LA), Ernest Polejewski. Bottom row left to right: Clyde Richards, Shane Whitmore, Leland Haynes (crew chief), Tommy Walton, Paul Hutto, Craig Meredith, Gerald Boyle, Roger Long. ***Pat Halloran***

He was always a very gracious and considerate individual when talking or working with our blue-suiters. However, there were frequent stories as to his short fuse with those in his employ at the Skunk Works when things didn't move fast enough for him. If he felt the occasion demanded it, he could show some of that side of his character with us. He gave me hell once, when I was the 9th SRW commander, for having Jim Sullivan and Noel Widdifield do an in-flight refueling in the middle of their record-breaking flight from New York to London in September 1974. Kelly wanted that record flight to be as pure as possible and an air refueling didn't fit into his vision of how the flight should proceed. Later, however, he was the first to tell me that it would have been extremely dicey not to do it my way, due to the weather in England. Of course, that conciliatory statement came *after* Jim set the record. Once the speed record was set, Kelly hosted our team to a tremendous dinner in London. He was obviously delighted, as we all were, to have finally had the chance to show the world what his marvelous creation could do.

In the Driver's Seat

Considering the time frame in which I checked out and flew the SR-71 in training and operations, I had an amazingly easy time of it. Things usually worked as designed and advertised. For all practical purposes, Mort and I had no real crises, no really close calls, nor any problems that put us into the emergency part of the checklist with any regularity. We had the usual unstarts (about four to five per flight in the early days), the normal fuel transfer screw-ups, and the fast learning curve on what was the real impact of things like a constant speed drive (CSD) failure. We had a couple of emergency landings at alternate airfields (who didn't?), and we were greeted with suspicion when we landed at Ellsworth AFB, South Dakota, two weeks in a row. We marveled at the ease of flying over downtown Hanoi, and we blessed Kelly for the splendid equipment that made it so. I compared this favorably with the unknown elements at play when I was making such flights over Cuba in the U-2 some years earlier.

Mort and I had some interesting incidents, but nothing really too scary. I remember one training flight when, just as I released the brakes to taxi from the hangar, my helmet face plate fractured into a thousand tiny glass segments as the heater element apparently malfunctioned. That would have been interesting 30 minutes later! On one occasion, we were in the holding pattern at 20,000 feet, awaiting clearance to begin our instrument approach from "Paradise" holding fix into Beale, when there was a very loud bang and a tremendous jolt throughout the airplane. For an instant I thought we had hit something, but all instrument indications were normal and the aircraft was flying smoothly. I pushed my periscope up to take a look at the aft sections of the plane and discovered that my drag 'chute doors were open. Our 'chute had mysteriously deployed at 250 knots and, as designed, departed the aircraft when a shear pin broke.

Another time, returning from a night transition flight very early in our training, we endured a number of unstarts during the descent (normal in

Centered at the front and top of the pilot's canopy was a periscope used for looking aft. By pushing the 3-inch periscope upward into the airstream, its 30-degree cone of view permitted the pilot to see both rudders and everything in between. We used the periscope to align each rudder individually, check for possible engine fires, confirm fuel dumping and termination, and to ensure we were not producing a visible contrail.

those days), resulting in an engine flameout. While trying to get the engine started, we experienced a "low tank pressure" warning light, indicating that further descent could possibly collapse the internal fuel tanks. We were frantically trying to maintain altitude to prevent this possibility, while still building enough airspeed to get the engine started. I forget how we managed that handful, but it all obviously worked for us, as Mort handled what seemed to be a dozen emergency checklists at the same time.

The SR-71's six fuel tanks used nitrogen gas to render the space above the heated fuel inert to prevent ignition. Gaseous nitrogen also provided positive pressure in each tank, preventing them from collapsing during descents from high altitudes. A very rapid descent could create too great a pressure change for the nitrogen to keep up with, illuminating the low tank pressure warning light.

I had a great time flying the B-model trainer with new pilots as they came into the program. Every flight was instructional for me as I taught the new guy the ins and outs of flying the Blackbird. It was fun to work the ANS navigation system in the trainer while still having a nice view from the elevated rear seat, unlike the RSO seat position in the A model. The view from the rear became far less enjoyable in the landing pattern, particularly on final approach, as the runway totally disappeared from view several miles out. Depth perception for landing was a far bigger challenge from the rear seat than the front.

Into the Frying Pan

The Yom Kippur War in 1973 was the first opportunity the SR community had to demonstrate a capability that Kelly Johnson held dear. This was to fly overseas operational missions *from* the continental United States and return. I was the 9th SRW commander when I received a call from Lieutenant General Bill Pitts, commander of 15th Air Force, with an alerting message that we were to be given the mission to perform reconnaissance flights over the areas of the conflict in the Middle East. Mission plans were already inbound to our Beale planning staff from the SAC Reconnaissance Center (SRC) at Offutt AFB, Nebraska.

A lot of activity was going on up and down the flight line at Beale. Maintenance was working feverishly getting planes ready, the crews were gathering at the squadron to plan and ask questions about something that had never been done before, and mission planners were busily trying to put it all together. This was to be a very big "first" for the unit and I prevailed on General Pitts to allow me to be the detachment commander. I felt the entire

The command and control of the SR-71 was extensive compared to most Air Force aircraft. The operational control began at the Joint Reconnaissance Center (JRC) in the Pentagon. The JRC obtained approval for all our operational flights at the State Department level and monitored them from takeoff until landing. It also determined the threat analysis for every mission and integrated other political factors, finally arriving at a numerical risk assessment number, deciding whether the mission should be flown or not.

The SRC at Offutt AFB was the unit our mission planners, commanders at Beale, and the detachments directly worked with in coordinating missions. SRC was the "execution" authority (go/no-go) for all of our operational reconnaissance missions. Global weather forecasts at Offutt AFB helped the Dets determine which suite of sensors would be used for specific target areas.

future of the SR-71 program could rest on the successful outcome of these very-high-level missions and I wanted to be in charge, and needed to be on the scene. General Pitts agreed with my request.

The plan was to launch the SR-71 from Beale, fly the operational mission, and land at RAF Mildenhall in England. We launched our first support package to RAF Mildenhall at midnight of the same day of the alert. Our KC-135Q was filled with minimal spare parts, maintenance, and operations personnel . . . including me. We were to expect the arrival of three SR-71s within 48 hours.

Upon arrival at RAF Mildenhall, we were a very tired and ragged bunch from 36 hours of intense duty. My first task upon arrival was to brief the British Minister of Defense (MoD) in London on our tasking and show him some of our routes. However, as I prepared to take my briefing to London, I received a call from SAC headquarters, advising that the British government had reversed its position. The British were denying us permission to operate out of their country into such a sensitive and unstable area as the Middle East. We were directed to immediately refuel our tanker, reload everyone and everything, and proceed back to the United States and prepare to operate from a forward base at Griffiss AFB, New York. It was the shortest TDY in the history of the 9th Wing!

By the time our exhausted group arrived at Griffiss, the SR-71s had already beaten us there. A small Palmdale test force team that happened to already be in place at Griffiss for an unrelated SR-71 project had initially taken care of them. Another advance support party from Beale had also arrived to begin setting up operations under the experienced leadership of Lieutenant Colonel Tom Estes, my operations officer.

This was going to be the kind of mission that Kelly had always hoped to show the world. A mission that demonstrated we didn't need forward operating bases (nor the money from Congress to prepare them) in order to perform our missions halfway around the world. Of course, it would take many tankers to support these long-range operations, but that was expected and an acceptable cost of doing business.

I made a "contract" with SRC about the amount of lead-time we required for tasking before a mission. Mission planning always included crew participation, and once that was completed, the crew still needed adequate crew rest before the flight. With takeoffs around 0200 hours, crew rest was going to be difficult, but sacrosanct. I also wanted it understood by everyone in the tasking chain that these were going to be very long, multirefueled missions, under the scrutiny of everyone from the president on down. Success was mandatory! I wanted to ensure we had the common sense to "fight like we trained." No shortcuts. This was fine with everyone. We did receive several mission taskings that incorporated the adequate lead-time we needed. However, the missions were canceled before takeoff time.

One day, after the agreed upon cut-off time for tasking had long since passed, an urgent call came to me from Colonel Ray Britton at SRC. The president had just been briefed on a critical mission that was needed and he had agreed with the powers that be to task it. Unfortunately, by the time the word got to us our crews had long since dispersed and were kicking back, doing things crews normally do while off duty. I was very unhappy to be given this tasking, but since we still had not flown our first mission, and this one was coming from the very top, I agreed we would take it on. Big mistake!

By the time we rounded up the crews and got them down for mission planning, we were already well into their mandatory crew rest time, yet they still had several hours of mission preparation to accomplish. They would only have had a couple of hours for crew rest with probably little or no sleep under these conditions. I spoke to each of the crews involved, trying to feel out their concerns with this short-notice tasking. It was obvious that they were so energized that they would have forfeited all crew rest. It was also very obvious that we had just pushed flying safety out the back door and were about to expose these crews to a totally unacceptable situation.

These were the longest operational missions we had ever attempted to fly, including more air refuelings than the crews had ever experienced before, and into a totally unknown operational environment. After reviewing the timetables again, I decided I had to bite the bullet and declare the mission a "no-go." I very reluctantly called Colonel Britton back at SRC and informed him that I was canceling the mission for safety considerations. There was a loud silence on the other end of the line. He cried, "You can't do that! It's already been approved at the White House." I replied that I understood all that, but it was still my call, as the on-scene commander, to cancel the mission for safety reasons. He said he would get back to me shortly. Shortly was right!

In about three minutes the telephone rang and General Meyers, the four-star commander in chief of SAC (CINCSAC) was on the other end. I'll never forget his first chilling comment. It was, "Halloran (that's always a bad start), tell me once again why you think you are in a position to cancel an operational sortie, of national significance, that has been briefed all the way to the White House." I guess I had two thoughts when he finished. First, I knew I was fired. Second, and more important, was that I was pissed off for being put into this position by the incompetence of his own SRC staff that knew we weren't supposed to be operating this way.

The acronym "CINC" (pronounced like "sink") stood for commander in chief. Thus, the commander in chief of Strategic Air Command would be abbreviated as CINCSAC, and pronounced like "sink sack."

He listened quietly while I gave him about a 10-minute detailed review of what our initial agreement had been with *his* headquarters. I gave him the sequence of what had happened during the past couple of hours, and my ultimate conclusion that what our crews were being asked to do, in a peacetime environment, was absolutely foolhardy. He was quiet for a moment and then said, "OK, Pat (that sounded better), I understand your position. We'll get back with you in a few minutes." Within a few minutes Ray called back and said that the mission was canceled and to expect the same tasking the next day. We all breathed a sigh of relief.

The next day we kicked off the first in a series of extremely successful operations, proving that the SR-71 could indeed perform those missions from the continental United States and do them safely, effectively, and within our well-established and tested operating rules. Jim Shelton and Gary Coleman flew that first sortie, with Al Joersz and John Fuller as backup crew. The flight was over 11 hours in duration and was the longest operational sortie ever flown to that date. In all, nine missions were flown from the East Coast to the Middle East; the spare aircraft was never needed. It was a great testimonial to our superb maintenance personnel, without whom none of us could have enjoyed the unmatched success of the SR-71 program. (P.S. I wasn't fired!)

Flying the Blackbird was *the* absolute high point in my 34-year military aviation career. I owe a lot to Kelly Johnson for the 17 years I was able to spend in the cockpits of his two favorite airplanes—the U-2 and SR-71. They were both magnificent, state-of-the-art machines that blended performance with beauty. Each, in its own way, outperformed every plane of its time, and did so while performing an operational mission that demanded the ultimate in design, engineering, maintenance, and flight skills. It all began with Kelly Johnson . . . the rest of us were just along for a wonderful ride.

CHAPTER FIVE

Lieutenant Colonel (Ret) Tony Bevacqua
Major (Ret) Jerry Crew
Lieutenant Colonel (Ret) Jim Kogler

Tony Bevacqua flew with two RSOs during his time in the SR-71: Jerry Crew and Jim Kogler. The first story is told by Tony, the second by Jerry, and the third by both Tony and Jim.

Tony Bevacqua, a high school graduate and son of a Sicilian immigrant, was born in Cleveland, Ohio; he enlisted in the Air Force on 29 February 1952 to avoid the Army draft. At that time, to get into pilot training, two years of college was the minimum requirement. Basic training was at Sampson AFB, New York. The day of the physical, they stopped everything

Tony Bevacqua, left, and Jim Kogler. The silver-colored pressure suits went through many transformations over the years. The next suit was all white in color, but created a tremendous amount of glare in the cockpit at 80,000 feet. To reduce glare they went to a dark brown suit for several years, then finally settled on the yellowish-gold color currently in use by the U-2 crews. *Tony Bevacqua*

for an announcement. "The Air Force needs pilots and navigators. Minimum requirement is high school graduation." In January 1953, Tony began the Aviation Cadet Pilot Training Program, Class 54-G, at Lackland AFB, Texas. After multiple moves and flying a variety of aircraft, Tony received his wings and commission on 14 April 1954.

Tony's first assignment was to Turner AFB, Georgia, to fly F-84F fighter-bombers. Turns out he was in the same squadron as Frank (Francis Gary) Powers, and later, rented a house with Frank and two other squadron members. While stationed there, Tony was asked, and volunteered to go into the U-2 program, although at the time, no mention of aircraft designation was made. In early 1957, he was assigned to "The Ranch" (now known as Area 51), to check out and instruct others in the U-2. When six U-2s were built, they were flown in loose formation in June 1957 to Laughlin AFB, Texas.

Tony flew U-2 missions from Ramey AFB, Puerto Rico; Eielson AFB, Alaska; Buenos Aires, Argentina; Upper Heyford, England; RAAF Laverton, Australia; Barksdale AFB, Louisiana (Cuba flights); Bien Hoa, South Vietnam; and Allbrook AFB, Panama Canal. In June 1963, the entire wing was moved to Davis-Monthan AFB, Arizona. In July 1965, Tony departed for Air Command and Staff College and arrived at Beale AFB a year later to fly the SR-71. Tony retired 31 March 1973 at Beale AFB.

Tony remained in the Beale AFB area after retirement and was (and still is) a key player in maintaining the outstanding civilian and military relationship between the local community and the base. As head of the Beale Military Liaison Committee (BMLC), Tony has kept the local community involved in Beale activities. When I was the wing commander, I thoroughly enjoyed working with Tony and the BMLC to build better relations.

Tony first flew with the RSO, Major Jerry Crew. As a farm boy, Jerry Crew entered the Air Force from ROTC at Iowa State University, graduating in 1956. After finishing navigator training in 1957 at Harlingen, Texas, and bombardier training in 1958 at Mather AFB, California, he was assigned to the 96th Bomb Wing at Dyess AFB, Texas, as a navigator in the B-47. Jerry really enjoyed flying as a navigator (especially in the B-47, as the navigator was the king) and decided to make the Air Force a career.

Knowing pilots run the Air Force, Jerry applied for pilot training. Well, something called a "spot promotion" (reserved for select crewmembers flying SAC bombers) got in the way, so he decided to pass on flight school. In 1963 he was sent to fly B-52 G bombers at Griffiss AFB, New York, for two years and then on to Air Command and Staff College in Alabama. That's when Jerry first became aware of the SR-71 Blackbird. He didn't like the B-52 and was about to return to the bird after school. He contacted his former B-47 pilot, who was assigned to the personnel department at SAC Headquarters. His friend, grateful for Jerry's earlier decision to remain a navigator, pulled a few strings and had orders cut for B-52s at Beale AFB. At that time, entry into the SR-71 program was by invitation only. His friend at SAC told Jerry not to report to the B-52 Squadron at Beale AFB, but to request an interview with Colonel Doug Nelson, the 9th SRW commander. The interview went well, and Jerry flew the SR-71s from 1966 to 1969.

Little did Jerry know that his decision to turn down pilot training was instrumental in his flying in the back seat of the Blackbird! If he had accepted pilot training, Jerry says he would have never qualified for the front seat in the Blackbird. After 308 hours in the SR-71 and an unplanned medical retirement, Jerry is now known as the "World's Fastest Active Farmer."

Lieutenant Colonel (Ret) Jim Kogler enlisted in the Air Force in 1952 at the age of 19. He applied for and was accepted into navigator training. Jim says, "I was always told I was too smart to become a pilot!" After training he became a B-26 bombardier and was assigned to Langley AFB, Virginia. He awaited orders to Korea, but the war ended, and he was assigned to Larson AFB, Washington, as a C-124 navigator. Little did Jim know that flying the C-124 ("Old Shakey") would help him out later as an RSO in the SR-71. He always computed the dead-reckoning (DR) navigation at 3 miles per minute in the C-124, and said it was an easy adjustment to go to 30 miles per minute in the Blackbird. Next, Jim spent over four years at Forbes AFB, Kansas, in B-47s. From 1960 to 1967 he was at Robins AFB, Georgia, as a radar navigator on B-52s. He joined the SR-71 program in 1967, and flew 568 hours in the Blackbird, until he retired at Beale AFB in 1973.

From U-2 to SR-71

By Tony Bevacqua

In the early spring of 1965, while flying the U-2 in the 4080th SRW, Davis-Monthan AFB, Arizona, I was notified that I had a one-year assignment to the Air Force's Air Command and Staff College (ACSC) at Maxwell AFB, Alabama, starting in August. I was at the peak of my flying career and thoroughly enjoying the U-2—*I did not want to go!* However, after trying very hard to get a waiver, I saw it was no use trying to avoid the inevitable.

I was very close to the 2,000-hour mark in the U-2, and wanted to achieve this milestone before leaving. As it got closer to August, they stopped scheduling me to fly the U-2. According to operations, I had 1,996 hours. I pulled out my flight records and counted 2,002 hours!!! Anyway, we left Davis-Monthan AFB in July after one helluva time trying to sell my house myself. The housing market at the time was very depressed, and I ended up selling it to an incoming U-2 pilot, Robert Hickman, who I believe had seven children. (He ended up crashing in Bolivia, on a flight from Davis-Monthan. Apparently he had a heart attack at cruising altitude, on autopilot, while heading south.)

Everyone's hero, movie star legend John Wayne, shaking Tony's hand in the U-2 Squadron at Laughlin AFB, Texas, around 1958. John Wayne was there to film the epic Texas movie, *The Alamo*. Behind John are his two sons, Patrick and Mike Wayne. *Tony Bevacqua*

In February 1985, *The Air Force Times* wrote an article on Tony, claiming that he might have been the youngest Air Force pilot to check out in the U-2, and also the youngest U-2 Instructor Pilot. Tony checked out in the aircraft on 14 March 1957 at age 24 and 5 months, and became an IP two months later, in May 1957. Can anyone beat that record?

Colonel DesPortes, commander of the 4080th Wing at Davis-Monthan, was transferred to Beale when the SR-71 program was first started. He and I got along very well, and he asked if I was interested in flying the Blackbird. I immediately replied, "Hell yes, Sir!" He said, "You've got it." While at Maxwell, around April 1966, I called him just to confirm that I still had a slot to train in the SR-71. He said that all was well and I was definitely coming to Beale. Trouble was, I hadn't received any orders for Beale yet, and most of my classmates already had their next assignments. The good part of that was, I didn't have orders to something else. When it was six to eight weeks before graduation, I started to get concerned about still not having orders, so I called him again. This time he must have gotten on someone's butt, because I immediately received my orders to Beale. Relief!

I arrived at Beale on 19 July 1966, and was fortunate to get housing immediately. I started my SR-71 ground school and simulator training soon after the T-38 checkout phase. My first flight in the SR came in November, with John Storrie as my IP. It was a good flight and seemed as if I could do no wrong. My second flight, however, wasn't until January 1967. Fog was the enemy! That winter had more days of fog than I can ever remember in my 35 years of living there. They call it the California valley fog; it occurs during the winter months and drifts as far north as Beale, where it stays for days on end. The wing was desperately trying to maintain the current rating for the few SR-71 crews who were checked out, and even that was tough to do.

The unclassified name for the SR-71 program was "Senior Crown." Only those personnel with the "Senior Crown" security clearance had access to our program. Coming from the U-2 program (called "Senior Year") into the SR-71, I found the security very strict, but nowhere as tight as when I was in the U-2 during the early years (1956–1960 particularly). Compared to the U-2 program, the SR-71 training was excellent. However, you have to remember that we had no U-2 simulator or training aircraft in which to practice! I much preferred the SR-71's full pressure suit versus the U-2 partial pressure suit—much more comfortable!

Anyway, after the January flight was finally under my belt, things seemed to run more smoothly, as far as training flights were concerned. I was teamed up with Major Jerry Crew for an RSO, and we were very compatible as far as I was concerned, although he was a lot more serious than I was. He didn't take to the jokes that I often dished out. Jerry was medically retired in 1969. I was later crewed up with Jim Kogler. Jim had survived a crash on the runway at Beale during takeoff in the SR-71 by ejecting from the plane. But that's another story! We were also quite compatible. Kogler was a jokester himself—it worked out well.

The Flight

By Jerry Crew

The morning of 26 July 1968 started as another typical day at our detachment on Okinawa. Major Tony Bevacqua, pilot, and I (Major Jerry Crew, RSO) formed Crew 013. We were hoping for a chance to fly an operational sortie over North Vietnam. We checked the schedule, hoping to be the primary aircrew. Instead, we were backing up the crew of Pat Halloran and Mort Jarvis.

Typically, our backup aircraft would taxi to the end of the runway and wait to either takeoff if the primary SR-71 aborted, or return to the hangar after the primary aircraft refueled and climbed successfully to Mach 3 cruise. Tony and the maintenance crew chief were idly chatting over the interphone when I told Tony to prepare for takeoff. He thought I was joking. He didn't know I was monitoring the High Frequency (HF) radio and had heard Mort's abort call. Something had happened during refueling that prevented them from climbing to altitude. Thirty seconds later, we were cleared for takeoff.

The HF radio is a long-range radio that transmits in either the single sideband or AM frequency spectrum. Surprisingly, the antenna for the HF radio was the SR-71's pitot boom and the insulated forward portion of the aircraft nose.

During operational sorties we were required to monitor the HF radio at all times to receive coded messages, warning us of events along our flight route. If we aborted a mission, the RSO transmitted a coded radio call over the HF to let the world know our intentions. I personally found the static coming over the HF radio very distracting and kept the volume control off at all times, leaving Don responsible for monitoring the HF radio.

We often received an HF call from other U.S. aircraft when flying through the Korean DMZ, heading southwest directly toward China. You could practically count on a call there because of our speed and heading (if continued!). The coded transmission was a reminder to "check our navigational accuracy." Little did "they" know we were about to make a left turn.

—Rich Graham

After the adrenaline rush, typical of takeoff with the SR-71, we settled down for a "routine" operational sortie. We rendezvoused with our KC-135Q tanker, and filled #976 with a full load of JP-7 for the mission taking us over Hanoi and Haiphong. We climbed to operational altitude and headed for [we hoped] a successful sensor take. North Vietnam had been "socked in" for two weeks by weather. Knowing that current, up-to-the-minute intelligence was necessary to conduct the ground war added urgency to our mission. We were assured during the weather briefing that *all* of Southeast Asia was CAVU (Ceiling And Visibility Unlimited).

Turning inbound on our first sensor run, I noticed the "R" light on my electronic counter measure (ECM) panel was illuminated. This meant that a North Vietnamese SAM [surface-to-air missile] site was tracking us on its radar. This didn't concern us because every operational sortie previous to us had reported an "R" light illuminating on the ECM panel.

What we *didn't* expect was the illumination of the "M" light, followed closely by the "L" light! This meant, quite simply, that the North Vietnamese had actually fired one or more SAMs at us. [The "R" light meant they were searching for you, the "M" light meant they were tracking you, and the "L" light meant they were launching at you.] I think it's fair to say the already tense atmosphere in the cockpit of #976 suddenly reached critical mass. I was scared out of my wits. Attempting to seem calm (I failed), I told Tony we had just had a SAM shot at us.

This news couldn't have occurred at a worse time. We had just started our first sensor take and evasive action was not an option. Tony asked how long ago was it launched, and I replied, "about five seconds." The time of missile launch was important because we were told countless times by our intelligence experts that the SA-2 missile's total flight time was only 58 seconds. In other words, if nothing happened by then, we were probably safe. Oh, the "experts" also told us it would take a perfect missile shot to hit us, as we were flying at the outer edge of their SA-2 missile's altitude limit. Somehow, those odds seemed much closer now.

We had practiced what to do in the event of a SAM launch many times in the simulator. My duty was to turn off the ECM jammer because we didn't want the missile tracking the jamming frequency during flight. The purpose of our jammer was to confuse the missile prior to launch. My other duty was to start the stopwatch to time the missile's flight.

When Iflying F-4s in Vietnam, we knew the bad guys could home in on our jamming signals and guide an SA-2 SAM directly at us. While flying fighters, it was a guts call whether to turn on your ECM jammer. Some pilots put a lot of faith in the jamming capability of our ECM pods, while the "manly man" fighter pilots thought they were merely excess weight and drag to carry around.

The SR-71's jamming equipment was state of the art . . . constantly being upgraded, modified, and improved to counter enemy threats around the world. The best in the business!

My reaction time seemed terribly slow. It took forever to turn off the jammer (actual time 5 seconds) and I never started the stopwatch. However, I did notice the position of the second hand on the clock when Tony asked how long ago the missile had been fired.

The next 50 seconds are in dispute! I thought the whole time was spent answering Tony about the length of the missile's flight. "How long has it been?" he asked. "Five seconds since the last time you asked," I answered. Interphone tapes show that Tony only asked four times. I do know it took much longer than the missile's predicted flight time to convince us of our safety.

We completed the sensor run and descended to our tanker over Thailand, preparing for our return run back over North Vietnam. We were surprised that we weren't recalled because everyone knew we had been fired at. I guess they thought since we weren't hit the first time we would try again. They were right, but believe me, our second pass was approached with a great deal of apprehension. It proved uneventful, as was the remainder of the flight back to Kadena.

Upon landing, we were met by the whole detachment wanting to know if we saw the SAMs or anything else exciting. We were the center of attention. We put up a good front, but the next day when we listened to the interphone tapes, I got spooked again! In reality, two missiles had been fired at us. Luckily, they shot early and below us—our cameras confirmed this.

The longest 60 seconds of my life occurred on 26 July 1969 in the cockpit of #976, flying over Hanoi at 83,000 feet at Mach 3.3!

Better Late Than Never!

By Tony Bevacqua and Jim Kogler

It was decided early on that all three Blackbirds on Okinawa would need changing out on an annual basis. Although our maintenance was quite extensive and sophisticated, our maintenance personnel could not accomplish a major overhaul inspection and repair. This could only be done at Palmdale, California. Here the planes were completely stripped down and refurbished by Lockheed maintenance personnel. Once they were finished, the planes were like new again. This changeover was accomplished by flying the first plane from Okinawa to Beale, followed shortly by its replacement doing the return trip from Beale. The rotation continued until the three planes were replaced.

On 21 September 1969, Jim Kogler and I were to fly Blackbird #974 over to Okinawa as part of this ritual swapping of planes. These missions were called "Glowing Heat"—I think this mission code word was in reference to all of us trying to fly at the "speed of heat." All was going normally throughout our final refueling. We had just started our climb and acceleration when a warning light illuminated in the cockpit, alerting us to a generator malfunction. We needed to divert. From this position, Midway Island was our emergency abort base. Having just taken on a full load of JP-7, we dumped fuel to reduce our gross weight and we headed directly for Midway.

The rule was that if you had an emergency, the plane and crews stayed at their abort location until all the other Blackbirds were flown to Okinawa. We ended up staying on Midway Island for practically *two weeks*. As the other SR-71 crews flew their Blackbirds over Midway, en route to Okinawa and Beale, they made remarks such as, "Tony was still at Midway, we could see the oil slick." (algae)

We were very fortunate that we arrived just after the "gooney birds" (Layson albatross) had departed. Judy Sides, wife of a U.S. Navy chief Petty officer (CPO) on Midway, a *noted* Layson albatross artist, was there. I asked if she would do some painting on our Blackbird. She put a tiny bird on the side of the cockpit, where painted Habus (miniature silhouettes of a coiled Habu snake) were lined up for each operational mission. Larger Habus were painted on the main gear doors and on each rudder. They remained on the planes until SAC decided that no "art" whatsoever was allowed on our planes.

Jim Watkins led the team that flew into Midway and repaired the generator. The entire two weeks was quite boring, since the Officers' Club didn't open until 1600 hours. However, we did have the opportunity to snorkel in their beautifully clear water.

CHAPTER SIX

Colonel (Ret) James H. Shelton Jr.

Jim was responsible for getting me into the SR-71 program. While I was flying F-4s at Kadena AFB in 1973, a mutual friend introduced me to Jim, at that time commander of the SR-71 unit—the 1st SRS at Beale AFB. At that time I was semicontent flying fighters, but have to admit, having just flown 210 combat missions in Vietnam, I was slowly becoming disenchanted with peacetime practice and training. We called it "flying around the flag pole." Jim's enthusiasm for flying the SR-71, and encouraging me to apply, put the wheels in motion. I assembled my application package, and the rest is history.

Tom Schmittou, left, and Jim Shelton. Notice the metal fitting on each side of the pressure suit at the stomach level. The tubular one on their left side connected to the cooling air supply to circulate throughout the suit. The disklike fitting on their right side is the critical pressure controller. In the event of a loss of cabin pressure, the suit controller sensed the loss and immediately inflated the suit. *Jim Shelton*

Colonel (Ret) James H. Shelton Jr.

On my arrival at Beale in 1974, Jim was still the 1st SRS commander. He had begun his Air Force career by entering aviation cadet training and received his wings in 1956. He then flew F-86Fs at Osan AB, Korea, and returned to the United States to fly the B-47 at McCoy AFB, Florida, and Lincoln AFB, Nebraska. In November 1964 he was selected to fly the supersonic B-58 Hustler at Bunker Hill AFB, Indiana, until October 1967, when he joined the SR-71 squadron at Beale.

Jim spent over nine years at Beale, six years flying the SR-71. He was the fifth SR-71 crewmember to reach the 900-flying hour plateau. Most commercial airline pilots would consider that a paltry amount of flying time, but few Habus ever reached that milestone. To put SR-71 flying time into perspective, our all-time-high crewmember was Lieutenant Colonel (Ret) Joe "J. T." Vida, who flew the SR-71 for 16 continuous years, yet amassed only 1,392.7 hours. Habus had a motto that succinctly tells the high quality of our limited flying time, "Subsonic time is a waste of time!" In June 1977 Jim was assigned as chief of reconnaissance at 15th Air Force at March AFB, California. He retired in January 1980 and went to work at Lockheed's Skunk Works on the F-117 stealth fighter.

I asked Jim if he would like to contribute to this project. His response told me immediately that he had some unique experiences just waiting to be told. Here are Jim's stories.

My Thoughts

I was sitting on my back patio deck looking over the Pacific Ocean channel toward Catalina Island, watching an aerobatics aircraft practicing for an air show. This started me reminiscing about my experiences as an Air Force pilot flying the SR-71. Piloting the SR-71 was the highlight of my flying career.

A T-38 belonging to the SR-71 Flight Test Division at Palmdale, California, with Ed Yeilding and J. T. Vida in the cockpits. All SR-71 pilots were dual-qualified to fly both aircraft. The T-38 was considered a low-cost alternative to maintain pilot proficiency. We flew pace-chase, formation, aerobatics, instrument, and cross-country training sorties in the T-38. *Lockheed Martin Skunk Works*

I took my first flight on 4 August 1968, and was fortunate to fly the aircraft for six years, accruing 911 hours in the SR-71 and 875 hours in the T-38 aircraft (the SR-71 companion trainer) while stationed at Beale AFB. There were many memorable flights during those six years, but three or four stand out.

All SR-71 crews (as well as U-2 pilots and wing staff personnel at Beale) flew the supersonic T-38 Talon jet trainer at Beale. In 1974, we flew 5 T-38s, eventually growing to a fleet of 14 aircraft as the U-2 unit relocated to Beale in 1975. I enjoyed being dual-qualified in two high-performance airplanes, a rare occurrence for most Air Force pilots.

We used the T-38 to maintain our flying proficiency, as we flew the SR-71 so infrequently. At Beale I probably averaged three SR-71 training flights a month, and at the Detachments, around four operational flights a month. The T-38 was also used as a "pace chase" aircraft with the SR-71, used frequently to monitor the Blackbird's performance and external conditions. Flying formation with the SR-71 was an extra perk. Its black beauty from all those in-flight angles was a sight to behold!

—Rich Graham

SR-71 Barrier Engagement—Kadena AB

The first was an operational mission that occurred on my initial overseas deployment with Major Tom Schmittou (RSO) to Kadena AB in May 1969. The operational tasking from SAC headquarters always had maintenance personnel generating a primary and secondary aircraft. On 13 June 1969, we were in primary aircraft #979 for an operational mission over North Vietnam. It was a typical four-hour flight, consisting of a single east-to-west pass across Hanoi, air refuel over Thailand, then a west-to-east pass just south of Hanoi, returning to Kadena AB.

The engine start, takeoff, air refueling, and acceleration to Mach 2.8 at an altitude of 77,000 feet went as planned. At the navigation checkpoint, Tom informed me that the navigation system was drifting and the mission should be aborted. Tom made the abort call, and I turned the aircraft back to Okinawa. The descent from altitude and approach for landing was normal. Moderate rain was falling, so I applied the rain remover fluid to the front windscreen, allowing me to see the runway about 2 to 3 miles out.

The touchdown on the runway went smoothly. However, as I retarded the throttles to idle, the cockpit began to fill up with fog (water vapor). I had forgotten to increase the cockpit temperature to 85 degrees or higher, to prevent the formation of cockpit fogging. I remembered one pilot had previously blown the canopy off on landing just to see the runway. I really didn't want to do that! I quickly flipped the cockpit temperature switch from automatic to

If you pushed a button on the right side of the control stick, it activated the rain removal fluid. When squirted onto a wet windshield it was supposed to clear the rain away, improving visibility. A later Service Bulletin deactivated the system because it was rarely used. Our flight manual stated, "The white fluid will stick to the glass and permanently obscure visibility if applied while the windshield is dry." Some Habus found this out the hard way!

manual hot. This eliminated the fog in the cockpit, but did nothing to slow the aircraft down. Being so engrossed with holding the temperature switch in the full hot position (spring-loaded), thereby fixing one problem, I inadvertently created another: I forgot to deploy the drag 'chute.

The drag 'chute must be deployed to slow the aircraft on landing, especially on a wet runway. In my mind, and in actuality, the aircraft was not slowing enough. I applied the brakes and the antiskid started cycling like crazy, so I turned it off, but to no avail. I then shut down one engine as I saw the end of the runway coming up very, very quickly (at about 120 miles per hour). Fortunately, the runway at Kadena had a cable barrier installed about 1,000 feet from the end, specifically for the SR-71. The barrier is designed to pop up in front of the two main landing gear and stop the aircraft in 400 to 500 feet. The barrier unit uses the B-52 aircraft brake system to slow the aircraft and bring it to a stop (hopefully!). Boy, was I relieved that the barrier

The BAK 11/12 barrier was installed at two of our operating locations—on runway 16 at Beale and on runway 05R on Kadena. The barrier was designed to stop the plane at a maximum speed of 180 knots. Arming and disarming the barrier was controlled in the tower. At both Kadena and RAF Mildenhall, we had a crewmember in the tower during all takeoffs and landings to make sure everything went smoothly.

When armed, the barrier was activated by the aircraft nosewheel and main gear as they rolled over pressure-sensitive switchmats located in the runway before the arresting cable. The switches energized a timing computer that caused the arresting cable to be thrown up to engage the main gear struts. On engagement, the arresting cable was pulled out with a relatively constant restraining force to stop the aircraft within 2,000 feet. This was all theoretical. In actual practice, the number of unsuccessful SR-71 engagements far outnumbered the successful ones. Besides Jim's successful engagement, I know of only one other.

worked as advertised! There was one unsuccessful barrier engagement on 10 October 1968 at Beale, where the SR-71 (#977) was destroyed. There were only two barrier engagements recorded at the time, and fortunately, ours was the successful one.

Well, I just knew my SR-71 flying days were over as I climbed out of the aircraft. This incident terminated my flying at Kadena AB for this tour. The maintenance personnel worked the rest of the day and all through the night replacing the gear doors, hydraulic lines, and electrical wires on the main landing gear damaged by the barrier cable. I owe a big thanks to those maintenance personnel, because the aircraft was ready to fly the next day. They sure saved my six o'clock position (butt).

Since this was the second fogging incident, Lockheed designed a lever that the RSO moved to stop air from entering the cockpit before landing, eliminating any chance of fogging the cockpit as the throttles were retarded. I call that handle the "Shelton lever." Needless to say, I was allowed to continue flying, thanks to the thorough flying evaluation the standardization crews administered to me on my return to Beale AFB.

Because of the dry climate at Beale, you seldom had to warm the cockpit air. Cockpit fogging was practically nonexistent. However, even with the "Shelton lever" installed, the hot, humid, tropical climate of Okinawa made it necessary to preheat the cockpit air prior to approach and landing.

Just to give you an idea of the difference the drag 'chute made on landing distance, the flight manual performance charts show a ground roll of about 6,300 feet, on a nongrooved, dry runway, with the drag 'chute deployed. Under the same conditions *without* a drag 'chute, the ground roll was around 9,600 feet. As I recall, the primary runway at Kadena was only 10,000 feet long.

KC-135Q Tanker Missed an Abort Call

On another tour to Okinawa with Tom, we were the backup crew on a periphery mission that was to fly just south of the Korean DMZ and then around the northeast edge of China. As backup crew, we were not expecting to fly, but to our good fortune, the primary aircraft aborted and returned to Kadena. We took off as scheduled, one hour after the primary aircraft, heading to the air refueling. I asked my RSO, Tom Schmittou, if he had contact with the tanker. He said there were no rendezvous signals from the tanker (no tanker, no mission). We contacted Okinawa Air Traffic Control (we normally did not do this on operational sorties) to see if they had information on a tanker out in front of us anywhere. They indicated there was a tanker aircraft heading toward us (our 12 o'clock position some 50–75 miles). I asked for a radar vector toward the tanker. Once the tanker was about 10 miles abeam us, I started my 180-degree turn to pull in behind it. There was still no radio contact.

At our slowest speed, we had a 25–30 knot overtake on the tanker and slid past the left side of the tanker (pilot's window) to get the aircraft commander's attention. I could just visualize the tanker commander yelling at the boom operator to quickly get into the boom pod, while telling his copilot to push the power up to increase speed: "There is an SR-71 that needs fuel, and somehow we have really screwed up!" We got our fuel and completed the operational mission. After we landed, the tanker aircraft commander apologized, admitting that he didn't hear the primary aircraft's abort call. He was just heading back to Kadena, thinking he was not needed for the mission. We told him "no harm, no foul," but his crew had to buy our dinner that night. Needless to say, we had lobster and champagne!

North Korea Overflight

The SR-71 program took over the North Vietnam and North Korea overflight mission commitments from the CIA's A-12 program in March 1968. The SR-71 was not tasked to overfly North Korea until May 1969, and there were very few of those sorties ever flown. Tom and I were tasked to fly one of the last ones, scheduled on 21 January 1972.

We took off in aircraft #979 and refueled northeast of Kadena, then accelerated to the northwest, turning north over the Yellow Sea west of the North Korean peninsula. Near the China-North Korea border we accelerated to Mach 3.15 and turned northeast, paralleling the China border, and made a right 180-degree turn over the Sea of Japan, rolling out southwest, paralleling the previous track. After reaching the Yellow Sea, we headed for the first air refueling, northeast of Okinawa. After refueling, we accelerated northeast toward the Sea of Japan. Once we were abeam North Korea, we turned southwest (left) to parallel the two previous tracks. This pass was different because the SAM sites in North Korea woke up and started to track us. They were so far behind in their reactions that they never attempted a SAM launch. That didn't make us too unhappy!

That night at the Kadena Officers' Club during dinner, a classmate of mine who was flying F-4s at Kadena said, "I know where you went today." He knew I'd been flying that day and he heard on the news that the North Koreans claimed a U.S. spy plane violated their airspace. I just smiled and changed the subject. About a week later, I received a letter from my father enclosing an article from the *L.A. Times* "News of the Day" section. The article read, "North Korea accused the United States of sending a high-speed, high-altitude SR-71 reconnaissance plane into North Korea airspace to conduct espionage and hostile acts" and further said, "it constituted a grave military provocation." When I wrote to my father I couldn't comment about the news article, but I thought it was quite a coincidence that he sent an article regarding my mission.

> Jim's mission over North Korea in 1972 must have been the last one. When I arrived at Beale in 1974, we were no longer flying over North Korea. We did fly routinely through the Korean DMZ, however, gathering intelligence on North Korea, until the Blackbird's retirement in 1990.
>
> **—Rich Graham**

Middle East Mission (Yom Kippur War)

The most memorable mission I ever flew was on 13 October 1973 during the Yom Kippur War. During this time our government wanted to know the battlefield situation between the Israelis and Egyptians. They could not move one of our spy satellites out of a Russian orbit due do to higher-priority targeting. However, Russia had one of its spy satellites monitoring the situation and was a step ahead of our intelligence community. The SR-71 was tasked to obtain the much-needed intelligence information.

Pat Halloran, the 9th Wing commander, presents the 1973 Reconnaissance Crew of the Year Trophy to Jim Shelton (center) and Gary Coleman. They received the award for flying the longest operational sortie ever flown by an SR-71: 11 hours and 19 minutes. Add about another hour for preflight and taxi operations. Imagine being firmly strapped into a seat that long without getting up! *Jim Shelton*

Colonel (Ret) James H. Shelton Jr.

The tasking arrived at Beale about 10 October, and as chief of the standardization section, Lieutenant Colonel Gary Coleman (RSO) and I were tasked to fly the first mission. We studied what appeared to be a relatively easy mission. The initial tasking was to take off from Beale AFB, fly through the Mediterranean Sea, down the Suez Cannel, make a right turn around the city of Cairo, Egypt, head northwest through Israel, back through the Mediterranean and recover at RAF Mildenhall, England. This would be about an 8-hour-and-45-minute flight. I knew I could handle a flight of this length. I had already flown a training mission of 10 hours and 30 minutes and had learned how to pace myself. The mission was scheduled to take off about midnight, planning to be over the target area close to either 1100 or 1300 hours. These two times provided the photo interpreter with the brightest light with some shadows so they could determine heights accurately.

Upon completing our mission planning, we obtained the intelligence briefing. We were informed that the State Department would not notify any country of our flight, other than the British, to request landing permission. The intelligence officer, in a matter-of-fact mode, advised us not to be surprised if the Egyptians or the Israelis fired SAMs or sent fighters up to attack us. My first thought was, "It's really nice to know who your friends are." Also, we were informed that if we had to abort the mission and land at an airfield that didn't have U.S. forces stationed on the field, one of us was to stay with the aircraft and the other crewmember was to seek an American embassy or a neutral country embassy. I decided that Gary would stay with the aircraft and I would hunt for the embassy. How do you search for an embassy in a pressure suit?

After reviewing the mission again in the morning, I went to the Flight Surgeon's office to get a Seconal sleeping tablet. I needed to go to sleep right after lunch in order to be at the Physiological Support Division (PSD) by 2100 hours, rested and ready to fly. Our mission briefing, preflight physical, and a high-protein, low-residue meal of steak and eggs went as scheduled. Can you believe, after all that preparation, the State Department canceled the mission? We were told to go home and rest for another mission the next day. By now it was around 0100 hours. Who could sleep after taking a sleeping pill 12 hours earlier? I was well rested and ready for a full day's work!

Earlier that same day, Colonel Pat Halloran (the 9th Wing commander at Beale) and our maintenance team had taken off from Beale AFB, heading for RAF Mildenhall, England, aboard a KC-135Q tanker, to be in place for our flight recovery.

The next day, we were informed that the British would not let the SR-71 land in England due to their dependence on Middle East oil. This action by the British changed our plans entirely. The *new* plan was to fly from Griffiss AFB, New York, through the Middle East and return to Griffiss. Well this was a great plan, but it meant that the mission was now 11 hours and 30 minutes instead of the original 8 hours and 45 minutes. We were told to go home and come back at 1530 hours to fly a Blackbird to Griffiss AFB. Colonel Halloran and the maintenance recovery team had departed England and were now en route to Griffiss AFB.

Lieutenant Colonel Ronnie Rice (a former SR-71 crewmember), the SR-71 program element monitor (PEM) at the Pentagon, selected Griffiss AFB because he knew that the SR-71 test force located at Palmdale Airfield, California, was scheduled to fly some test missions from there in a few days. The test force had a tank car full of JP-7 (the SR-71's special fuel) parked on a railroad siding and a Lockheed civilian recovery team was already in place.

We took off from Beale AFB in aircraft #979 at about 1700 hours heading for Griffiss AFB, with one in-flight refueling over Nevada. As we headed east at Mach 3 and 80,000 feet, our route took us south of Chicago and north of Indianapolis, then directly to Griffiss AFB. Passing south of Chicago, I said to Gary, "I can see the lights of Chicago out the left side window and the lights of Indianapolis out the right side." It was so clear that night. I commented, "We must be creating quite a sonic boom that's touching the ground and disturbing a lot of people."

The weather was clear at Griffiss AFB for the night landing. I turned the landing light switch on about 10 miles out, according to the checklist, and continued my approach. As I started my flare for landing there was no landing light reflecting on the runway. I moved the landing light switch to the "taxi" position to obtain some light. After the Lockheed recovery team got us out of the aircraft, the base commander came up and said that he was told by SAC headquarters, "This was a high-priority Top Secret mission." He really knew it was secret, because I'd waited until I was over the runway in my flare before I turned on my landing light. I didn't want to ruin his illusions by telling him that I didn't know the landing light was burned out until I was in my flare for landing and just switched on my taxi light.

We worked with the base commander to obtain quarters for the second flight crew, plus Colonel Halloran, and the maintenance team that would soon be arriving from England. The sonic booms we created were so severe that SAC headquarters instructed the flight planners at Beale AFB to change the route of the second aircraft that was following us to Griffiss AFB. I knew we had created quite a sonic boom. However, it turned out to be worse then I thought, as indicated by the articles that appeared in newspapers on 12 October 1973. The shock wave stretched from Indiana to New York state.

I always laugh when the news media quotes some Air Force individual who says he is investigating a sonic boom. In this case, Lieutenant Colonel Rice knew exactly who, why, and what caused the sonic booms. When Dr. Shelton Alexander, a Penn State geophysics and seismology expert said, "It conceivably could have been a meteorite entering the earth's atmosphere," do you think Ronnie was going to tell the world that the professor was wrong, and it was really an SR-71 going into Griffiss AFB?

At Beale there was an office that handled sonic boom complaints on a full-time basis. All of the SR-71 training missions in the United States had to avoid major cities, national parks, ski resorts, and a long list of other noise-sensitive areas. The office received boom complaints from everyone and anyone. Farmers claimed their cows wouldn't give milk any more, chickens wouldn't lay eggs, and minks that wouldn't breed. All sonic boom incidents attributed to SR-71s had to be thoroughly investigated and claims paid if found justified. From the time an SR-71 passed directly overhead at 80,000 feet, it took around 1 minute and 20 seconds for the sonic boom to reach the ground. The actual noise level was very similar to hearing a thunder clap about 15 miles away.

For most sonic boom complaints we merely altered our route of flight. For others, the Air Force was forced to compensate for broken windows and cracked ceilings. It even made newspaper headlines when Captains (Ret. Brig. Gen.) Buck Adams and (Ret. Lt. Col.) Bill Machoreck flew the return speed run from London to Los Angeles (5,446.86 statute miles) in 3 hours, 47 minutes, 36 seconds. Unstarts forced them to start their descent earlier than planned. Their low-altitude sonic boom broke the windows (supposedly) of movie star Zsa Zsa Gabor's house, creating a public relations nightmare for the Air Force. Surprisingly, Buck and Bill were invited to Zsa Zsa's house, and the Air Force ended up receiving favorable publicity from the event. Buck says she was a gracious host, and they gave her an autographed picture of the SR-71.

At midmorning on the 12th, Gary and I studied the mission route one more time. I then went to see the base flight surgeon to obtain a Seconal sleeping tablet. I was dressed in my orange flight suit with all the unit and SR-71 patches displayed, so he knew I wasn't stationed on the base. The flight surgeon said he could not supply me with a Seconal tablet, because he didn't know my medical condition. I told him to call the SRC at Offutt or the flight surgeon at Beale to obtain permission if he couldn't make that decision for himself. After about 10 minutes he finally relented and supplied me with a tablet.

After a late lunch, Gary and I went to our room for crew rest. I took my Seconal tablet and fell into a very deep sleep. Gary didn't use sleeping tablets, so he didn't rest as soundly. Speaking of sound, I have been known to snore, and that night, unbeknown to me, I let out some loud snorts. When Gary and I were eating our preflight meal, he admitted that he didn't sleep very well due to my snoring. He said, "My mind is at rest, because I know you were sleeping well by the supersonic sounds you were making."

SR-71 crewmembers were permitted to take "uppers" and "downers" if they needed them. We were drug-tested during our initial training by the flight surgeon to determine which medication suited your physiology best. The pills were tightly controlled by the flight surgeon and very few SR-71 crews ever used them.

We knew the pressure was on us to accomplish this mission, as there would be no backup aircraft. When maintenance personnel recovered the second aircraft coming from Beale AFB, they damaged the wing tip on the hangar door while backing the aircraft into the hangar. It was going to take several days to obtain a replacement wing tip.

The takeoff in aircraft #979 at 0115 hours was normal for the SR-71, but rather noisy for the locals. We leveled off at 25,000 feet, heading for the first air refueling. There was a little clear-air turbulence at level off, and the turbulence increased as we got closer to the rendezvous point. Once I connected with the tanker I knew I had to stay in the contact position for 19–20 minutes to obtain the required amount of fuel needed to get us to the next air refueling. As the aircraft got heavier, the turbulence caused me to work harder to stay in the contact position. Near the end of the air refueling, turbulence actually bounced me off the boom.

As I worked to get back into position, the flight control stick shaker activated, warning me that I was near the edge of the flight control envelope. Combinations of weight, airspeed, rate of nose movement, and turbulence cause the activation. I got back in position and had full tanks by the time we reached the end of the air-refueling track. We accelerated to Mach 3, climbing to 79,000 feet heading for the second air refueling east of Portugal. Because of our tremendous speed heading eastward, the sun began rising very quickly over Greenland . . . you go from night to day almost instantaneously.

The second air refueling went smoothly. While connected to the boom and using the boom intercom (interphone between the SR-71 and tanker), the tanker crew told us that the Portuguese air traffic control was concerned about a high-speed, unidentified plane closing on them quickly. What a surprise! The tanker crew denied seeing any such aircraft in the area. Strange how the radar blips merged and joined together for 20 minutes before separating!

After reaching cruise altitude and speed, I decided it was snack time. I had two 16-ounce containers of water and two NASA-made tubes of strained apricots. Oh, yummy! I'd been offered many types of food, but I passed on strained meats and settled on fruit. I remembered deceiving my son by telling him how good the strained meats were, but would only eat a small amount myself. The tube food resembled a large tube of toothpaste. It had a thin metal seal that was punctured as you screwed on the feeding tube. The feeding tube is then inserted into a small hole, located on the right side of the pressure suit helmet. Well, when I screwed the feeding tube onto the tube of apricot, it penetrated the seal, and suddenly, apricot was spraying everywhere. Thinking quickly, I stuck the tube into my pressure suit pocket desperately trying to contain the mess. I'd forgotten one essential principle of physics, "as altitude increases, outside air pressure decreases." That tube of apricot was manufactured at sea level. Opening it at my cabin altitude of 26,000 feet caused the apricot to spew wildly.

After satisfying my hunger with food and water, I was faced with the problem of a full bladder. The pressure suit has a urine collection device (UCD) built into it. The urine is collected in small plastic bags, nicknamed "piddle packs," in the lower left pressure suit pocket. When you fill one piddle pack, you can put it into the lower right suit pocket. When you fill the second one, you can leave it in the lower left suit pocket. However, when you need to start using a third piddle pack, the problem becomes what to do with pack number two in the left pocket. I improvised by hanging the pack on the canopy emergency jettison T-Handle, located on the left-side console. It worked fine as long as I didn't have to raise or lower the ejection seat.

I only had three more air refuelings to complete before I would be back at Griffiss AFB. Each time you refuel, you have to lower your seat about 4 inches to enable you to see the bottom of the tanker aircraft. Fortunately, the seat adjustment switch was on the right side of the seat. This freed my left hand to protect the pack as I raised and lowered the seat. I almost had more than just apricot to clean up by the end of the flight!

The rendezvous point for the third air refueling was located near the island of Crete, in the Mediterranean. From my perspective, the rendezvous was normal. We obtained mileage information over our secure radio, about 150 miles from the tanker. The tanker was offset 21 miles to my left, abeam the rendezvous point and heading toward us, just as required, when he made his 180-degree turn to roll out four miles in front of us. After we hooked up the tanker, the commander said, "I had the pedal-to-the-metal just getting to the rendezvous point. The Spanish Air Controller held me on the ground for 30 minutes." This robbed him of the opportunity to establish a normal orbit 30 minutes before the rendezvous time. He barely had time to proceed past the rendezvous point by about 6 miles and start an immediate 180-degree turn back toward us. From my perspective, this turned out to be a perfect textbook rendezvous. From the tanker's perspective, it was a "wing and a prayer" maneuver!

The success of the SR-71 program owes a big, big thanks to the KC-135Q tanker force. Without their expertise, creativity, and dedication to the mission, many SR-71 missions would have been aborted. Like they say, "It takes two to tango." Without in-flight air refueling, the SR-71 would need to land after a two-hour flight.

Jim is 100 percent right. Without the professionalism of our tanker crews at Beale we would be flat on our faces. I cannot recall a mission being aborted because the tankers were not there to refuel us. I've heard lots of stories, and know of many others, where tanker crews went out of their way and above and beyond the call of duty to rescue a Blackbird crew in distress.

Beale had 35 KC-135Q model tankers that were devoted to the SR-71 refueling mission. The tankers and aircrews went TDY everywhere with us. We worked hard together, and partied hard together, all around the world. There was a definite camaraderie between the KC-135Q crews and the Habus. I've truly had some of my worst hangovers due to the tanker crews. Thank you! The last one was while I was the wing commander visiting Det 1. At about midnight I was coming down the back stairs of 318 from a Habu party when I saw the tanker crews partying in room 101. Three of my favorite activities were going on in that room. They were playing "liars dice," watching a Fleetwood Mac video starring Stevie Nicks, and the booze was flowing. I was in "hog heaven" and partied with them until the wee hours of the morning. I can still feel the effects of that night!

—Rich Graham

After successfully completing the third air refueling, near Crete, we turned southeast and headed for the Suez Canal, accelerating to Mach 3.15. As we headed down the Suez Canal, Gary informed me that a SAM site in Egypt was tracking us. We did nothing but maintain speed and heading. There was no real threat from just being tracked. I remembered what the intelligence officer had told us. No country was informed of our flight, and we could, therefore, expect someone to take a shot at us. Fortunately, as we continued south over the Suez Canal, the SAM site stopped tracking our plane.

Eventually, we turned west to circle around the city of Cairo, Egypt. Starting my turn I pushed the power up to maximum afterburner to maintain Mach 3.15, because as the aircraft turns, the wings lose lift and require more thrust to maintain speed and altitude. To make matters worse, the outside air temperature was warmer than standard (minus 55 degree C), requiring additional thrust. However, I was already at maximum thrust! I had two choices. Lower my altitude or let the Mach decrease. There is really only one answer. Ask any fighter pilot, and he will tell you, "Keep your Mach up."

While descending to maintain my Mach, the red "High KEAS" (knots-equivalent air speed) warning light came on, indicating my equivalent air speed (EAS) was too high for the altitude. I quickly checked the compressor inlet temperature (CIT), making sure I was not exceeding the 427-degree C maximum limit. I maintained my Mach, altitude, and kept the "High KEAS" warning light on throughout my 270-degree right turn around Cairo. After rolling out wings level, heading northeast perpendicular to the Suez Canal, I converted my excess thrust into altitude and finally gained enough altitude that the "High KEAS" warning light went out.

Once again, an Egyptian SAM site started tracking us. Through the side window I spotted high-altitude condensation trails approximately 40,000 feet below us. Now we had fighter aircraft trying to track us or attempting to shoot us down, as well as the threat from the SAM site. Based on our location, I believed they were Egyptian aircraft and not Israelis.

Once across Israel, we started a left turn back to the air refueling near Crete. Our route of flight back to Griffiss was a reverse course of the one that got us to the Crete air refueling. The fourth air refueling went off without a hitch.

After leveling off at Mach 3 and heading to my fifth air refueling, I was hungry. However, I didn't want to add to the apricot mess already in my pressure suit pocket. Then a flash of inspiration! I thought if I partially screwed the feed tube on the apricots, but didn't break the seal, and then insert the tube through the feeding port in my helmet I could avoid the spillage this time. Once the tube was in my mouth, I finished screwing on the feed tube. It worked! Sure enough, I squirted apricot in my mouth, not in my pocket. I shared this technique with other crewmembers who had feeding problems. The fifth air refueling off the coast of Portugal went as scheduled. All I could think about was one more air refueling and we would be back, landing at Griffiss AFB.

I had one other concern. Where would I put my fourth piddle pack? I decided to use the container that held our approach charts and maps and lay them on the cockpit instrument panel. I worried that I might inadvertently puncture the bag, allowing the urine to run over the electrical circuit breaker panel, creating an electrical short or fire.

As I passed 10 hours and 30 minutes of flying time, I remembered just how tired I'd been flying a training mission of the same length. However, I was not tired. I attributed this to two factors. First, the adrenaline generated by this mission had kept me going. Second, I remembered pacing myself too stringently on that practice training mission. I flew at precisely Mach 3.00—not 2.99 or 3.01—this required constant small throttle adjustments. Realizing how tired I became by trying to maintain Mach 3.00 precisely, I reduced the throttle adjustments. On this mission I let my cruise Mach vary anywhere between 2.95 and 3.05 before making a throttle adjustment.

Our sixth air refueling was over Canada. We took on a small load of fuel, all I needed for a short subsonic flight back to Griffiss AFB. On the final leg back, knowing the weather at Griffiss was clear, and we wouldn't need any extra fuel, I pushed the throttles up to full military power (just before the afterburner range). This increased our speed to around Mach .98. While cruising at Mach .98 the Canadian air traffic controller kept asking us what type of aircraft we were. I responded, "As filed on our flight plan." After landing, I questioned our mission planners as to the type of aircraft they had indicated on our flight plan. They replied, "A KC-135 tanker." No wonder the traffic controller wanted to know the type of aircraft—a KC-135 flies almost 150 miles per hour slower than I was going. Perhaps a new breed of supertanker?

I landed back at Griffiss AFB after 11 hours and 19 minutes, tired and hungry, but thrilled with the mission success.

Admiral Moore, chairman of the Joint Chiefs of Staff, called Gary and me to the Pentagon to personally thank us for flying this important mission. While there, we were shown photos from the mission. The photos clearly showed that the Israelis had moved farther into Egypt than Golda Meir had admitted. The State Department used these photos to convince Golda to withdraw from Egyptian territory. I saw one photo I would like to have a copy of, for my own collection, but it had *Secret* stamped all over it. The photo had both the pyramids and the sphinx in the same picture frame, shot from 80,000 feet.

Epilogue

The epilogue to the story occurred in September 1974 at the Farnborough Air Show in England. The SR-71 had just completed the New York to London speed run in 1 hour ,55 minutes, and 32 seconds, landing at the Farnborough International Air Show. The day after the landing, our maintenance personnel were setting up for public display and towed the aircraft across the runway. As the crowd control fence was moved, allowing the aircraft to be towed into position, a large group of spectators crowded around. Colonel Halloran, maintenance personnel, and I were attempting to move the crowd back behind the barricades, when I found a person with his head in the nose wheel well opening. I asked him to move behind the barricades, when in broken English he said, "Tell me about the SR-71 flights over the Middle East in 1973 and 1974." I said, "I have no idea what you are talking about." He replied, "Don't bullshit me, I am a MiG-21 squadron commander from Egypt." For security reasons, I denied all knowledge of any such flights. Later, I wondered if he was flying one of the aircraft creating the condensation trails I had seen below me on that day in October 1973.

CHAPTER SEVEN

Colonel (Ret) Alan B. Cirino

Al received his commission through the AFROTC program at San Francisco State University, graduating as a distinguished military graduate. Al attended pilot training at Reese AFB, Texas, and received his Air Force wings in August 1966.

Al's first operational flying assignment was to the 417th Tactical Fighter Squadron, Ramstein Air Base, Germany, as an F-4D pilot. He returned to the United States in July 1968 when his entire F-4 squadron was relocated to Mountain Home AFB, Idaho. In 1970, Al was selected to be a Forward Air Controller (FAC) in Vietnam, flying the OV-10 out of Bien Hoa Air Base, Vietnam. During his one-year tour of duty, he flew 204 combat missions.

Returning to the United States in March 1971, Al was selected to be a B-52D aircraft commander at Carswell AFB, Texas. He flew 130

Al Cirino gets ready to de-suit at the Physiological Support Division (PSD) facility. This was the Air Force's entire repository for all pressure suit operations, and consequently, had a high level of experienced personnel. Although not considered a military uniform, the David Clark Co. model 1030 pressure suit was *the* most prized uniform for all Habus. *Al Cirino*

B-52 combat missions, including missions over Hanoi during Linebacker II, from Guam and Utapao Royal Thai Air Force Base, Thailand. He subsequently served as a standardization/evaluation instructor pilot until March 1974.

In April 1974 Al was selected to fly the SR-71, also serving as the squadron operations officer. He accumulated 456 hours in the Blackbird. Following a one-year stint at school, Al was assigned to the Office of the Joint Chiefs of Staff, Washington, D.C., in 1979. He served a four-year tour there as an operations staff officer in the Joint Reconnaissance Center (JRC).

From July 1983 to August 1985, Al was commander of the SR-71 squadron at Beale AFB, and later served as assistant deputy commander for operations and as director of operations, 14th Air Division. In 1986, Al was selected as the deputy commander for operations at Grand Forks AFB, North Dakota, with the B-52 and the B-1B bombers. Al retired after 26 years in the Air Force, as the 3rd Air Division vice commander, Hickam AFB, Hawaii. He retired with 4,400 flying hours and 477 combat missions, and now flies for United Airlines.

After more than 17 years of flawless operational flying from Kadena AB, Okinawa, Japan, #974 crashed near the Philippines on 21 April 1989. Al tells the story of what happened.

Another Lost "Habu"

Life was good. The entire 3rd Air Division, Strategic Air Command, had just been relocated seven months prior from the remote island of Guam in the Marianas chain to the beautiful paradise of Oahu, Hawaii. As an element of SAC, our charter was to monitor all bomber and tanker activities in the Pacific and Indian Oceans. Before the Gulf War, operations in our theater of command were fairly routine. On 21 April 1989, all of that was about to change . . . particularly for me.

My boss, Major General Don Marks, received a phone call that afternoon from SAC headquarters in Omaha that an SR-71 had just crashed off the northern coast of Luzon in the Philippines. Normally, the Blackbird operation at Det 1 fell under the purview of SAC, without any interference from us. We did not maintain any day-to-day liaison with Det 1. This notification from SAC was therefore unique.

I was called in to discuss the situation with General Marks. All the while I was thinking what an unprecedented occurrence this was . . . having not lost a Blackbird since 1972, some 17 years earlier. We were told immediately that the SR-71 crew, Dan House (pilot) and Blair Bozek (RSO), were rescued unharmed, so we settled into the discussion of action to take as time was of the essence due to the political nature of the crash. Here was the premier, Top Secret U.S. reconnaissance aircraft, full of state-of-the-art surveillance equipment, sitting on the ocean floor in waters accessible to any foreign power. Because of the sensitivity of the aircraft, and its relative accessibility (owing to the crew report of the crash site), the decision was made to try to salvage the entire aircraft.

We didn't discuss anything with our PACAF hosts other than to advise them of our involvement, as this was being treated strictly as a SAC matter. I was given orders to be the president of the Accident Investigation Board. I was to proceed to Kadena, as quickly as possible, assemble a cadre of Det 1 maintenance experts, and formulate an investigation plan. We would then proceed to Clark AB in the Philippines and be joined by a team of experts from Air Force safety, Lockheed, and Pratt & Whitney. Two days later I was winging my way to Kadena for the beginning of a two-month saga. Everything proceeded according to plan, and after our arrival at Clark, with a good night's sleep behind us, our team of 15 headed north toward the unknown.

Before we get to the recovery, I asked Dan to describes his fateful flight. Here is his account.

> "Blair Bozek and I spent the day prior to our flight at the Det. Our mission planning and preparation took longer than usual, as this was not going to be a routine flight. Using the word 'routine' to describe anything we did in the SR-71 is slightly misleading, but this was a mission we didn't do very often, and required extra preparation. We were to take off from Kadena, turn south, and climb immediately to cruise speed and altitude of Mach 3 and around 75,000 feet. Then we would rendezvous and refuel with two KC-135Q tankers off the west coast of the Philippines before climbing back to altitude and working several targets in Southeast Asia. On the trip back, we would rendezvous and refuel with the same tankers before returning to Kadena. We reviewed the route, the turn points and timing, scheduled sensor actions, area threat assessment, and several possible emergency divert fields.
>
> "Normally, we refueled shortly after takeoff, but with an immediate climb after takeoff, we would be considerably lighter than usual and would climb much more rapidly. We called this a 'rocket ride.' Our call sign was Kobe 25, and we were scheduled to fly aircraft #974, my second-favorite plane in the fleet. Each plane had its own personality, and #974 and I got along fine.
>
> "On 21 April 1989, we departed Kadena in some rain showers, turned south and climbed to 74,000 feet and Mach 3. After settling into our cruise, we began ranging with our tankers. They were 400 miles away and directly in front of

us. Twenty-four minutes into the flight, I heard and felt a slight 'thump' in the airframe as the nose yawed gently to the left, and the plane began to roll left.

" 'Alpha within limit . . . unstart?' Blair asked, giving me the required procedure for an unstart, then checking to confirm that we'd actually had one.

"Unstarts were fairly common in the SR-71 and could cause significant yaw and pitch-up movements. The first step of the unstart procedure was 'Alpha within limit.' It was a reminder not to let the nose of the airplane pitch up excessively and approach a stall. 'Alpha' is aerodynamic engineering shorthand for angle of attack (AOA).

" 'Don't know,' I replied as I pushed on the right rudder pedal and moved the control stick to the right to stop the uncommanded left turn.

"My eyes went immediately to the inlet control gauges on the lower instrument panel directly in front of my left knee. It did not appear to be a typical unstart, as the inlet had not cycled automatically. It took a few seconds to convince myself that the inlet control system spike and bypass doors had not moved from their cruise positions, and that the unstart indicator light near the top of the instrument panel was not on. Then I looked at the upper right side of the instrument panel where the engine instruments were. The left engine had quit, and in fact had seized—rpm was zero, oil pressure zero, afterburner nozzle open, and EGT dropping rapidly. The master warning and master caution lights were on, as were several other lights in the cockpit.

"I told Blair the engine had failed. We would later learn that oil starvation due to a leaking oil seal had caused bearings in the left compressor section to fail. This allowed spinning compressor blades to contact stationary blades and break apart. These broken blades caused massive damage in the rest of the compressor, and it literally exploded, slinging pieces of metal in all directions. Checking the periscope, I could see that there were several large, jagged holes in the top of the left engine nacelle. The damage was severe enough to stop the engine from turning. It had been a deceptively gentle process from where I sat, yet was obviously cause to immediately abort the mission and land as soon as possible. We quickly decided to divert to Clark AB, in the Philippines.

"Each engine turned its own accessory drive system (ADS), which contained an electrical generator, a fuel-circulating pump, and two hydraulic pumps. One hydraulic pump was for the SR-71's flight controls (crucial for flight), and the other one for auxiliary hydraulic systems. The left ADS turned the 'A' flight control hydraulic system pump and the right ADS turned the 'B' pump. Either system was capable of moving the flight controls.

"When an engine fails, it usually keeps turning (windmilling in the airstream) enough to keep the ADS generator and hydraulic pumps working down to at least 15,000 feet. But when an engine quits turning, so does the ADS, and everything else associated with it. Loss of 'A' flight control hydraulic pressure caused the 'A' channel of the stability augmentation system (SAS) to disengage along with the roll axis of the 'B' channel. The single remaining 'B' pitch and yaw axes remained coupled but operated at reduced effectiveness. The plane became difficult to fly.

"An engine failure at Mach 3 is bad enough. A simple ADS failure or SAS failure is also bad. All because the failed left engine was not turning, we were dealing with three major emergencies.

"We had decided to divert to Clark Air Base in the Philippines, our only realistic choice, but it was still well over 300 miles away. We called our tankers, told them to come north to meet us on our way to Clark, then ran our engine shutdown and divert checklists.

"Step 2 of the engine shutdown and descent checklist is to manually turn the restart switch on. When I did this, the left spike moved forward, inducing enough yaw to cause our 'B' yaw SAS axis to drop off the line. The plane now became *very* difficult to fly. It yawed a bit more, then began an uncommanded roll to the right. I pushed in full left rudder and full left forward control stick to stop the roll, which grudgingly slowed, then stopped at nearly 60 degrees of bank. As it rolled back through wings level, I centered the rudder pedals and control stick, but the plane kept rolling to the left. Once again, I had to use full travel of the stick and rudders to stop it. This went through four cycles, then quit. We were slowing down with our speed at just over Mach 2. I could hear myself breathing heavily and feel my heart pounding. From Mach 3 to Mach 2.5 I felt that I had very little control over the aircraft. This concerned me as I didn't immediately recognize and understand the cause and didn't know if it would happen again. I had been totally focused on looking outside and controlling the airplane, not on watching the instrument panel.

"Analysis of the flight recorder data showed that the yaw induced when the left spike went forward was also enough to cause the right engine to unstart. A series of four unstarts had created huge asymmetric thrust changes. All this with five of the six flight control SAS axes failed.

"With a little skill and a good amount of luck, we flew out of that series of gyrations and continued our diversion to Clark AB. Now 10 miles left of our last course, we reestablished a new direct course. We descended and slowed to subsonic speed, calculating that our single-engine level-off altitude should be around 18,000 feet and that we should have plenty of fuel to get to Clark. When things appeared to be settling down, the master warning light came on again. Checking the annunciator panel, I saw a flashing 'B' hydro light in the middle of the cluster of steady lights. This meant either low pressure or low quantity. The gauge showed we still had full pressure, suggesting that our only working flight control hydraulic system was losing fluid and would eventually fail. We later learned that when the compressor exploded, a piece of broken blade had nicked a 'B' hydro pressure line, causing it to crack. We were steadily losing fluid from our only working flight control hydraulic system and had no idea how long it would last. We were at about 400 knots and 15,000 feet, still descending and unable to hold altitude.

" 'Aw, &#$%!!' I said out loud.

"Blair immediately asked, 'What is it?'

" 'We've got a 'B' hydro light, Blair.'

" 'Oh, &#$%!!' was his reply.

"Our discussion of this turn of events went something like this, 'Well, if we lose the 'B' hydro system, we'll have to bail out.'

" 'Yup.'

"We continued heading toward Clark AB, which was still over 200 miles, or 45 minutes, away.

"As we neared the north coast of the main Philippine island of Luzon, 'B' hydro pressure began to fluctuate, then it dropped from 3,000 psi to 2,000 psi. The system was obviously failing rapidly and would not get us to Clark. We began to see some small islands and desperately looked for any kind of runway to land on. Blair searched our maps, but there are few cities on the north coast of the Philippines, and fewer still with a runway. Normal operations required a runway length of at least 7,000 feet. I was hoping for at least 5,000, and probably would have made an attempt on 4,000. We agreed to remain over the water as we continued even though that was not a direct path to Clark. If we had to eject, we didn't want to do it over mountainous jungle just inland from the coast, and we didn't want classified material falling into the wrong hands. 'B' hydro pressure fluctuated again and dropped to 1,500 psi.

"I turned left to parallel the coast and flew east, still looking for any suitable piece of concrete to land on. Despite the low 'B' hydro pressure, the plane was still controllable. Blair found a potential field on one of his maps and asked me if I could turn right. At that point, the 'B' hydro gauge dropped below 700 psi and I was holding full left rudder with the control stick full left and forward. The plane pitched up and began to roll hard to the right. I replied, 'No, I can't! BAIL OUT. BAIL OUT. BAIL OUT!' The pilot and RSO ejection systems are completely separate and one person cannot eject the other under any circumstances. I flipped the RSO BAILOUT switch to 'GO' and pulled my ejection seat D-ring. As a backup to the verbal command, the switch turned on a BAILOUT light in the rear cockpit, commanding the RSO to bail out. We went out at about 300 knots and 10,000 feet. Elapsed time from engine failure to ejection was 16 minutes.

"I remember the D-ring hitting its stop and the sensation of light coming into the cockpit as the canopy blew off. The ejection seat fired and the next thing I recall is some serious opening shock as my parachute slowed me from 300 knots to zero very quickly. I tried to visually check my parachute, but found it difficult with a full pressure suit and helmet on. I managed a quick glimpse and it looked OK. Then I started looking for Blair. I was oriented to our final easterly course as the land was to the south and the ocean to the north. I was facing west, and could not spot Blair immediately. With some difficulty, I turned the 'chute so that I was facing east and saw him under what looked like a good parachute. In relation to our flight path, he was ahead and above me. I saw that he had deployed his survival kit, so I knew he was conscious and probably uninjured. He'd had to delay ejection because he wasn't in proper position for a safe bailout when I gave the command. He now claims to be the only RSO with solo time in the SR-71. I like to remind him that although that may be true, he was totally out of control the entire time.

"I looked for the airplane and finally spotted it. It was slightly to the east of me and looked like it was falling straight down. It was upside-down and wasn't spinning or tumbling at all. When it hit the water, there was a splash, a brief fireball, and it was gone.

"I prepared for landing in the water by deploying my survival seat kit. This releases the seat kit attached to the parachute harness, and inflates a one-man life raft, which both remain attached to a 20-foot nylon lanyard. Then I inflated the life preserver unit, which is built into the parachute harness assembly. The descent rate under a 35-foot-diameter parachute is very slow, so I had plenty of time to look around. It was a sunny morning, with no wind, the land was lush and green, and the ocean was absolutely calm. I could see boats turning toward me as I neared the water. My feet hit the water and I released the risers on my parachute to help separate from all the lines and the canopy. But, it was so calm, that the edge of the 'chute fluttered down on top of me anyway. By the time I'd pulled it off of me, a 'banca' boat had arrived.

"A 'banca' boat is a 20-foot dugout canoe with outriggers on either side and is powered by a two-stroke engine mounted on the end of a long shaft that goes through a pivot point in the transom. This simple setup allows both propulsion and steering from the same mechanism. Not a very elegant ride, but since one of the rules I try to live by is never to give up a free ride when I'm shark bait, I gladly accepted. One of the two men in the boat was wearing a Notre Dame T-shirt, the other was wearing a New York Yankees baseball cap. I took this as a good sign that they might help me. They spoke no English, but somehow I knew they were asking me if I wanted a ride. They helped get me and my survival gear into their boat. The gear and I were still tangled up in the parachute, and the front half of their boat looked like a large bowl of spaghetti.

"We went over to where Blair had entered the water. He'd gotten into his life raft and was just climbing into another banca boat. We tried our survival radios but couldn't hear anything because the search and rescue forces were still too far away and the low mountain range a few miles inland was blocking our signal. We went to the scene of the plane's impact, where there were only a few pieces of debris and a fuel slick on the surface. More boats arrived and added to our flotilla. As more and more people showed up, the English-speaking improved steadily.

"We asked the fishermen to take us ashore, but they shook their heads and said, 'No. No good.' They didn't want anything to do with that particular turf, as it was controlled by the New People's Army (Communist insurgents). They suggested we go to their town, a two-hour ride to the east, and since we really weren't in a position to argue, we agreed.

"After a brief stay at their residences (literally, thatched huts), we were handed over to two men who appeared to be a local police officer and a military member of some type. We went to the town's communications center (one phone, one telegraph key) and asked to call Clark Air Base, but no one knew how to do that and the number wasn't listed in the book. We found the number for the U.S. Consulate, in Manila, but had to wait our turn behind about 30 other people waiting to use the one phone.

"They eventually decided to take us to some 'local officials.' We'd taken our pressure suits off and were wearing the dark-green nylon lining over our long underwear. We entered a large building, carrying our survival gear and emergency radios, and were introduced to the mayor and town council. They were very concerned for our well-being and asked if we needed to see a doctor. When we told them that it wasn't necessary, they invited us to have lunch with them.

"They shared their simple meal of rice, pork, vegetables, pickled squid, and the best ice-cold bottle of Coca-Cola I've ever tasted. The men were very curious as to what happened and what kind of airplane we'd been flying. When we told them we couldn't say, the subject was immediately dropped. I imagined the men of the council to be World War II veterans and that U.S. servicemen were welcome, especially under these circumstances. The mayor, who appeared to be about our age, insisted we have coffee with him at his home after lunch. It amused me that our survival radios were automatically sending out distress signals while we sat on the mayor's patio drinking coffee. We asked if there was a radio transmitter anywhere and they eventually took us to one. As we were en route, a U.S. Navy P-3 flew overhead. We stopped and made radio contact, but the reception was poor. On reaching the short-wave radio, we identified ourselves to the P-3 crew and were told that a helicopter was on its way to pick us up. We drove back to the mayor's house and Blair positioned himself in a dried-up rice field to greet the helicopter crew. Meanwhile, I went back to the mayor's house for a final cup of coffee and to thank him and his countrymen for their wonderful hospitality. I also picked up our mission gear, which we'd left on the patio.

"The HH-53 rescue helicopter took us back to Clark. The crew would rather have taken us to the Officers' Club for some refreshments and that sounded good to us. But postaccident procedures require immediate medical evaluation and an interview with the safety investigation team. We went from the helicopter to an ambulance and were strapped to stretchers and fitted with neck braces. This seemed rather ironic to me after five or six hours of activity in various modes of transportation. In all fairness to the medical establishment, head and spinal injuries are common when ejecting from any airplane, and they can take some time to show up. The procedures are designed to avoid compounding the severity of any hidden injury. Once in the ambulance, the doors were closed and the driver backed up no more than 100 feet to the doors of the emergency room. We were thoroughly examined and extensively X-rayed before being kept overnight for observation.

"Once in our rooms, we gave written and verbal accounts of the accident to the safety investigation team. Before cleaning up and going to sleep, we got to call home to assure our wives and families that we were OK.

"The next day, we returned to Kadena and received a warm welcome home from all the people of Det 1. Spontaneous applause broke out as we stepped off the plane, and I think we shook hands with, and hugged, every person there."

The Recovery

Side-scanning sonar operations of the crash site took place on 29 and 30 April 1989, revealing the debris field of #974. The 280-foot-long salvage vessel USS *Beaufort* was dispatched to the site to lift the wreckage with its 10- and 15-ton cranes, fitted on the bow and stern of the ship respectively, and to find the sensors and defensive systems. Due to the proximity of the Communist New Peoples' Army, a number of Navy SEALS (Special Forces) were onboard the *Beaufort* to provide protection to the divers and crew. An order for "general quarters" was sounded at 0400 hours one morning during the search. Crewmen rushed to their action stations in readiness for an immediate confrontation. They saw a large number of small vessels (which had been detected on the *Beaufort*'s radar) heading for the ship. Tension mounted until it was discovered that the would-be attackers were really fishing boats. They came toward the bright lights of the naval vessel because a very large school of fish had congregated around it! The local fishermen were expecting to take full advantage of the unique situation.

When the inverted #974 impacted the water, both engines, the sensors, and other onboard equipment smashed through the airplane's upper surfaces. These were scattered on the ocean floor at varying distances away from the main wreckage. Cables were attached to one of the J-58 engines. The late-evening movements dislodged the engine's ignition tank, containing the highly flammable triethylborane (TEB). This created a small leak, which released tiny amounts of the chemical throughout the night. As a result, small amounts of the volatile chemical were released and bubbled to the surface, where it mixed with ambient air, exploding in small green puffs. The magic of the "Yankee" engineers caused quite a stir among the native fishermen who saw the eerie "TEB-bubble show" that night.

The next day both engines were lifted and brought aboard the *Beaufort*'s fantail, and two days later, many of the sensors were also recovered. When the ship's crew attempted to lift the main section of the aircraft, the crane operator found that the large delta-shaped wing greatly exceeded the lifting capacity of his crane, and the wreckage refused to budge. A yard-derrick was sent from the naval base at Subic Bay in the Philippines, and the forward fuselage section was recovered on 7 May, while the main structure was lifted aboard the *Beaufort*'s fantail the following day. Despite Dan's skillful and valiant efforts to save the plane, the black wreckage was a sad ending for a once-proud Blackbird.

I was based in the Pacific at the time as the vice commander of the 3rd Air Division. We were responsible for all SAC activities in the Pacific Theater and had just been moved from Andersen Air Force in Guam by the then CINCSAC, General Chain, to Hickam AFB, Hawaii. This move was designed to make SAC's presence more responsive to the commander in chief Pacific and to the Pacific Air Force commander, who were both based in Hawaii.

On 21 April 1989 I was called into my boss' office and informed of the crash of #974. Because of my previous experience in the SR-71, and because of my proximity to the crash site, I was assigned as president of the Accident Investigation Board. SAC headquarters had identified a team of investigators, including representatives from Lockheed and Pratt & Whitney, and tasked them to proceed directly to Clark Air Base in the Philippines. Since I was closest, I was among the first to arrive. It took a couple of days to get the first 15 or so team members assembled. We received thorough briefings on the accident, followed by a helicopter ride to the crash site off the north coast of Luzon. An interesting side note to the incident was that a Russian trawler had picked up the Mayday call of #974 and was proceeding to the scene. Fortunately, the U.S. Navy also had a destroyer in the area, and it proceeded at full steam to the crash site to provide protection and security for the site until a salvage effort could be mounted.

When we arrived on the scene two days later, the USS *Beaufort*, having been immediately dispatched from Subic Bay, was in position over what was thought to be the debris field (approximately 1/2 mile off shore, and in 200 feet of water). Our destroyer was hovering nearby, providing the cover we needed against prying eyes or salvage attempts by unfriendly forces. There was a contingent of Navy SEALS on the beach providing protection from the Communist Insurgent forces lurking in the nearby jungle. We had to land on the beach and be taken to the USS *Beaufort* via rubber rafts through the pounding surf—a new experience for Air Force personnel! As we boarded, we were greeted by the captain and settled in for what was about to be a very interesting two-week adventure at sea, albeit tethered to the bottom in one location.

From a national security standpoint, we were desperate to recover as many of the highly classified sensors on board as possible. A sophisticated side-scanning sonar system towed behind a small vessel was used to locate the debris field. The major factor aiding the search for the aircraft was that the sea bottom 1/2 mile off shore was flat and sandy, providing excellent contrast with large aircraft parts. As luck would have it, the aircraft struck the water in a flat "planform" attitude. Upon impact, the engines were ripped from their mountings and like two torpedoes side by side, continued their trajectory to the ocean floor, imbedding themselves there. That's precisely how they were found. The sensors aboard the SR-71 also ripped through their chine mountings and headed directly to the bottom.

The divers were hampered by the clouds of sand that they kicked up while walking around on the bottom looking for parts and pieces. Net loads of aircraft debris were lifted to the surface. It was also possible with the cranes on board the *Beaufort* to bring the engines to the surface. One mystery that puzzled the divers, and those of us on the surface listening to their radio commentary, was the location of the main fuselage. While they had found the main wing, they were at a loss to explain the whereabouts of the fuselage. Even the sonar scans did not produce a sighting. It wasn't until one observant diver reported seeing a thin pencil-like protrusion extending aft from the tail that we determined what had happened and solved the mystery. Apparently, on impact, the long diving board–shaped fuselage had split open and literally folded under the main delta wing, making it invisible to sonar and to the diver's limited vision at that depth. The clue to its whereabouts was the pitot boom extending from the *rear* of the aircraft.

Up to this point, we had recovered all of the important classified pieces that had been ripped out of the airplane. All that remained was to raise the aircraft itself. Cables were attached to the fuselage but the weight of the entire aircraft, even buoyed by water, proved to be too much for the cranes on *Beaufort*. A yard derrick was called for from Subic Bay and had to be towed up the west coast of Luzon by tug. We spent two more days on board waiting for the vessel to arrive.

It didn't take long for this mammoth-floating rig to do the job. We all gathered by the rail of our vessel and watched in disbelief and sadness as this once-proud and beautiful Blackbird was hauled from its watery grave. The light of day revealed a twisted mass of titanium and wires, only vaguely

The unrecognizable forward fuselage being hoisted aboard the USS *Beaufort*. The impact with the water had to be tremendous, especially considering that each SR-71 was built with over 90 percent titanium. As you can see, it's nothing more than a twisted mass of titanium. *Al Cirino*

recognizable as the fastest jet in the world. The aircraft and all its precious cargo now littering the entire deck of the *Beaufort* and the yard derrick were carried back to Okinawa for analysis and final burial.

Now, our work as the accident investigation team really began. The engines were flown back to Pratt & Whitney in Florida for complete teardown and analysis. Lockheed technical representatives examined the airframe with a fine-tooth comb on Okinawa. During the subsequent investigation, it was determined that a materiel failure in one of the compressor main bearings caused a catastrophic seizure of the left engine. One of the sheared compressor blades ripped through the flight control hydraulic lines in the wing, creating a small hole in the right, "B" backup system. Fortunately, the hole was small enough to prevent loss of all fluid in that system until such time that the aircraft had safely decelerated to subsonic speed. Then, when all the fluid was gone, the compete loss of flight controls ensued.

It took us about five weeks to get the engine and airframe analysis results and to prepare the findings briefings for CINCSAC.

CHAPTER EIGHT

Colonel (Ret) Don Emmons

Don entered the Air Force in October 1964. After completing navigator and bombardier training, he was assigned to the 96th Bomb Wing, Dyess AFB, Texas, where he flew B-52E/D aircraft. Flying B-52s out of Guam, Utapao, and Okinawa, Don ended up with 225 combat missions over Vietnam, 5 of which were over downtown Hanoi during Linebacker II sorties. He amassed over 3,500 hours in B-52s.

The "Snake and Nape" team on Okinawa: Don Emmons, right, and Rich Graham. We had a requirement that all operational sorties had to be flown with a formed crew. If one crewmember was too sick to fly, then the mission passed to the next crew on the ladder. Don and I flew the SR-71 together for 5-1/2 years. *Rich Graham*

In September 1974, Don arrived at Beale AFB. Over the next seven years he flew 69 operational sorties in the SR-71 as an RSO and chalked up over 700 hours in the Blackbird and 117 hours in the T-38. In August 1980 Don was selected to be the squadron operations officer and was the acting Det 4 commander at RAF Mildenhall on a periodic basis. He left Beale AFB in July 1981 for the Pentagon, where he was the program element monitor (PEM) for the SR-71 program. In October 1984, Don was chosen to be the commander of Det 6, 2762 Logistics Squadron at Norton AFB, California, which was uniquely responsible for total worldwide logistics support of the SR-71. He remained at Det 6 until the SR-71 program closed down on 30 September 1990. After that, Don was chosen to be the commander of Det 8, 2762 Logistics Squadron, Robins AFB, Georgia, which had the same responsibility for the U-2.

He retired in August 1992. When Congress directed the SR-71s back into service, Don's expertise was sorely needed. In November 1994, Don was hired as a consultant to resurrect the Blackbird program. In my opinion, only he could handle the job of "putting Humpty Dumpty back together again." The newly formed SR-71 unit was located at Edwards AFB, California, as Det 2 of the 9th Reconnaissance Wing at Beale AFB. After President Clinton line-item vetoed the SR-71 program in October 1997, Don closed the door to Det 2 for the last time on 9 October 1999, ending the final chapter of Blackbird's unique history. Here are his stories.

Bomb Scare

We were the new crew-in-training at the time with less than 50 hours apiece in the Blackbird and at the far end of our training route. We had just disconnected from the tanker at 25,000 feet after topping off all of our tanks when it happened. I didn't need any cockpit instruments to tell me that the muffled bang and instantaneous yaw to the right meant that we had lost our right engine. Although Rich had immediately performed all the necessary emergency procedures, he called for the checklist as we descended. After several unsuccessful attempts at restarting the engine, we both knew that we would not be returning to Beale that day.

Our nearest abort base was 100 miles to the south, which would require a 90-degree turn to the left. The aircraft was at its heaviest weight, so we were continually losing altitude with only one functioning engine. Rich had his hands full executing a left turn with an opposing engine while in a descent. All the while we were dumping fuel to get down to a reasonable landing weight. The situation had our complete attention—it was our first emergency and land-away in the SR-71. At 18,000 feet the aircraft was able to maintain level flight as we threaded our way toward Blytheville AFB in Arkansas. Rich did a superb job of flying and landing the aircraft with an engine out. We were met on the ground by a very large base contingent. It was the spring of 1975 and curiosity was still abounding with the mystique of an SR-71. (Actually, that mystique never did dissipate.)

The recovery crew from Beale AFB, with the spare engine and support equipment, did not arrive until late the next evening. The plan was to spend the next day changing the engine and performing all of the necessary operational checks and preflight, with a departure on the following day. At 0230 hours we were roused out of bed by Colonel Samay, who was in charge of the Beale recovery team. He had received a call from the Blytheville AFB command post that the entire team from Beale was to report ASAP to the hangar in which the SR-71 was housed. Upon arrival, an irate base commander informed us that a bomb threat had been received. One had supposedly been placed on the "spy plane which the base was hiding" and was scheduled to detonate at 0400 hours. We didn't see how this was possible since security police guarded the aircraft the entire time. However, the guard on duty could not avow that no one else had had access during his watch. The explosive ordinance disposal (EOD) dog sniffers found nothing, so prudence prevailed, and at 0330 hours all personnel withdrew 100 yards away.

An hour later it was determined that it was a hoax and the base commander asked how much longer we would be around. When told it would be another day he went into a tirade and demanded that we be "off the base" by 1000 hours that day—knowing that request was totally unrealistic. Apparently, our warm welcome was immediately terminated by the potential of more bomb threats. Our commander endeared himself to all of us in earshot when he informed the base commander that he wasn't in the position to demand anything from us, and we would leave on our terms, not his. The base commander left in a huff, and Colonel Samay asked the chief master sergeant in charge how soon he could have the aircraft ready to go. The chief asked, "Do we have to follow tech data?" Without missing a beat, the colonel's *challenge* was "My question is, in your opinion, how soon can we safely launch the aircraft?" To which the chief smiled with that tacit understanding and replied, "We'll show this base what the 9th Wing professionals are capable of!" Rich and I launched with a new engine and flew back to Beale without further incident. Our takeoff time was 0957 hours. Take that, Blytheville!

Diego Garcia

It was the best of times. It was the worst of times. No, I'm not referring to the French revolution, but to the summer of 1980. Things could not have been better for me in early June of that year. I had been flying the SR-71 as an RSO for six years. This alone was the ultimate thrill for any navigator. I had been overly blessed, as the average tour to fly the SR-71 was four years. For the past two years, I had held the esteemed status of senior RSO in Stan/Eval division as both an instructor and evaluator. I had been promoted to lieutenant colonel, and my pin-on date was 1 July. I was preparing to go TDY to Kadena AB for my last operational tour flying the SR-71. Upon return from that tour of duty, I was to become the squadron operations officer, only the second navigator in SAC to ever hold that position. Yes, things could not have been better; life was indeed good.

I arrived at Beale AFB in June of 1974 and started my checkout in the T-38 before beginning SR-71 training. The squadron commander told me that the next RSO to enter training was an officer called Don Emmons, and I would be crewed with him. The first time we met was at the Beale AFB flight line, during a ceremony to welcome the return of the crew that just set the London to Los Angeles speed record. Little did I realize at the time, I would have the privilege of flying with Don for the next 5-1/2 years in both the SR-71 and T-38.

While flying the SR-71, Don and I had the nicknames of "Snake and Nape," respectively. Snake and Nape was the abbreviated name given to my favorite bomb load flying F-4s in Vietnam . . . six "snake-eye" MK-82 bombs and two cans of "napalm." In January 1980, the Snake and Nape team finally broke up when I was selected to be the squadron commander. For the next six months, Don continued flying with another pilot, Bob Crowder, until I asked the powers to be if Don could be my squadron operations officer. The Snake and Nape team was back in action!

—Rich Graham

Our TDY tours at Kadena went normally for six weeks. At that time three SR-71 crews were on Kadena. One crew replaced another every two weeks. In all my worldly travels with the Air Force, Okinawa was my favorite location. The island was absolutely beautiful, offering some of the best touring, dining, shopping, beaches, snorkeling, boating, and diving. The flying was superb, with missions ranging anywhere within the South China Sea, the Taiwan Straits, the Yellow Sea, the Korean Peninsula, the Kuril Islands, the Sea of Okhotsk, to the Kamchatka Peninsula. Summer not only offered the best weather for operational flying, but also was the perfect time to enjoy what Okinawa had to offer. Since this was my last tour, I planned to thoroughly savor each of the 42 days awaiting me. My first letdown came when I discovered that we would be deploying later than planned.

One of the SR-71s at Kadena had developed an unresolved, annoying chatter with one of its inlet doors. This was so bad that it degraded the imagery taken in flight. The decision was made to replace the Det 1 Blackbird with one from Beale AFB. This meant that Bob Crowder and I would be ferrying a replacement aircraft over rather than taking the usual passenger flight on a KC-135Q. Don't misunderstand; ferrying an SR-71 to or from our Detachments was a relished task and highly sought after by Habus. After all, this reduced your travel time from 19 to 5 hours. Any flight in the Blackbird is nothing less than wonderful. However, the ultimate is flying an operational sortie . . . a reconnaissance mission against the "bad guys." So, in addition to missing eight days of island offerings, I would also be forfeiting the opportunity to fly one or two operational missions. Of course, the crew we were replacing was elated over *their* extra time on Okinawa, and then having the luxury of flying an SR-71 back to Beale AFB. This was only the first of several setbacks.

The flight over went as planned. Our great circle route took us south of the Aleutian Island chain and down the Russian and Japanese coasts into Okinawa. We refueled shortly after takeoff, accelerated to Mach 3 for a hot leg, and descended for another refueling off the Alaskan coast. The next hot leg flew us along the Russian coast to another refueling just west of Japan, and then a short supersonic leg into Kadena AB. The time en route was a little over five hours.

While waiting our turn on the crew "ladder," Bob Crowder and I spent the next few days getting acclimatized to the time change and enjoying the island fare. SR-71 operational missions were levied by SAC headquarters and were randomly scheduled. The unit acted on the "tasking" as it was received from SAC. We referred to them as "ops" sorties, and each crew flew every third mission, as defined by their turn on the ladder. Habu crews loved ops sorties. This is what we trained to do. Most Air Force aviators spend their entire flying career training to accomplish their particular combat mission in case of war. Most never experience it. Flying reconnaissance during the cold war was the real thing for us. We flew against our adversaries, and bringing down an SR-71 would have been the ultimate coup for them. Of course, the SR-71 offered us the relative peace of feeling impervious to any hostile reactions. Still, you always experienced that euphoria of having tested the enemy's defenses and bringing back the "take," as we referred to the intelligence data we gathered.

The "ladder" determined who flew next. With three crews at our detachments, one crew became the primary fliers, another crew was the backup fliers and performed mobile duties, and the third crew had the day off. Once the primary crew completed the mission, they dropped down to their day off, and the other two crews moved up the ladder. The ladder was never violated. Well, practically never!

Arriving on Kadena later than planned, I was busy planning my promotion party for 1 July. The food had been ordered, the booze was purchased, and over 50 invitations had been sent out for my big event. Life was just getting good again when our Det 1 commander, Colonel Ray Samay, called the unit together for a special meeting. We knew something out of the ordinary had been levied on us. The excitement level was high. He briefed us that an SR-71 was to be deployed for a few days to the remote island atoll of Diego Garcia to "show presence" in the theatre. If tensions in the Middle East heightened, this island would serve as a staging base, 5,000 miles closer to the area of conflict. The philosophy was, being seen there now would decrease any suspicions of military intent if we arrived at a future date.

The advance support team of over 50 personnel, led by Colonel Samay would leave on 29 June, and the aircraft would follow on 1 July. Bob and I were not next on the ladder—this meant we would not be the assigned crew. I sat back in the briefing room and breathed a sigh of relief, smiling as I envisioned more ops sorties for us in that crew's absence. Things were good again. My party could occur as planned, I could make up for lost sorties, and not lose any more of my remaining precious days on Okinawa. My elation was short-lived.

At the end of the briefing, Colonel Samay announced that Bob and I had been selected as the "lucky" crew for the deployment. Oh no! I spent the next day, to no avail, trying to wrangle ourselves out of the flight. It turns out that our selection had been decreed from the 9th Wing commander at Beale AFB. The good news was that the plan was for us to fly down one day and return the next. OK, I could live with that. Everyone on the party invite list was notified of a 24-hour delay. Being a Saturday, it would work just as well.

That Friday morning I proudly showed up at the ops briefing sporting my new rank. We were scheduled to be back by 1700 hours the next day. I left the keys to my BOQ room and told the other Habus that if we were delayed, to start the party without us, we would be there shortly. Now that we were committed, I was looking forward to my new adventure. After all, this would give me the opportunity to see the Southern Cross, a treat for any navigator who had gone through celestial training. This is the most spectacular of constellations, but it can only be viewed south of the equator.

We refueled shortly after takeoff and accelerated to our cruise of 80,000 feet and Mach 3. Our 4-1/2-hour course went south-southwest between Taiwan and the northern Philippines, into the South China Sea, to a southeastern heading below Vietnam, and toward the isthmus separating Malaysia and Burma. This was the only land we flew over and it didn't last long traveling at 30 miles a minute. Diego Garcia is a small atoll in the middle of the Indian Ocean, 1,200 miles directly south of the southern tip of India. We were instructed to pass over the island first with cameras on to get some photos "suitable for framing." Reproductions of this shot later adorned the hallowed

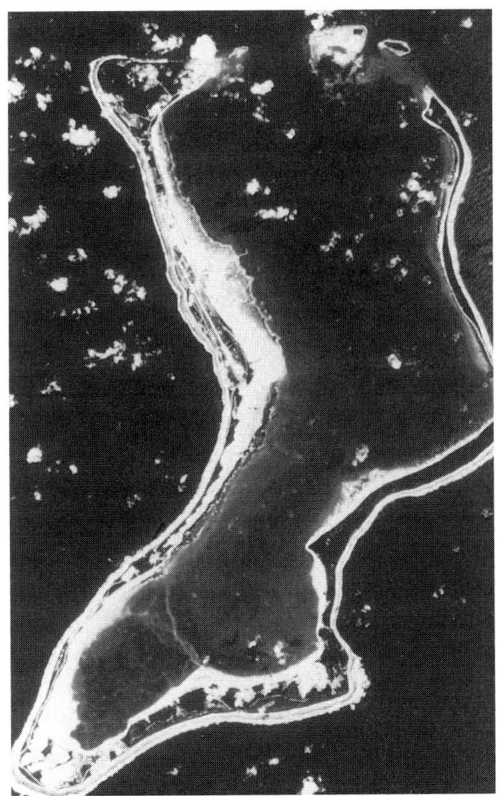

Aerial view of Diego Garcia, located in the middle of the Indian Ocean. It wasn't until the early 1980s that the United States realized the strategic importance of the coral atoll. At the time, the United States was extremely limited in locations its aircraft could use if tensions rose in the Middle East. The runway was lengthened to support B-52 operations, and Diego Garcia is now a major base supporting the war on terrorism in Afghanistan. *Don Emmons Collection*

halls of SAC headquarters and the Pentagon. The horseshoe-shaped island is 19 miles long and separated by a 5-mile lagoon. Its widest point of land is less than a mile. At anchor in the middle of the lagoon was a U.S. submarine tender with two nuclear subs moored on one side and a destroyer on the other.

Upon landing, Bob and I were unaware of our impending reindoctrination to life in the boonies. Colonel Samay welcomed us to the rock. He proudly stated that Bob and I were in luck. He had wrangled rooms for us in the *only* air-conditioned building on the island—a luxury even he and the support troops did not share. Our new living quarters turned out to be a recovery room in the base medical clinic. Our first order of business was to doff our pressure suits, shower, change, and check out the surroundings. Fortunately, we noticed the lack of soap before getting wet. It took awhile for one of the medical personnel to locate some for our use. However, we were not as lucky in noticing the lack of towels. Dripping wet, and yelling down the hall for assistance, brought a disgusted "You didn't bring those, either?" We had to make do with some 1-foot-square, blue surgical cloths.

We then went to Base Operations for the in-country briefing, which was standard military procedure upon first arriving in a foreign country. The

United Kingdom controlled Diego Garcia. The entire native populace had long ago been relocated, making this a pure military outpost. The U.S. Navy had over 500 Seabees living there in a tent city. We were informed that special care should be taken in driving because of the 25-British-pound fine levied if any of the Queen's subjects were struck by automobile. In addition to the five British military personnel who managed the island, this also included all goats and soldier crabs, both of which were in abundance and considered the roads to be for their sole usage. Unfortunately, the briefing stressed not to venture into the surrounding waters under any circumstances. The shark population was aggressive and plentiful. Just two weeks earlier, a man who disregarded this warning was hit and severely injured by a shark, while wading in water below his thigh.

We spent the afternoon touring the area, intending to be at the Officers' Club when it opened at 1800 hours. Having frequented these habitats during tours to England, I was always impressed by their great settings for socializing and drinking. However, this "Officers' Club" was essentially a grass hooch, just large enough to house a 15-foot bar and several tables. It reminded me of *Gilligan's Island*. It was located on the very tip of the atoll, affording a beautiful view of the beach on three sides. Since there was no capability to lock the club doors and windows, the nightly alcohol fare had to be brought over from the "ship's store" on base where it was kept secure. The crowd was eagerly awaiting the arrival of the pickup truck carrying the spirits, mix, and ice. After unloading the stock, the truck driver then became the bartender for the evening. The drink of choice for SR-71 crewmembers was vodka and tonic, which we referred to among ourselves as a "basic hook." However, the only offerings that night were beer, bourbon, and rum. It was hard to make a match since the only mixes were tonic and Sprite. But, "when in the war zone," we learned to make do when necessary. It was

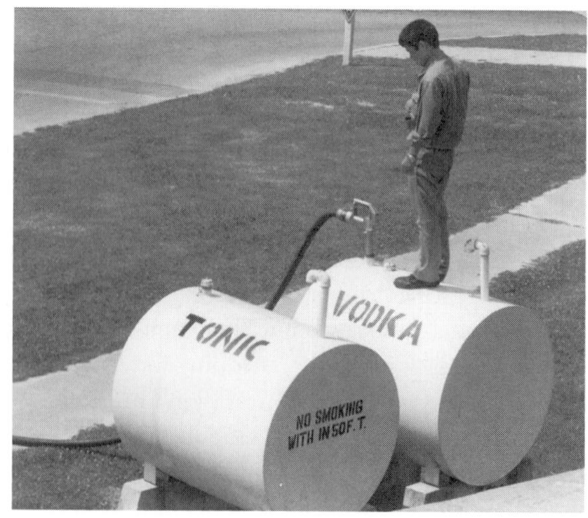

Local Okinawan refilling our monthly supply of vodka and tonic! There were many days when we all felt as if we *had* drained the tanks. These are actually kerosene tanks beside our quarters to run the air conditioning units. We were also known to spray-paint black SR-71 silhouettes around the bases. *Rich Graham*

more humorous than anything, since we had had a long day and would soon enter crew rest for our flight back to Okinawa.

The Habu term "hook" referred to any alcoholic beverage (because like a hook shot in basketball, a drinker "hooks" his arm as he drinks). If you asked for a "basic hook," that was our term for a popular drink among Habus–vodka and tonic. My first Det 1 commander, Col. (Ret) Tom Estes, was even more specific about a basic hook–it had to be made with Gordon's vodka and Schweppes tonic, with a twist of lime. Any Habu worth his salt had a plentiful supply of Gordon's vodka and Schweppes tonic behind his bar ready for a no-notice party or a visit by the Det 1 commander. It's hard to imagine, but on Okinawa, in the mid-1970s, tonic water was actually more expensive than the vodka!

–Rich Graham

When Bob and I returned to our room, we were met with another surprise. There were no sheets or pillows on the hospital beds. We somehow knew the incredulous answer would be "You didn't bring your own?" so we didn't even bother to ask. I've always found hospitals to be too cold for comfort and this one proved to be no different. We didn't dare complain. However, we knew where they kept the surgical cloths from our prior experience in the shower. We "borrowed" several to cover ourselves as best we could, just to keep warm.

The next morning we were met with more bad news. During the maintenance preflight, it was discovered that one of the SR-71's auxiliary drive systems (ADS) needed replacing. Basically, the ADS uses a drive shaft from the engine and powers the generators and hydraulic systems. Det 1 had already been apprised to send a replacement to us. This would necessitate a 48-hour delay. Now, what were we to do? We had already toured the small island. The answer promptly presented itself. The SR-71 was always a natural attraction. We had the perfect static display. Maintenance had completed all its work on the Blackbird, and we were certainly available. It didn't take long for our "Tours-R-Us" operation to start. It was our way of saying thanks to the local inhabitants for their hospitality.

The rest of the day zoomed by as Bob and I and several maintenance personnel fielded questions in front of the aircraft from the hundreds of Navy personnel on hand. Most crewmembers will agree that it is questionable which is higher—the excitement of those viewing the airplane for the first time, or the pride exhibited by those giving the tour. Everyone was in a great mood and a big Saturday night at the club was anticipated by all. More groans were emitted, however, when the evening's bar stock was again unloaded. This time it was vodka, scotch, Coke, and 7-Up. Didn't the Navy know the proper alcohol and mix protocol? The locals even joked that it must be the Navy's answer to its charge to "de-glamorize" alcohol—a bureaucratic buzzword for reducing alcohol consumption by the military. Regardless of this nuance, the evening was thoroughly enjoyed by all and we made many new friends. Moreover, the Navy had graciously offered to entertain us the next day with tours of their ships.

At 0800 hours the next morning Colonel Samay, Bob, and I were picked up by a launch and taken to the destroyer. There we had a lovely breakfast with the captain and his officers, followed by a tour of the ship. I was fascinated by it all. From there, we were taken to one of the subs for a tour and a light lunch with the captain in his cabin. They had been at sea for five months and were in to replenish their food stock. It was a most interesting sight. You cannot imagine the closeness of quarters in the living and working space. Everyone has visualized it, but one has to experience it firsthand to appreciate it. No claustrophobia would be allowed here! There was absolutely no space wasted. Every nook or cranny was filled with dry goods or loaves of bread and pastries. The sub's Command Center held the latest in technology and looked as if it came out of the *Star Wars* movie. My highlight was playing with the periscope. Then we were off to the sub tender itself. This was a very large vessel with 1,100 people aboard. It was literally a floating service garage. Its machine room alone would draw envy from any U.S. manufacturer. Its video library of 1,200 movies astonished us all. Remember, this was in 1980, and before VCRs and Blockbuster Video Stores were common entities. This impressive tour of several hours culminated with one of the finest dinners I have eaten. It was a fantastic day, and one I will never forget. It left me with a greater appreciation of our Navy cohorts. Note that I said appreciation—not envy. It reminded this lad, who grew up in a Navy town, why he joined the Air Force. It offered a quicker means of travel, a daily opportunity of being on terra firma, and a continual change of horizon scenery.

Our takeoff was scheduled for 1000 hours. At that time, the sub tender was to have a Fourth of July ceremony on deck with all hands attending. They requested we fly over as low as possible as we departed. Everything proceeded normally. After engine start we were notified that the ANS was having problems. The astro-tracker portion was inoperative and several power dropouts had occurred during the alignment. At best, we would have inertial guidance only, with an unknown amount of drift during the 5,000-mile trip. It was recommended we shut down and order another unit from Okinawa. I recommended to Bob over the interphone that we press on, and he agreed. A couple of minutes later Colonel Samay came up the ladder, and over the engine noise asked if we were sure we wanted to accept the aircraft. I gave him a thumbs-up to which he smiled, patted my back and gave his thumbs-up to the maintenance staff below. I looked down and saw smiles on everyone. They all wanted to leave as badly as we did!

After takeoff Bob took it out of afterburner and turned toward the sub tender. I could see hundreds of sailors on the deck just waiting for our pass. He lit the burners again as we passed over them at 100 feet. Bob was particularly good at making impressive high-speed, low-altitude passes with the SR-71. This is a favorite at air shows, but it's usually accomplished at 500 feet or higher. I looked down through my view sight and witnessed numerous personnel hitting the deck and diving for cover. I thought to myself we are going to catch hell over this, but what the heck, anything for the troops. We owed them for their gracious hospitality. They requested low and that's what they got!

We proceeded to our tanker waiting for us about 100 miles away at 25,000 feet. The ANS began having power dropouts, requiring automatic hot-air starts. This would probably not continue for long before it shut itself down completely. Well, no problem I thought, I'll just do a cold-air start, which involves shutting the system down completely and doing another complete alignment. I don't know of anyone ever doing a cold-air start successfully, but it was an emergency procedure that we practiced in the simulator. To initiate the alignment would require the KC-135Q tanker navigator to give us precise geographical coordinates of our present position and an accurate heading while we were refueling on the boom. I tried numerous attempts to enter the data into the ANS, but to no avail. The ANS was now totally inoperative. There was no backup navigation system in the SR-71 at that time.

Around 1985, the SR-71 fleet was upgraded with an accurate backup means of navigation by adding a ring-laser Inertial Navigation System (INS).

Well, it was decision time. I had 15 years' experience as a navigator, consisting of 3,500 hours in a B-52 and 700 hours in an SR-71. Dead reckoning (DR) was taught way back in Chapter One of my navigator training. This method of using only time and heading had been the mainstay of navigation for decades before modern technology prevailed. It was time to earn my pay and go back to basics. I was confident of success and explained the situation to Bob. He agreed to press on.

The tanker navigator gave me a current position and heading as we dropped off the boom to start our acceleration to Mach 3 and 80,000 feet. I started a stopwatch as Bob and I compared that heading to the heading reflected on each of our small whiskey compasses. I had planned on a visual fix as we passed over the Malaysian isthmus, but as my luck had it, it was undercast below. An hour and a half, and almost 3,000 miles later, should have placed us due south of Vietnam. Although I was confident of my navigation, prudence still prevailed. To avoid any possibility of an inadvertent overflight, I had Bob turn an additional 10 degrees to the right for a safety factor. The rule of thumb is that one degree of heading change will displace an airplane 1 mile for every 60 miles traveled. We were traveling at 2,100 miles per hour, or 30 miles per minute. This equated to us veering south of course five miles every minute that elapsed. This is precisely why SR-71 crews joke about how fast one can get lost at Mach 3.

A whiskey compass is required in all aircraft by the FAA. It was a *very crude* instrument to provide aircraft heading. Errors in magnetic lines of variation, aircraft deviation, and internal compass errors all have to be taken into consideration when computing aircraft heading. There are so many errors in using a whiskey compass, particularly at 2,000 miles per hour, that we considered it a true emergency procedure!

It was called a "whiskey" compass because during aviation's pioneer days actual whiskey was used as the stabilizing fluid inside the compass.

A rendezvous with the KC-135 is accomplished using an ARC-50 radio communication system. It locks onto the tanker and gives a distance and relative bearing. A few minutes later our electronic rendezvous equipment showed the KC-135Q tanker 212 miles away. We started our descent. Instead of being dead ahead, the tanker was 10 degrees left. Perfect! The correction had not been needed after all; we had been on course all along. A sigh of relief was in order. After refueling we again started the stopwatch as we received our position and heading from the tanker navigator and started the acceleration back to altitude. An hour and a half later we locked onto Kadena 225 miles straight ahead. That DR stuff does work. We had done it.

Upon landing, everyone informed me that my promotion party was a great success. We never heard one complaint about the flyover from the Navy. Moreover, I did see the Southern Cross. An SR-71 never again landed in Diego Garcia.

Burial At Sea

After being recovered from the bottom of the South China Sea in 1989, the wreckage of SR-71 #974 was moved to Kadena AB. Its wreckage was placed back in the same hanger it departed on its ill-fated flight months earlier. Although this was an ideal place for the Accident Investigation Board to examine the wreckage, it didn't do much for the morale at Det 1. Imagine the tremendous satisfaction and pleasure of working daily on a larger-than-life machine, and then later, viewing it daily in a destroyed state. Consequently, when the board completed its investigation, the wreckage needed to be removed ASAP. The highest of esprit de corps, held for 25 years, was already waning due to the announced termination of the SR-71 program. As the commander of Det 6, 2762 LS, I held all the logistics responsibility levied on the Blackbirds by Air Force Logistics Command (AFLC). Removing the wreckage fell under this purview. Unfortunately, my staff and I had already been diligently working this issue for some time, to no avail. There were only four viable options for disposal but as each was pursued, a brick wall emerged.

The wreckage could be turned in as salvage to the military's Defense Reutilization and Marketing Office (DRMO). They would in turn, sell it as scrap metal to the highest bidder on Okinawa. It could be transported back to the United States for the same type of disposal. Another option was to bury the aircraft remains on Kadena. It could also be disposed of at sea.

Det 1 aircrews in their "orange bags," and staff personnel in front of an SR-71 hangar. Left to right: Rich Graham, Bill Groninger, Don Emmons, Dave Nicola (maintenance officer), Jay Murphy (director of operations), George Chumbley (intelligence officer), Chuck Sober, Barry MacKean, and Lee Shelton. *Rich Graham*

Extenuating circumstances precluded any of these as being possible. The quickest and least costly option was to bury it. Precedence had already been set. Over 25 years earlier, an SR-71 had been buried on Kadena after its local demise. However, we could not receive approval from Pacific Air Force (PACAF), the operating command. With the ongoing closing and consolidation of U.S. military bases on Okinawa, Kadena AB was constantly constructing facilities for its new tenants. The possibility of continually having to dig it up and move it elsewhere on the base was not something they relished.

Using the local DRMO was never really an option. Although this is the standard procedure for the disposal of aircraft wreckage, this situation was different. The local economy consisted of foreign nationals and we had no control over the buyer. This was an SR-71 and its technology was still highly classified. Titanium is the strongest of metals and there were still large pieces of the aircraft intact. It simply would not do to have a Blackbird tail section found mounted in front of some Japanese business establishment, or worse. I tried having it flown back to the States but couldn't get approval to use Air Force transport or expend any monies commercially to do the same.

Burial at sea seemed the best remaining option, but we needed Navy assistance. The word from the Air Force side of the Pentagon was a "No can do!" Apparently, it required approval from no less than the Chief of Naval Operations (CNO). At that time, the SR-71 was a curse word among the Air Force general officer corps. Getting the Air Force to even start the coordination by our SR-71 representatives in the Pentagon was out of the question. Pressure was continually mounting to have the aircraft debris removed from the premises, but I had no place to put it. Moreover, I could find no Air Force agency even sympathetic to my plight. It was merely the times. The entire SR-71 program was in the process of being dismantled—much to the delight of the Air Force bureaucracy. Solving this dilemma suddenly became the highest priority of Det 6 and its 159 employees.

One of my program managers, Cynthia Hernandez, asked if she could personally work the Navy issue. Although her primary responsibilities lay with the SR-71 flight simulator and the Astroinertial Navigation System (ANS), she already had a reputation for great success in the "hard to do" category. She was tenacious in her ability to handle any obstacle presented her, doing so with great aplomb. I sensed at that moment that resolution was at hand. She started by totally bypassing the Air Force. Using one of my Pentagon phone books, she started calling around to various Navy offices until she found the right venue. Her verbal and persuasive skills enabled her to move right up the chain of command. She even had admirals calling her and offering their assistance. Just when success appeared imminent, a new glitch presented itself.

The U.S. Navy honors the "Law of the Sea," which is a voluminous listing of universal maritime laws to be adhered to by all nations. This was in the late 1980s, and the environment had suddenly become a paramount issue, even within the Law of the Sea. Refuse could no longer be arbitrarily dumped at sea without an environmental impact study and written permission from the Environmental Protection Agency (EPA) itself. The CNO's permission could not be garnered without this square being filled. Not to be denied, Cynthia started calling EPA offices around the country until she found the responsible office. Finally, resolution seemed in reach. However, disaster struck again as a massive earthquake rattled San Francisco. One of the badly damaged buildings was, you guessed it, the one that housed the Regional EPA office coordinating our paperwork.

None of the EPA personnel were allowed access back into the building until it was certified as safe. The original paperwork was not retrievable. Daily calls to their temporary offices produced the same response. No one knew when access would again be allowed. This aptly reminded me of the saying "So close, and yet so far." After several weeks, we were finally told that it would be at least six more months. Cynthia explained the gravity of the situation to as high a supervisor as could be found, and asked if he envisioned any problem with our obtaining the needed approval, whenever that may be. He told her to proceed as necessary and he would personally attend to the follow-up paperwork. The question was, would a verbal approval satisfy the Navy? This would be the proverbial, "The check is in the mail!" When she called the Pentagon, the Navy only asked if the EPA had granted approval. She could honestly reply in the affirmative. Fortunately, official copies of the approval were not required on their sign-off sheet—just that it had been obtained. It sailed through the Navy's system and the CNO granted his permission to use a Navy ship. Thank you again, Cynthia.

The wreckage was subsequently transported to the harbor and transferred to a waiting vessel. The captain later sent a classified message to my personal attention. It stated that the remains of SR-71 #974 were buried at sea with full military honors. The occasion occurred at 1157 hours on Christmas Eve of 1989. The coordinates given placed it several hundred miles from Okinawa. The final resting place was in 25,597 feet of water, in an area known as the Mariana Trench.

CHAPTER NINE

Lieutenant Colonel (Ret) John J. "Jack" Veth

Jack began his military career in 1963 as a student pilot at Williams Air Force Base, Arizona. Following completion of flight training, Jack received an assignment as an F-4C Phantom pilot. After upgrade training, Jack was assigned to the 480th Tactical Fighter Squadron, and in February 1966 deployed with the squadron to Da Nang Air Base, Vietnam, to participate in the ongoing Vietnam conflict.

After flying combat missions in Vietnam, Jack was assigned to the Air Defense Command as an F-101 fighter interceptor pilot. He flew the F-101 out of Dow AFB in Bangor, Maine, and Otis AFB, Massachusetts, until 1970.

Jack attended Squadron Officer School at Maxwell AFB, Alabama, and remained there as an instructor until 1975. While at Maxwell AFB, he flew both the T-33 and T-39 aircraft. Jack applied to the SR-71 program in 1975. He began flying operational sorties with the Blackbird in 1977. The SR-71 proved to be the last operational aircraft Jack

Crew of Jack Veth, left, and Bill Keller. Notice the pull-down strap attached to the neck ring on Bill's suit. If the pressure suit inflated, it was possible for the metal neck ring and helmet to actually rise up and cover your face. If that happened, the pull-down strap allowed crewmembers to pull the neck ring back down into position. *Jack Veth*

flew, as he was assigned to March AFB, California, as the director of reconnaissance at 15th Air Force in 1982.

Jack retired in 1984 and joined Northrop Corporation's development and production team for the advanced technology (Stealth) bomber, the B-2. At the same time, Jack began law school in the evenings to pursue a second career as an attorney.

In 1987 he graduated from Western State University College of Law and was admitted to the California Bar the same year. Jack currently combines his experience in aviation and his legal education in a law practice, including aviation and complex tort law, personal injury, and product liability litigation, specializing in aviation crash litigation. He is currently the managing partner of the California office of Speiser Krause.

The SR-71 was not designed with night flying in mind. I knew he flew the first operational night sorties after many years of no night flying, and asked him to write about his experience.

First Post-Vietnam Night Operational Mission

At precisely 2105 hours on the night of 19 September 1977, a tower operator at Kadena flashed a green light to an SR-71 (#960) sitting on the runway, indicating it was cleared for takeoff. This flashing green light also indicated the beginning of a new era in peacetime reconnaissance operations for the men and women of Det 1 who flew and maintained the Blackbirds. The previous operational night mission flown by an SR-71 out of Kadena occurred five years earlier, on 28 December 1972, during the Vietnam War. Following the war, all operational missions from Kadena were flown during daylight hours.

The cameras used at that time required daylight. The majority of our takeoff times were based on arriving in the target area around noon for high sun angles to produce good pictures. It wasn't until later that our side-looking radar imaging system (called CAPRE) produced satisfactory intelligence, allowing us to fly at night or with cloud cover over the target area. By 28 December 1972, the air war in Vietnam was quickly ending. On 18 December 1972, President Nixon authorized a massive air campaign, called Linebacker II, bringing the air war directly to the heart of North Vietnam–Hanoi! Many losses were incurred during Linebacker II, but it was something that should have been done years before.

Little did I realize, while flying Wild Weasel missions over Hanoi during Linebacker II (also called "The 11 Days of Christmas"), SR-71s were overhead gathering valuable intelligence.

—Rich Graham

As the green light from the tower flashed, Bill Keller, my RSO, and I began the takeoff roll. Ten seconds later, #960 left the ground to begin a 4-hour, 5-minute night sortie. The mission was scheduled to include two Mach 3 cruise legs through the target area for radar imaging, two descents from above 80,000 feet for refueling, and a landing back at Kadena at 0110 hours the following morning.

The mission used radio-silent procedures from taxi until just before our landing clearance. During the mission, we rendezvoused with the tanker through our special radio ranging system, providing us with the azimuth and distance information from the approaching KC-135Q. All our refueling procedures were designed so that as we ended the refueling track, the SR-71 had a full load of JP-7. After disconnecting from the tanker's boom, I flew the aircraft to a safe distance away from the tanker and lit both afterburners, beginning our climb to operational speed and altitude.

Our route took us northwest from Kadena toward the Korean peninsula. The mission included four passes through the target area. We were to make one pass to the northeast and one to the southwest on each loop through the demilitarized zone (DMZ) separating North and South Korea. At the end of the first pass we made a wide 180-degree turn over the Sea of Japan to retrace our path over the DMZ from the opposite direction. After our second pass through the target area, we returned to the refueling track to refuel for the second loop. Our descent into the refueling track was a standard-descent approach used during our day missions. It involved a 90-degree turn and a descent from above 80,000 feet to an altitude of 25,000 feet, the optimum refueling altitude.

Jack after completing a mission. You can see on the sleeves of Jack's suit a written checklist. Only those who have ejected from an aircraft truly know the state of disorientation and total confusion you can find yourself in. The checklist on the left sleeve had steps to take during the parachute ride down, and the right sleeve for a water entry. *Jack Veth*

At 25,000 feet, Bill advised me of the tanker's location. It was in its preprogrammed turn, rolling out about three or four miles in front of us. The weather in the refueling track had deteriorated markedly during the preceding hour. In fact, the absence of forward visibility made it almost impossible for me to see the flashing lights of the tankers. Thanks to the perseverance of the tanker crews, and our own persistence, the night weather rendezvous proved successful. I was able to slide the SR-71 into position behind the extended boom of the KC-135Q tanker, stabilize in the precontact position, and move slightly forward to the contact position. The tanker's boom operator ("boomer") plugged into our refueling receptacle, located just behind Bill's cockpit. We took on our fuel at a rate of approximately 6,000 pounds per minute. By the end of our refueling track, which was shaped like a racetrack, we were full and ready for our second run through the DMZ.

After the second loop through the DMZ, I turned the Blackbird to the southeast, and at the appropriate time began our long descent to an uneventful landing. All systems on our bird performed flawlessly, allowing us to successfully complete the mission.

The purpose of our mission was intelligence gathering to evaluate indications and warnings (I & W) of troop increases and supplies in North Korea. Flying the mission at night caught the North Koreans totally off guard and resulted in a more complete picture of their military activity. The North Koreans, having been caught by surprise, filed a complaint with the State Department, claiming we overflew their territory. A check of the onboard sensors and navigation system of the SR-71 disproved their claim.

If you fly reconnaissance missions over the same targets on a frequent basis, intelligence analysts are able to determine (to some degree of certainty) a country's intentions, based on a massing of troops, planes, supplies, and other key military indicators. These were called I & W sorties.

Subsequent night missions proved highly successful in keeping the North Koreans off balance. The night flying techniques developed during the early night missions were applied in later missions to minimize the potential of pilot vertigo and improve overall safety procedures.

Eight nights later, on 27 September 1977, the crew of Joe Kinego and Larry Elliott flew the second operational night mission. Again, the mission was scheduled as a two-loop (four passes through the target area) sortie, including two air refuelings. The first refueling was directly after takeoff and the second one was after the first loop. Following the mission, Joe, Larry, Bill, and I discussed our night flying procedures with the Det 1 commander. As pilots, Joe and I shared the same concerns. Our night training sorties at Beale

AFB generally involved a single refueling after takeoff, then a one-loop Mach 3 cruise leg, returning for a night landing. The first two night sorties at Kadena added a high degree of complexity and safety concerns during the night descent into the refueling track.

Vertigo, or spatial disorientation, is a common pilot concern in any aircraft. It's compounded while flying the SR-71 at night during rapid descents from above 80,000 feet to the 25,000-foot refueling altitude while making a continuous 90-degree right turn. Both Joe and I had experienced vertigo during our night missions to the point where we were both concerned for the safety of the crew and aircraft for future night missions.

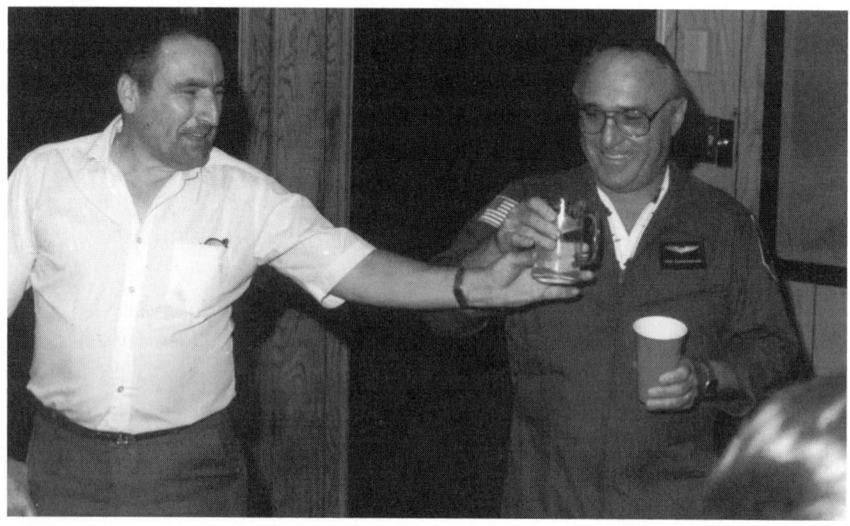

Tony Bevacqua handing a drink to Bob Cunningham in the 1st SRS Heritage Room at Beale AFB. Bob was one of our Det 1 commanders and innovative thinkers on how to employ the SR-71. He was instrumental in making the SR-71 a 24-hour operation with the introduction of routine night flying. *Rich Graham*

As a result of our discussions with the Det 1 commander, the flight profile for future night missions was changed. They were reduced to a single loop and a single refueling immediately after takeoff. Further, all descents from Mach 3 cruise were kept as straight as possible until the aircraft was well below subsonic speeds, in a "friendlier" night environment. Lighting changes to the front cockpit were made to increase the pilot's spatial awareness. Night flight training at Beale was also increased to better prepare the crews for the night environment.

Flying operational sorties at night soon became a common event. As a result of the lessons learned during the early night missions in the fall of 1977, the flexibility of the SR-71 was increased to a 24-hour operation.

When we began flying night operational sorties, the Det 1 commander was Lieutenant Colonel Bob Cunningham. He was noted for his boundless energy and creative mind. Bob's trademark as our Det commander was his nervous pacing, back and forth, directly in front of the pitot tube just prior to engine start. As a former Habu, Bob had the foresight to realize that the SR-71's days were growing short unless we could "compete" with other reconnaissance assets that worked around the clock.

After the first few night sorties there was a hue and cry among the crews claiming that these were a dangerous proposition. Cockpit visibility wearing the pressure suit helmet was minimal at best. Add to that the lack of any discernable horizon at 75,000 feet at night, the criticality of bank angles beyond 35 degrees, and the ever-present possibility of unstarts . . . these were all real concerns to the aircrews. Habus were convinced that the next incident or accident would involve operational night flying.

Knowing night flying was going to be a long-term commitment, we took positive steps. We began flying night simulator missions and beefed up our night training sorties to encompass all the techniques we learned from our operational experiences at Kadena. However, vertigo was still a major concern at night. The SR-71's cockpit was not well suited for night flying, so we asked the Lockheed people if they could improve its layout to reduce the possibility of vertigo. The prototype they came up with was evaluated in a T-37 by Habus and retrofitted into each Blackbird. The result was a gyro-stabilized laser beam, projecting a bright red horizon line across the entire front cockpit panel. It was called the peripheral vision device (PVD), and added another layer of "comfort" to our night operational sorties.

Christmas Tree Smuggling—Christmas 1977

Since there were a limited number of SR-71 crews in the program at any one time, the publication of the crew deployment schedule was an event everyone awaited with anxious anticipation. This was especially true for the schedules that covered crew deployments during the Christmas season. We deployed for six-week periods, always keeping three crews on Kadena at any one time. That meant three crews, or approximately one third of the total SR-71 crew force, spent Christmas on Kadena every year.

At the time, we were authorized only 9 combat-ready crews. After Det 4 at RAF Mildenhall became a permanent operation, we were authorized 11 crews.

Bill and I were scheduled to be at Kadena for Christmas 1977. In preparation for the holiday season we decided it would be appropriate to take a fresh Christmas tree with us from California to Okinawa, adding Christmas cheer during our time away. Our challenge was getting the tree onto the KC-135Q tanker for the flight over and getting it past U.S. Customs officials, who inspected the plane. Bill purchased the tree and arranged to have it delivered to Beale on the night of our deployment. Somehow, we managed to get the tree onboard the aircraft without attracting anyone's attention.

The tanker was to take off from Beale, land and refuel at Hickam Air Force Base in Hawaii, and then continue on to Kadena. The first leg of the flight went smoothly without anyone uncovering the secret cargo. However, upon arrival at Hickam, U.S. Customs officers inspected the airplane, discovering the tree. Despite our protests, customs officials held to their position that the tree could not go on to Okinawa. To our disappointment, the tree was confiscated. Christmas on Okinawa proved to be an enjoyable event that year, despite the fact that our plan was derailed by an official who became known as the "Grinch Who Stole Christmas."

Giant Barnacle—1977–1978

In late 1977, the SR-71 was tasked with a mission in support of the U.S. Navy. The name of the program was "Giant Barnacle." The mission was to provide high-altitude photography of the Eniwetok Atoll. Eniwetok is an uninhabited atoll in the Marshall Islands. It's located approximately 12 degrees latitude north of the equator in the western Pacific Ocean. Eniwetok was the site of 43 atomic and thermonuclear explosions during the development of America's nuclear weapons arsenal. Tons of radioactive sand and debris remained on the island, which the United States undertook to clean up between 1977 and 1980. The information the SR-71 was requested to gather would help the Navy evaluate the extent and location of the radioactive debris and determine the effect radioactive material had on the coral surrounding the atoll.

Three missions were flown out of Det 1 in support of Giant Barnacle. The first was flown in October 1977 and the second in December 1977. Due to the cloud cover over Eniwetok at the time, neither of these missions successfully obtained the information desired by the Navy. A third mission was scheduled on 19 May 1978, and Bill and I were tasked to fly it.

The flight from Okinawa to Eniwetok presented some unique challenges. The flight was to include two air refuelings with a recovery at Anderson AFB, on the island of Guam, at the southern tip of the Northern Mariana Islands. The Guam recovery was scheduled so that the SR-71 could participate in the annual Anderson AFB open house. Aircraft were flying into Anderson from all over the world to participate.

Bill and I quickly realized during our premission planning that we were about to traverse a large portion of the western Pacific Ocean. Flights over water presented no particular danger in the SR *unless* a major aircraft emergency, such as an engine failure or inlet malfunction, forced a descent to lower altitude and a recovery at the first available airfield.

As a result of our planning, Bill and I also realized that once we passed abeam Guam, heading southeast toward Eniwetok, we would eventually get to a point where if we lost an engine, our only possible landing strip was the runway on Eniwetok Island. This thought did not sit well with either one of us. We knew that if aircraft problems occurred, it would take a long time to deploy support equipment and personnel to get us off the island. In addition, the length and quality of the landing strip did not give us confidence that we could land safely, and eventually, fly the SR-71 off the island and return to Kadena.

At 0638 hours on 19 May 1978, we took off from Kadena in aircraft #967. Anderson AFB was our final destination, following a high-speed, high-altitude pass over Eniwetok. We joined with the tanker for an uneventful refueling. Following refueling we accelerated to cruise speed and altitude and headed over the western Pacific. Once again, the cloud cover over the Pacific Ocean appeared as if it might preclude our accomplishing the mission. Miraculously, as we approached Eniwetok, the cloud layer far below us opened up, revealing the Pacific Ocean, and, ultimately, our island target.

In accordance with our mission plan, as we reached the island, the aircraft rolled into a 30-degree bank and the onboard sensors began to operate. Bill monitored sensor operation while I monitored aircraft performance. However, we had come a long way in a short time and neither of us could forgo looking out the cockpit to see the island that had eluded discovery on two prior missions. Bill confirmed that the sensors were operating properly and it was apparent to me that we were accomplishing the mission. I was struck with a sense of history, knowing that this was the place where so many of our atomic tests had occurred between 1948 and 1954. At that moment, I realized the contribution I was making and was thankful for the opportunity.

Due to the success of the mission Bill and I flew, the Giant Barnacle program was canceled and no further missions were flown. During our 3.3-hour flight we had gathered the information requested by the Navy and had successfully recovered at Anderson AFB. Our Detachment commander, Lieutenant Colonel Bob Cunningham, was there to greet us along with representatives of the Guam press and TV media. Bill and I were interviewed on the flightline before we could even get out of our pressure suits. We participated in the open house and met many local military and civilian personnel. The maintenance support personnel led by Lieutenant Colonel Cunningham provided all necessary maintenance on the aircraft and prepared it for its return flight to Kadena on 21 May.

With the success of the Giant Barnacle mission and the successful participation in the Anderson AFB open house, the SR-71, maintenance personnel, and Bill and I, all returned to Kadena with a tremendous feeling of accomplishment and pride in our ability to get the job done despite any operational or environmental difficulties.

CHAPTER TEN

Colonel (Ret) Lee Shelton

Lee had an exceptional career with the SR-71 program. He's probably been associated with the program in more jobs than most Habus can think about. I met Lee and his RSO, Colonel (Ret) Barry MacKean, at Beale when they entered the program in December 1977. Somehow, when you first see a crew together flying the SR-71 simulator, swamping them with emergency after emergency, you form lasting impressions of future expectations. I knew instinctively that both Lee and Barry had what it took to be

Don Emmons (left) presents Lee Shelton his citation for the Meritorious Service Medal at Det 1. As the last Det 1 commander, Lee wanted to leave a permanent legacy of the SR-71. Det 1 personnel put their squadron fund together and had an inscribed plaque mounted on a stone pillar. This was erected on "Habu Hill," a notorious viewing spot for SR-71 departures. Future generations can now read about the Habu that once roamed the skies of Okinawa. *Lee Shelton*

accomplished Habu aviators, commanders, and full-time supporters of the Blackbird program.

Lee was an outstanding AFROTC graduate in 1966 from Oklahoma University. His operational experience includes tactical airlift in the C-7A Caribou, flying out of Da Nang AB, in Vietnam, undergraduate and graduate flight instruction in the T-38, and nuclear alert in the FB-111. He had staff tours with Air Training Command, Strategic Air Command, and the Pentagon.

During his career of 27 years, 16 were devoted to the SR-71 program as a pilot, 1st SRS operations officer, program element monitor (PEM) in the Pentagon, Det 1 commander at Kadena AB, and the Strategic Reconnaissance Center (SRC) at Offutt AFB. He has 740 hours in the SR-71.

Lee retired in 1993, joined the international workforce of SITEL Corporation, and spent the next seven years as an executive with postings in Nebraska, Australia, and Michigan.

Not only does Lee have some interesting Habu stories, but he also tells them with exceptional flair. I am sure you will enjoy his words.

Beginners' Luck

If you were one of the select few fortunate enough to be a part of the SR-71 program, it was easy enough to be the object of "professional" envy from *outside* the ranks of the squadron. At one time or another, almost everyone with wings (all air services of all the earth's nations) wished they were flying our jet and wearing the "orange bag" (our flight suit). As the object of that heavily cloaked male envy, the challenge was to maintain a modest, humble, ah-shucks attitude in the presence of those lusting over our ultimate boy-toy. This attitude-maintenance routine could be a full-time job.

It was far more difficult to be the object of envy from *within* our squadron. Our equal access to the black jet, our relative skills, the challenging missions, the exciting travel, and the professional and personal prestige associated with belonging to a small, elite group of aviators made for a very level playing field, void of the most basic emotions. Almost.

Flying high-value, high-risk, one-of-a-kind operational sorties, approved by the National Command Authority (NCA), from an overseas operating location was about as much fun as you could legally have in a uniform. Getting *to* that forward location, from Beale AFB, routinely involved some of the longest, coldest, most uncomfortable, and boring commutes known to mankind. We were transported as "live cargo" in the back of our supporting KC-135Q model tankers to either Europe or Asia. There were 35 Q-model tankers stationed at Beale to support our worldwide operations. Barring a maintenance problem, these trips routinely required a stop en route and consumed between 12 and 24 hours of your life. If en-route maintenance was required, all bets were off. However, there was an alternative to this death-by-a-thousand-cuts, and it was called "Glowing Heat."

Periodically, a forward-deployed SR-71 was returned to the United States for scheduled maintenance. It would be replaced with an SR-71 from the Beale flight line. To ensure the most effective use of the aircraft swap-out, an operational sortie was generally flown in conjunction with the deployment. "Glowing Heat" was the code name applied to these sorties, and everyone in the squadron prayed to the god of the crew ladder for this Mach 3 reprieve from riding in the back of the tanker. The men of the 1st Squadron envied "Glowing Heat" missions.

In keeping with the squadron's commitment to develop and maintain almost telepathic crew coordination, Barry MacKean, my RSO, and I were joined as an inseparable pair from our entry into the program. Our first operational deployment as a mission-ready crew was to Kadena via a tanker to Hawaii (and then via Guam due to unfavorable winds), and required a mere 23 hours and a few odd minutes. We were much too excited to feel the pain and continued to wonder how those *other* guys in the Air Force were spending their time.

This first Kadena tour was immediately followed with a deployment to RAF Mildenhall, England. These twice-yearly SR-71 deployments were timed to the seasonal rotations of the Warsaw Pact troops in Eastern Europe and the Balkan states. Due to their infrequency, these England deployments were highly prized in the squadron and the crew ladder god had awarded this one to us, "the new guys." The permanent detachment (Det 4) had not yet been established at Mildenhall, so the aircraft needed for this deployment would have to be ferried to and from Mildenhall via Glowing Heat. Glowing Heat . . . us. We were rookies . . . and we were envied! And it gets even better!

At the close of our 20-day Mildenhall deployment, we flew the jet through the "area of interest" and then across the Atlantic to Beale. Including the time dedicated to intelligence collection, the trip took less than seven hours. Six weeks later, it was time for Barry and me to return to Kadena . . . and the deployment was scheduled as a Glowing Heat! Oh, Lord . . . the air dripped with envy. We ate breakfast at Beale, lit the burners, and less than seven hours later, ate breakfast again at Kadena. Six weeks later, as our second Okinawa tour was drawing to an end, it was determined that a maintenance-plagued SR-71 would need to be rotated to Beale. Oh, be still my heart . . . a third *consecutive* Glowing Heat! Barry and I were again too excited (and perhaps too dense) to recognize that the prevailing atmosphere in our peer group had changed from one of good-natured envy, to subtle hostility and thinly veiled threats of great bodily harm. We made it back to Beale in just under five hours . . . the only way to fly!

Over the years on Okinawa, the outside surface of a closet door in room 220, Building 318 (our bachelor officers' quarters home on Kadena) became a priceless archive of squadron lore. On it were recorded the signatures of many famous guests, records of significant events, and other memorabilia associated with our program's illustrious history. The Magic Marker inscription on the top left corner of the door read, "Absolute World Record—Mildenhall to Beale to Kadena to Beale—18.3 hours—crew E13—Shelton & MacKean."

When the CIA financed the OXCART program and planned its deployment to Kadena in 1965, construction of the detachment facilities began immediately. Building 318 was part of this plan for housing the OXCART and tanker crews in a separate facility. The objective was to minimize scrutiny and maximize security.

The crews had rooms blocked off in building 318 that no one else could use. Consequently, crews modified the rooms to suit their own taste. Over the years a lot of time, money, and energy was spent making each room more "livable." As you can image, many traditions and room decorations were passed down from each generation of crews. A closet door in room 201 was also famous for its scribbled signatures and quotes, by many generations of Habus. Unfortunately, unbeknown to us, the rooms were scheduled for refurbishment. One day, while we were out flying, Okinawan painters were performing their duties and painted over the door. We were devastated! Another piece of our traditions and history was lost forever.

Beak-to-Beak Over Vladivostok

When we were deployed to overseas locations, the "operations ladder" strictly managed the flying schedule for individual crews. In a sequential rotation, one crew flew as primary, the second crew served as backup crew, performing mobile duties, and the third crew, which had flown the last sortie, slept late, watched the Habu takeoff, and went to the beach. The ops ladder kept all things orderly and simple. It presumed that all Habu crews were equally qualified and that the crew sitting number one on the ladder would fly the next sortie, regardless of its difficulty or their relative experience. I know from personal experience, as a rookie crewmember, and later as a detachment commander, that this one-size-fits-all philosophy could generate some anxiety, but it was eminently fair and universally respected. We had no "conditionally qualified" SR-71 crews. Once you achieved 100 hours in the SR-71, you were as qualified (theoretically) as a Habu with 1,000 hours.

There were occasions when a particularly desirable sortie would be laid on, and the ops ladder presented the mission to someone else and you *knew* you would never again get the chance to fly such a mission. There were even times (and I speak only for my RSO, Barry, and myself) when the ops ladder placed us in the backup or spare position, when we literally prayed that some minor, but temporary debilitating, flaw would affect members of the primary crew or their aircraft and permit us to fly in their place. Seldom happened, but we continued to pray. Generally, however, the ops ladder had a way of ensuring things were evenly distributed over the course of your time in the program. Virtually everyone got at least one sortie that would provide them with memories for a lifetime.

In September 1980, Tom Alison and J. T. Vida were at Beale AFB preparing to deploy to Okinawa as a replacement crew. Rather than ride the KC-135Q model to Det 1, they were scheduled to ferry a fresh SR-71 to Kadena, permitting an aircraft to return to Beale, and eventually to Palmdale, California, for major refurbishment. This swap-out sortie, "Glowing Heat," was almost always flown as an operational sortie, collecting intelligence on the trip down the Soviet east coast and the Korean peninsula en route to Okinawa. To maximize the potential for "take," the mission planners proposed flying an opposing mission from Kadena, precisely converging the two sorties on Vladivostok, home of the Soviet Far East Fleet and a target with the solid reputation for rich contributions to our intelligence database. According to the ops ladder . . . Barry and I would fly the opposing aircraft from Kadena.

The mission planning by both Habus and Q-model guys on both sides of the Pacific was extensive. At Mach 3, the variations in ground speed are pretty insignificant, so the SR-71 cannot lose or gain much time over a set course. If your brake release and takeoff is on time, and each of several end-refueling points is on time, your time-on-target (TOT) is fairly well assured. Conversely, if you fall behind on your timing, you are unlikely to make it up en route. Our expert maintenance troops generally controlled the takeoff time, but a host of gods and minor spirits affected the myriad factors associated with multiple, en-route air refueling. The ability of the SR-71 crew to affect either the maintenance troops or the demons was generally nil. On this mission, to preclude that one-in-a-million chance for a truly spectacular rendezvous, Tom and J. T. would have a not-lower-than-altitude "floor" on their sortie and Barry and I had a not-higher-than cap. This would ensure our vertical separation.

Due to the relative distances involved, Tom and J. T. would depart Beale and even refuel several times before Barry and I would get airborne at Kadena. Reports of these key en-route events, broadcast over high-frequency (HF) radio, would allow us to follow their progress and, if necessary, adjust our scheduled takeoff to guarantee our precise TOT. The objective, of course, was to have two very-high-speed, very-high-altitude "penetrators" converging on Vladivostok from opposing directions at *exactly* the same moment, significantly compounding their air defense solution . . . acquisition, tracking, and response. In addition to our onboard sensors, and in anticipation of a fairly robust Soviet response, a host of "other collectors" were scheduled to participate in this sortie and record the Soviet reaction to our two aircraft.

On 1 April 2001, a Navy reconnaissance EP-3E Aries II was gathering electronic intelligence (ELINT) off the southern coast of China when a Chinese fighter intercepted it. A routine event for "other collectors" of intelligence. However, they made world news headlines when the two planes collided and the Navy EP-3E landed on the Chinese island of Hainan.

The EP-3E and other collectors have a complex array of antennas, computers, and software onboard to scan a broad frequency spectrum. Even though the SR-71 had an excellent ELINT collection capability in its own right, it was sometimes necessary to fly what was called a "coordinated" mission. These involved other collectors, better suited for highly sophisticated ELINT collection. In our case, the other collectors were typically Air Force RC-135 or EC-135 aircraft.

If you want good ELINT collection from the bad guys, first and foremost, you have to persuade them to activate their electronic equipment; otherwise it's a waste of time. The SR-71 was excellent at "stimulating" the electronic order of battle (EOB) in any country it flew over or around. That's what our coordinated sorties were all about. With precise timing, we stimulated the electronic environment with the SR-71, while other collectors sucked up electronic signals for recording and analysis.

The SR-71's Electromagnetic reconnaissance system (EMR) had the capability of locating electronic signals in a 650-nautical-mile swath along its flight path. After processing and analysis of the recorded signals, accurate location of the emitters could be determined.

Tom and J. T. were about the best in the business; their flight times were spot-on. Barry and I turned our jet loose and streaked down Kadena's runway 05 Right and began climbing toward our refueling point. Maintenance had done its job to get us off on time, but the gremlins that oversee air refueling were also airborne. Our rendezvous with the tanker was terrible! Lots went wrong and by the time we finally had our gas, we were beyond the EAR (end air refueling) point and *several minutes late*. A sortie like this is approved at a very high level in the nation's government and its progress is monitored in near real-time throughout the National Command Authority. We were late and everyone knew it!

I mentioned earlier that at Mach 3 it was difficult to make up much time en route. You also know that the modifier "Mach 3-plus" is always mentioned in the same sentence with SR-71. At Mach 3-plus, you can make up *heaps* of time. The SR-71 is limited not by Mach number, but by the temperature of the air ramming through the engine, the compressor inlet temperature (CIT). So, as two aviators whose names were about to become household words throughout the intelligence community for blowing their mission timing, the choice was simple. Push it up and fly CIT versus Mach!

We gradually gained more and more precious time in our dash to the point in space where we were to meet Tom and J. T. Each of the two aircraft had our air-to-air TACAN set to range on the opposing jet. We were closing at Mach 6-plus, and the TACAN miles-to-go counters were spinning like the wheels in a slot machine. It is incredibly clear at the Habu's operating altitude, so even at this awesome rate of closure we eyeballed Tom and J. T. as they ripped by several thousand feet above us and slightly to our right . . . and within only *seconds* of the agreed-upon time! Piece of cake!

OK, Lord . . . I'll take the stick now.

It got even better when we returned to Okinawa (it's amazing how simply legends can be explained when you are there at the making). Despite our opposing tracks, the remainder of our respective missions placed Tom's aircraft and ours within several miles of each other when we entered the Kadena traffic pattern. Just a few hours earlier the tower had cleared *one* SR-71 to take off and now he was receiving a request to clear *two* for landing. Tower cleared us both for the break and even advised Tom his "wingman" was three miles in trail. We taxied together to the T-hangar. The "locals" were *still* telling the story of one Habu taking off and two coming back seven years later, when I returned to Kadena as the Det 1 commander . . . replacing Tom Alison.

Good to the Last Drop . . .

Of the 29 SR-71A models constructed, the program normally kept only 10 in active service at any one time. Some of those not in the operational lineup were going through an extensive, periodic, take-it-apart-and-put-it-back-together refurbishment by the Lockheed wizards at Palmdale. Still others were in Lockheed's "deep storage." To keep the airframe time balanced across the fleet, ensuring that the jets "aged" at the same rate, they were periodically rotated into and out of storage. This shepherding worked so well that when the aircraft was being considered for retirement (the first time), the average age across the fleet was something like 2,300 hours per airframe, with only a few hundred hours separating the high- and low-time birds. Additionally, this incredible aircraft was retired by the Air Force with only a fraction of its original service life cycle consumed. There were even some that advocated that the original estimates of the SR-71's service life cycle were far too conservative.

They proposed that the extreme heat generated with each sortie had the effect of annealing the jet's titanium shell, rejuvenating it and actually extending its serviceable life. We'll never know.

Suffice to say that when an aircraft returned to the active inventory from deep storage, it was the subject of an extensive refurbishment effort by both Lockheed's civilian force and our guys in the maintenance squadrons. As with most machines, it was not the constant hard use that could be the most destructive, but long periods of inactivity. When the maintenance troops finally released the jet, it was required to pass an extensive series of airborne examinations during a Functional Check Flight (FCF). In many Air Force squadrons, there are select crews, trained and designated to accomplish an FCF. In the 1st Squadron, all of the crews were qualified to conduct this type of flight, but most often FCFs fell to the instructor crew assigned to the SR-71 crew training simulator. On Good Friday, 9 April 1982, Major Bill Keller and I, the "sim crew," drew the task of flying a two-loop (two supersonic legs, separated by an air refueling) FCF on aircraft #973. The jet was coming from several years in deep storage, with a serious side trip through the maintenance bays. Pretty normal. No sweat.

An FCF is accomplished with reference to a special additional crew checklist. Many more things are extensively exercised, deliberately failed, or "pressed" than on a normal SR-71 sortie. The numeric results of all this pushing and pulling, qualitative and quantitative, are dutifully recorded in the checklist by the aircrew for subsequent digestion by the maintenance guys. An FCF is not a particularly challenging assignment, but the SR-71 was inherently a challenging aircraft. When something went wrong, it did so at an alarming rate, so you rapidly got yourself into unexplored territory. For that reason alone, flight testing an SR-71 that has spent the last several years cocooned in a hangar caused you to focus on the job at hand.

Ground operations were good, takeoff was normal, and we climbed out for our first air refueling in the vicinity of Boise, Idaho. Several routine tests of the stability augmentation system (SAS) and the autopilot en route, and of the air refueling system during the onload, and it was time to "go hot." All subsequent activity at Mach 3 cruise and altitude was also normal, and soon we were ranging on our next tanker and descending from above 70,000 feet to 26,000 feet for refueling. One loop down and one to go and the aircraft was delivering a flawless performance. The second hot leg took us out over the Pacific Ocean, exiting the California coast near Eureka, prior to turning back in for descent and landing at Beale.

It was very soon after level off at Mach 3 and 71,000 feet that the master caution light illuminated, with Bill confirming its presence from the back seat. The master caution was the big light on the instrument panel at eyeball level that told us something evil was happening. You then looked on the pedestal between your legs and read one of the 40-odd individual lights on the annunciator panel to determine exactly *what* evil was happening. Normally, this second step was unnecessary as you were highly attuned to every little flicker, rumble, wiggle, and nuance in the aircraft. Normally you were reacting to the malfunction *before* the master caution light fired off. This time Bill and I had not felt or anticipated anything.

The SAS does precisely what the words imply: It augments the stability of the aircraft throughout all flight regimes. By using triple-redundant sensitive gyros in the pitch, roll, and yaw axis, it dampened out the flight controls. Without the SAS operating correctly in all three axes, the SR-71 was *very* unstable at supersonic speeds. The SAS was particularly useful for cruising at Mach 3 speeds, where just *one degree* of pitch up or down is equal to a 3,000-feet-per-minute rate of climb or descent.

Following strict crew coordination procedures, my job following Bill's challenge "master caution light," was to recycle the light (in the event there was yet *another* evil that wants to turn it on), identify the appropriate light on the annunciator panel, and call for the corresponding emergency procedure from our extensive checklist. I did all that and Bill heard me say, "System 'A' flight hydraulic failure."

You should know that in most modern jets, two independent, redundant hydraulic systems, "A" and "B," power the movement of the flight controls. You should also know that the emergency procedure for loss, or impending loss, of 50 percent of your flight control hydraulics, is to get your butt on the ground ASAP! We started to do just that.

An emergency was declared with ATC, we requested an immediate turn to Beale and immediately began dumping the fuel we had just worked so hard to pack into the beast. We watched the pressure in the affected system bleed to zero. Fortunately, we were heading west over the Pacific Ocean when all this occurred, so the public relations nightmare that normally accompanies an unplanned, supersonic descent over an urban area was, for the moment, avoided. Considering the circumstances, however, things seemed under control. Then the master caution light illuminated again. Bill confirmed it.

I said, "System 'B' flight hydraulic failure," and Bill said, "I just gave you that." I say, "No, you gave me 'A' system failure. I now need the checklist for 'B' system failure." Bill said, "Oh, shit."

Additionally, you need to know that the emergency procedure in the SR-71 for a second, subsequent, and final flight hydraulic system is to immediately

EJECT! I tell Bill we will press for Beale, but that he should run the checklist for ejection and, if the pressure continues to fall, be prepared to go on my command. He repeated his earlier comment.

We watched the gauge for the "B" system and the pressure seemed to hold. As long as there is pressure, we are both flying and avoiding the big "E-word." I was now heading for Beale like a scalded cat. The checklist called for significantly reduced airspeed in conjunction with hydraulic malfunctions, but I figured we had a serious leak, and a leak means x-fluid loss over x-time period and I was doing everything I could to reduce the time afforded to the drips.

About then, our mobile crew, alerted by both ATC and the Beale command post that we were returning with a malfunction, came on the radio with "Hey, Aspen (our call sign), what's up?" That day, due to some scheduling anomaly, Lieutenant Colonel Al Joersz, our squadron commander, was handling the mobile duty. Bill told him we were 30 miles north of Beale . . . with a dual flight control hydraulic failure. At first, Al said absolutely nothing and then tentatively asks, "Say again?" Bill repeated himself to Al, and Al repeated Bill's earlier, "Oh, shit." Seems this was the phrase of the day.

Major General (Ret) Al Joersz set a world speed record over a straight course on 27 July 1976. Al and the RSO, Major George T. Morgan, flew aircraft #958 at a *Federation Aeronautique Internationale (FAI)* certified record speed of 2,193.167 miles per hour.

The flight controls were beginning to feel a might sluggish and there was some "chatter" in the control stick. (Or was it my imagination?) As late as possible, on a very short final approach, we slowed to a speed that permitted the gear to safely extend. As we crossed over the runway threshold, the remaining pressure in "B" system was virtually zero. Touchdown. 'Chute deployed. We taxied clear of the runway, maintenance pinned the gear, and we shut down #973's engines.

Subsequent findings by maintenance revealed that a set of seals in the flight control hydraulic system failed and allowed the fluid to escape. The combined capacity of the "A" and "B" hydraulic system is 5.79 gallons. System "A" was bone-dry and System "B" contained literally "cups" of fluid. The hydraulic shop chief figured we had less than a minute of flight control authority [ability to control the plane] remaining when we shut down.

Scrunched-Down in a Little Bitty Ball

The generally accepted maxim in aviation is that ambient air temperature decreases at a standard lapse rate from the Earth's surface up to a certain altitude, and then it stabilizes at a constant temperature. For all practical purposes, and for flight in normal air vehicles, this is true. For the SR-71, neither practical nor normal, this was not true. The temperature of the atmosphere is not constant, but constantly varies. In 1977, when I began qualifying in the aircraft, my Habu instructor, Major Bob Helt, explained it as if we were very rapidly flying through Swiss cheese, wherein the cheese and all the holes were at slightly different temperatures. Air masses at different temperatures have different densities and when you are streaking through these pockets of air with varying density at 33 miles per minute, it manifests itself as turbulence. So, at altitude above 70,000 feet, where there should have been nothing but smooth air, it was often a very rough ride. Sometimes violently so.

One scenario in which you could always anticipate this turbulence, á la temperature differential, was passing from land to water, or vice versa. One place where you always passed from land to water and back again was entering and exiting the airspace over the Korean peninsula, something we did quite routinely. Anticipating areas of possible turbulence was just good mission planning, because the critical dynamic balance maintained by the Habu's temperamental inlets could be startled by the change in airflow and a startled inlet could ruin your whole day.

On a beautifully clear, "you-can-see-forever-from-up-here" Friday, 21 January 1983, we entered the Korean airspace just south of the DMZ in SR-71 #960. We were flying a "bow tie" sortie. The profile was to cross the peninsula west-to-east, do a big 180-degree turn out over the Sea of Japan and recross the land mass east-to-west, do another 180 for a second pass through Korean airspace, and then turn south and return to Okinawa. If you flew just a single loop, with only one 180-degree turn, it was dubbed a "lollipop."

The initial trip across was routine and very stable, essential for good imagery from the sensors. As we coasted out over the land and went "feet wet," the airplane was violently shaken by a single, terrific blow that lasted only a fraction of a second. Coincidentally, the master caution light illuminated, and I immediately focused my attention on the condition of the inlets and engines. All normal. As I began to sweep the cockpit for the source of the warning light, I saw both a red light in the landing gear handle and the "canopy unsafe" light illuminated. Had the turbulence been of sufficient severity to unlatch a gear or crack open a gear door *and* lift the canopy from its down-and-locked position? Or, more likely, had the rapid application of positive and negative Gs caused both the gear and the canopy microswitches to "float" momentarily, declaring an "open" status to the warning light? A Dirty Harry asked, "How lucky do you feel?"

We rolled out on a southerly heading toward Okinawa, the engines out of afterburner, and began an equally gentle manageable altitude and airspeed. It was a long drive back speed that would not damage the gear should it choose to extend, or damage us if the canopy chose to separate. Maintenance later confirmed that the microswitches had been given just enough room to turn the lights on and both gear and canopy had been locked for the duration.

Looking back on these events a few hours later, with my feet firmly on Okinawan soil, I realized all my concern, beyond the first few seconds, was pure wasted energy. If, at Mach 3, the canopy had separated, or if a gear/gear door had presented itself to the slipstream, the result would have been both instantaneous and most likely catastrophic. At the time, however, if only in my mind, I had willed myself to scrunch down in the nose of that airplane into a little bitty ball . . . to present the smallest possible surface area to the "big wind" I knew was coming at any second.

I did not know it at the time, but this single pass across Korea and subsequent air abort was to be my last operational sortie in the SR-71. On 24 January, I was named as the operations officer for the 1st Squadron. I would continue to fly instructional sorties in the SR-71B model and FCFs in the A model, but I would never again enjoy that very special sensation of taking an SR-71 into harm's way. I had flown 78 operational missions in 10 Kadena deployments, 4 rotations to RAF Mildenhall, and 5 Cuban sorties. I hated to quit.

So, Ya' Want To Be a Habu?

Application for entry to the SR-71 program and the subsequent qualification phase was considerably more difficult than flying the airplane. In the first place, it was not a widely known or discussed facet of the Air Force's operation. You knew they were out there and that someone had to be flying them, but you never thought that someone was someone like you. I learned of the program and applied only because a fellow pilot in my FB-111 squadron had applied, and failed to gain entry. I figured I was *at least* as good as the other guy and could certainly do no worse than he did. Besides, I was looking for some form of divine intervention to save me from a pending staff assignment to SAC headquarters. You see my point.

Any "special duty" assignment is associated with literally tons of paperwork—arcane forms ad nauseam, copies of all existing flight evaluations, certified records of flying hours, preliminary physical exam, copies of all existing flight physicals, copies of your *family's* medical history, written endorsements by carefully selected senior officers, etc., etc., etc. When you exercised the complete application drill for a special duty assignment like the SR-71, you "by god" wanted to fly the jet just to recoup some of the man-years invested in the process.

On average, two or three pilots *per year* were selected from among all of those who aspired to enter SR-71 training. If your personal mountain of paperwork cleared the gatekeepers at the Military Personnel Center and those SAC headquarters, it was forwarded to Beale AFB for review by a panel of

Every year the 9th Wing commander held a Det Commander's Conference at Beale. The dates *just happened* to coincide with the Blackbird Reunion in Reno. Pictured (L to R) are Barry Mackean, Lee Shelton, Don Emmons, Rich Graham, Geno Quist, Nevin Cunningham, Jay Murphy, Tom Alison, Gil Bertelson, and J. T. Vida in the commander's base house in May 1988. *Lee Shelton*

senior SR-71 crewmembers. Without a doubt, this last stop was the point of toughest scrutiny. If you cleared this last hurdle, both intensely objective and admittedly subjective, you were invited to Beale for a week-long interview: one-on-one discussions with senior officers and group "hangar flying" sessions with the crew force, T-38 flight evaluations, an SR-71 simulator evaluation, social events . . . and *the* physical examination.

The physical requirements and the associated physical examination stopped many a good man from even considering application to the program. It was widely held that you needed to be in pretty damn good shape when you reported for the interview. Additionally, it was widely believed that the qualification physical for the SR-71 was the same one administered to astronaut candidates. (NOTE: The original crews selected for the SR-71 program took the actual astronaut physical.) The physical was far more "severe" than any routine annual Air Force exam and had a reputation for identifying otherwise undetected flaws in a pilot's physiology. Once identified, these new physical glitches could result in one's *removal* from flying status . . . forever! You could travel to Beale to become a flying god and return to your home unit grounded a week later!

The physical examination was usually scheduled early in the interview week at Beale. Logic being that if you busted it, there was little invested in you at that point and you could go home without consuming a lot of local resources. There was a 24-hour fast preceding the all-day physical, conducted at the large USAF hospital at Travis AFB, Fairfield, California. So, you arrived very early in the morning, tired, anxious, and hungry as hell, about to play "You Bet Your Wings" with the doctors.

The menu seemed endless: pints of blood tests, quarts of urinalysis, glucose tolerance tested, lung capacity measured, ocular probing of the eyes, aural bombardment of the ears, reflexes, height, weight, body fat, EKG via stress treadmill (aptly named), visit with the "shrink," and somewhere during the day, an EEG. This last evaluation was done to measure "normal brain wave activity" by means of numerous, nasty little tacks on wire leads driven into your head. I arrived for my EEG appointment sometime in the late afternoon, drained of most of my bodily fluids and dehydrated, hungry enough to eat the back end out of a possum, and totally exhausted trying to outlast the treadmill. (We all tried to kill the treadmill. It was the manly thing to do.)

A very cute, starched, and white-clad medical technician immediately begins the ritual of pressing these thumbtacks into my skull. I flinched with the first couple and let out an audible groan when about number six or so entered my scalp. This darlin' little med tech stopped what she was doing, took a step back to look me square in the eyes, smiled, and said, "Don't pass out on me, Hot Shot, or I'll ground you right here."

Over the years, we would all have occasion to ponder what a "normal brain wave" really looked like and, more to the point, what the brain wave of a Habu looked like compared to that normal one they were searching for.

Whole Lot of Shakin' Goin' On

As the reader turns the pages in this book of collected memories, he could get the impression that logging flying time in the SR-71 was simply an extended series of white-knuckled emergency procedures. Far from it. Considering the environment in which we routinely operated the plane and its attendant extremes of speed, altitude, temperature, and physiology, the Habu was an unnaturally reliable machine. When a malfunction *did* occur, however, those factors usually interacted geometrically to produce some memorable moments. When things begin to go wrong at Mach 3-plus, you move away from *normal* at an alarming rate.

People unfamiliar with the SR-71, laypersons and even other pilots, would often ask us "how does it look up there" or "how far can you see" or "do you really have a sense of speed when you are flying at Mach 3?" These simple questions were difficult to answer, for most of us rarely looked outside the cockpit for more than a brief peek. You see, it was common knowledge

While Lee was commander of Det 1, he wanted to celebrate the 20th anniversary of the first ops sortie, flown by Jerry O'Malley. Through Lee's initiative, and Pat Halloran's two-star influence, we were able to use a Beale KC-135Q to take a large group of former Habus over to Okinawa to join in the festivities. They dedicated a dormitory called O'Malley Hall. Lee on the left and Tom Pugh on the right talking, while Ken Collins listens. *Lee Shelton*

among our crews that the Habu *knew* when you were not paying attention to it. The SR-71 was a jealous honey and if you lingered on a sunset, a moonrise, or a brilliant thunderstorm far below, it *knew* . . . and recaptured your complete and full attention in ways unlike any other jet. It was unwise to take anything for granted until the Habu had been returned to the chocks.

The following is an exact copy of an incident report I completed for inclusion in our aircrew read file at Detachment 1, Kadena AB, Okinawa, Japan:

Date: 4 March 1982
Reply to Attn of: Majors Shelton and Keller (Z-14)
Subject: Narrative of Landing Roll Incident (SR-71 SN 975)

1. Approach to Runway 23L was normal, with about 10,000 pounds of fuel at 155 Knots. Winds were reported on short final to be 180/16, for a computed crosswind component of 11 Knots. Actual landing was accomplished with little or no "cross-control" input as crosswind appeared to have washed out at the low end of 23L. For this reason, drag 'chute deployment was initiated prior to "flying the nose to the runway" as is the procedure for crosswind landings. Drag 'chute deployment

and activation of nose wheel steering were normal and conformed to the cockpit cadence/pacing of other flights. About two or three seconds after nose wheel steering was selected and as the main wheel brakes were being checked at 100 Knots, a violent vibration began in the aircraft.

2. Vibration was of medium frequency (4–5 cycles per second), but very intense amplitude with each input. Onset of vibration was instantaneous and did not vary in intensity, frequency, or amplitude until it abruptly ceased at approximately 10–15 knots.

3. Within the cockpit, the motion seemed both vertical and lateral, combining in a rapid rolling or torsional sensation. Rolls seemed almost 5 degrees left and right. Nose wheel steering remained "On" throughout, but was not totally satisfactory in maintaining ground track (perhaps nose tires were not in full contact with the runway). It was quite difficult to feel the effect of wheel braking due to the vibration (antiskid had been selected "Off" immediately), so the drag 'chute was retained well into the landing roll and may have jettisoned below 55 knots. Right elevon and brake were used to augment nose wheel steering and back-stick was held to relieve weight on the nose gear.

4. The vibration began and ended sharply and with no indication of onset or termination. Sensation was as if the cockpit was literally being shaken like mechanically mixing a can of paint. As aircraft rolled to the crown of 23L, the crosswind seemed to play a more active role. The aircraft began to weathervane and to drift toward the left edge of the runway. There was some real concern by both crewmembers that the aircraft might depart the hard surface.

5. When the vibration ceased, it was as if nothing had occurred. All systems were operational; nose wheel steering, braking, and ground handling characteristics were all nominal. Maintenance personnel inspected the aircraft, pinned the landing gear, and indicated it was clear to proceed to the T-hanger. Both crewmembers were a bit uncomfortable about taxiing the aircraft, but continued in a cautious (but highly suspicious) manner. In hindsight, I feel taxiing in showed less than good judgment on my part and I wish I had not done so.

6. In summary, I am curious and thankful. Curious because I have absolutely no idea as to the why or what of it (nor does maintenance). Thankful because in spite of all my actions/reactions during the rollout, I am not sure I was any more than a passenger for the duration of the event. Speaking of passengers

> . . . throughout the incident, Major Keller maintained radio contact with Mobile, describing "for the record" the nature of the vibration, provided me with his "best guess" corrective actions, and maintained a truly professional attitude. Thanks, Bill.

Signed
Lee M. Shelton II, Major, USAF

As is the custom among all aviators, serious aircraft incidents that do not result in bent metal or busted bodies always produce humor. Adrenaline is funny that way. Anyway, the legend that endured long after this brief moment of terror was not a maintenance solution (they never provided one) or the collective aircrews' preparation to respond to a future reoccurrence (never happened), but rather the telling and retelling by the Mobile crew of Bill Keller's radio transmission to them as they chased our herky-jerky progress down the runway. To do it correctly, you have to rapidly strike yourself in the chest with both fists while loudly repeating **"M-m-m-m-m-oooo bile, a-a-ar-re-e yy-y-y-o-o-u-uu, gg-g-gge-eting a-a-a-all tth-th-is?"**

Maybe you had to be there . . . but maybe it's better you weren't.

Two Trash Haulers at Mach 3-Plus

As my September 1967 graduation date from undergraduate pilot training drew closer to the time when we would select our first operational aircraft, based on final class standing, everyone in the class *knew* their assignments would take them to Vietnam. At that time in our history, everyone in every pilot training class knew their assignment would take them to Vietnam; you just weren't sure what you would be flying when you arrived there. Maybe not immediately, but eventually we were all sure to go.

My "first choice" in the block of available aircraft was an F-100 Super Saber, a single-seat, single-engine jet fighter. My second selection, for reasons known only to me and perhaps God, was the Canadian-built DeHavilland C-7A Caribou, a piston-powered, STOL (short takeoff and landing) tactical transport aircraft. Perhaps God also knew that I would have killed myself in the F-100, so He and I settled on the C-7A. I was a "trash hauler."

If any aircraft matched its nickname, it was the Caribou, with its high wing, sweeping high tail, exposed butt, pug nose, and cranelike main landing gear. The real beauty of all this airborne ugliness was its unmatched ability to deliver 5,500 pounds of literally anything into abysmal Special Forces airstrips less than 1,000 feet in length. In accomplishing its singular skill, the Caribou droned between deliveries at an indicated airspeed of 125 knots, making it the *slowest* retractable gear aircraft in the entire Vietnam Theater of

Operations! Proves God was still looking out for me, since you could walk away from most Caribou crashes.

Umpteen years later, I am an IP and flight examiner (FE) in the SR-71, flying operational sorties in the A model and instructional missions in the B model. When I joined the 1st Squadron in 1977, my squadron commander was Lieutenant Colonel Pat Bledsoe, who had been an 0-1 "Bird Dog" forward air controller (FAC) in Vietnam. He did his combat flying at 115 knots. As a result, Pat clearly held the "record" for the man who had flown the slowest and the fastest in his career, but Pat's 0-1 had a *fixed* gear. My Caribou credentials clearly qualified me for the claim to fame as the "slowest to fastest" human in manned, air-breathing aircraft with *retractable* gear.

Colonel (Ret) Pat Bledsoe established and still holds the FAI-certified world record for absolute speed in a manned, air-breathing jet aircraft over a closed course. On 27 July 1976, Pat and the RSO, Colonel (Ret) John Fuller, flew Blackbird #958 to a sustained speed in level flight of 2,092.29 miles per hour. That record, and the other speed and altitude records set by the SR-71 in 1976, remains unchallenged today!

In 1981, Major Les Dyer was accepted into our squadron and began his training as a Habu pilot. Many years earlier, Les had begun his military flying career as a trash hauler—a Caribou pilot in Vietnam. (You can see this coming, right?) Significant academic and simulator requirements were accomplished and Les was certified to begin the flight instruction phase. History records that at 1115 hours, Friday, 29 January 1982, in SR-71B #956, Les Dyer, Habu student, and Lee Shelton, Habu instructor, dropped off their assigned KC-135Q model tanker with a full, 80,000-pound load of JP-7 and began the acceleration to Mach 3-plus above 70,000 feet. Never before, and never since, had two aviators, previously qualified in the *slowest* retractable gear aircraft in the USAF inventory, flown *together* in the world's fastest aircraft! We were a rags-to-riches pair, and we joke about our "history-making mission" to this day.

CHAPTER ELEVEN

Master Sergeant (Ret) Steve Koren

From our standpoint, maintenance produced a flyable plane and we flew it. However, maintenance and operations were united with our love and devotion to the Blackbird.

Steve enlisted in the Air Force in 1970. Following his basic training at Lackland AFB, Texas, and maintenance training at Sheppard AFB, Texas, he was assigned to Luke AFB, Arizona, where he worked on the F-100, F-104, and F-4 aircraft as a crew chief. In 1972, Steve went to Incirlik AB, Turkey, where he worked on C-141s, F-4s, and Turkish F-84s and F-86s. A year later he was assigned to Randolph AFB, Texas, as a flight line crew chief/expeditor on T-37, T-38, and T-39 aircraft.

Centered in the camouflage uniform is Steve Koren. He and the other maintenance troops wanted a final picture standing in front of the last SR-71 remaining at Beale AFB in 1990. Because of maintenance troops such as these, and those who went before, we could fly the SR-71 on the edge of the envelope. *Fred Carmody*

At this point in his military career, Steve was diagnosed with a rare form of cancer. He spent the next seven years at Randolph, winning this battle and fully recovering. He was released from assignment restrictions in 1980 and spent three years at Hahn AB, Germany, as a flight line expeditor on F-4 and F-16 aircraft, in support of NATO. Steve was handpicked for his assignment to Beale and arrived there in 1983. At Beale, Steve was one of the last "official" production superintendents (better known as "pro supers") of the SR-71s. When the Blackbirds retired in 1990, he transferred to the U-2 program as a pro super. Steve retired at Beale AFB in 1992. Here is his story.

What exactly did it take to get an SR-71 airborne? "Kick the tires and light the fires" is one phrase that definitely did not pertain to this 55-ton aviation marvel as she sat in her shelter awaiting an aircrew. On average it took 18 to 20 hours of preflight preparation by the crew chief and assigned ground crew to get the bird "crew ready." Then the avionics specialists had to perform uploads of equipment or preflight "ops checks" of their particular systems.

What Steve calls "shelters" are the individual taxi-through hangars for the SR-71. These were small in comparison to larger military aircraft hangars.

From a maintenance standpoint the name of the game was "beat the clock." Launch time was critical, with only a "plus" or "minus" 10-minute window from scheduled take off. That only gave a 20-minute spread to fix any last-minute problems.

To make this happen, it took a lot of people who knew their particular specialties, determination to make things work, coordination, preplanning, and two or three sets of eyes, constantly monitoring everything, ensuring that each step was accomplished and nothing was overlooked, or out of place.

SR-71 Flight Line Operations

Each Blackbird had a crew chief. This is the one person who knew the airplane best. He orchestrated the work of the people assigned to him, and coordinated who he needed working on his plane with the roving "expeditor." People can say what they want, but in my opinion, the crew chief was the mainstay of the ground operation. From hangar housekeeping to having aircraft forms in order, preplanning specialists, launching, recovering, inspecting, and servicing—*the crew chief made it all happen!*

Weather was not an excuse. We could be making an aircraft recovery at Beale in 110-degree heat, making the titanium skin hot enough to fry an egg, or standing at the end of the runway in a monsoon doing last-minute checks before our bird took off. We could be working in 20-degree weather on an open ramp (windchill *minus 22 degrees)* in South Dakota, fixing a broken Blackbird that was trying to make it home—*the crew chief was always there.* Everyone worked together, from the assistant ground crew members, to the specialists who were there to fix a particular problem—everyone pitched in, directed by the crew chief.

Just so we don't perpetuate another myth about the SR-71, when Steve says you could fry an egg on the skin of the SR-71, he is referring to the heat from the sun. Many people believe the skin was so hot on landing (because of the searing Mach 3 temperatures) that you couldn't touch it. In reality, the plane cooled off quickly during descent and arrival. About the only place you might still find heat after landing was in the main gear assembly, and that depended on how far out you lowered the gear.

The expeditor drove constantly around the hangars, observing, monitoring, and calling in job requests from each crew chief. He used a Plexiglas "status board," set up in his vehicle to monitor each Blackbird, annotating all jobs in progress, with estimates of completion times. The expeditor was the main "radio contact point" coordinating all flight line maintenance. He was in constant contact with maintenance control, who dispatched whomever he needed for a repair.

Finally, there was the production superintendent or, "pro super." This was the overseer of *everything!* He watched over the entire flight line, monitored all maintenance radio transmissions, sometimes overriding decisions when time became a critical factor. About an hour before flight, the pro super went through the aircraft forms, ensuring that all maintenance was complete and properly documented, no "Red X" (grounding conditions) existed, the weight and balance form was complete with all scheduled equipment uploads documented, and no inspections were overdue.

After reviewing the aircraft forms thoroughly, the pro super then signed off on what is called the "exceptional release." His signature acknowledged that according to what he had just checked and observed, all maintenance was complete and the aircraft was "crew ready." The pro super did get help from two other roving supervisors. The FMS super (field maintenance) monitored all his personnel and critical jobs in work such as hydraulics, sheet metal, aero-repair, electrics, engines, machinists, and coordinated with the pro super. Likewise, the AMS super (avionics maintenance) did the same thing with comm/nav, autopilot, ANS, SLR (side-looking radar), instruments, ECM (electronic counter measures), MRS (mission recording systems), and photo shop. However, in the end, the pro super had the final call on all maintenance decisions.

It was so busy on the flight line, it was impossible for one person to track it all. In a nutshell, the pro super received inputs from the AMS and FMS supervisors. They all monitored the expeditor, who was coordinating everything, and complied with the requests of the crew chief and his assistants who were *doing* the work. That's why they said, "If you ever want to know what's happening with a particular Blackbird, *ask the crew chief.*"

So now you know how it all worked. You can imagine, when you had one crew chief, three ground crew assistants, and two or three members from each shop, all in the shelter working simultaneously, you tended to bump into each other. A prime example was sitting in the front cockpit performing a "power on" preflight inspection while six other specialists were screaming they also needed to get in the cockpit to ops check the systems (or little black boxes) they had uploaded, while a seventh specialist is saying he needed "power off" to install his particular component—where's the crew chief?

Blackbird Preflight

Everyone knows what a "preflight" is. When you had 105 feet of center body length, plus 55 feet of wing width, made up of titanium and composite materials, strapped on to two Pratt & Whitney J-58 jet engines, that was a *lot* of area to cover.

The aircraft was divided into four basic areas of inspection:

Area 1: Front cockpit, canopy, windshield, nose, nose strut, and nose wheel well

Area 2: Rear cockpit, canopy, drag 'chute compartment, and center of main fuselage to tail cone (top and bottom)

Area 3: Entire left wing area and control surfaces (elevons), left wheel well, left strut and tires, left engine tailpipe, flameholder, A/B liner, variable exhaust nozzles, engine nacelle, and left rudder

Area 4: Same as Area 3 *except* substitute the word right for left

Now assign these four areas to four people and we'll see you in about four hours. Once the four areas were inspected, the crew chief picked (any) two areas and reinspected them. This was called a "supervisory follow-up" inspection. Yes, it was done on every preflight. Whether an operational sortie or training flight, all preflight inspection criteria were the same.

Hydraulic test stands, or "gigs," were hooked up to the SR-71 to supply hydraulic pressure to the four individual hydraulic systems. That's right, *four hydraulic systems!* That also meant four hydraulic pumps, two each located on the accessory drive of each J-58 engine. Letters identified the pumps. A and B hydraulics powered the flight controls. L and R went to the utility hydraulic systems, operating the nose-wheel steering, landing gear, brakes, inflight refueling door and boom nozzle locks, and both spikes.

There was also a maintenance procedure called a "hot gig." Whenever we came back with a flight control write-up, it was typically a problem with one of the flight control actuators. However, the left and right elevons had 20 hydraulic actuators on *each* side, and each rudder had 4 actuators. Maintenance could only troubleshoot and isolate the culprit by heating the hydraulic fluid up to inflight Mach 3 temperatures and circulating it throughout the plane. That was called a "hot gig."

What Is a Spike?

Okay, just what are the spikes? Remember seeing those cone-shaped, pointy things sticking out of the inlets (you might call them *intakes*) of the SR-71? These were the crucial aerodynamic components that worked in conjunction with the J-58s, enabling the Blackbird to achieve such incredible speeds.

Each spike was mounted on a huge hydraulic actuator, mounted directly *in front of the engine* on what was called the centerbody frame. As the SR-71 surpassed Mach 1, the shock wave formed was literally *held in place* by the spike cone so it was not ingested into the engine. Both spikes had the capability of moving horizontally 26 inches. So why do we need them to move? Remember those J-58 engines? Not only did they need fuel to operate, they also needed air. At 80,000-feet altitude (or 15 miles up), the air is beginning to thin out. In addition, the faster you went, the more fuel and air the engines needed. As the spike retracted, the inlet area around the spike cone increased, allowing the engine to ingest more air.

The spikes basically performed two functions: regulating the amount of ingested air for required engine performance, plus keeping the shock waves from being engulfed by the inlets. *If* the shock waves went down the inlets, they would hit the first rows of compressor blades with such force that not only would the blades be wiped out . . . well, just think of it as an *instant* catastrophic failure of one or both engines . . . acute structural failure of the nacelle and airframe integrity . . . hydraulic and generator failures, *plus*, add to that, traveling at over 2,000 miles per hour at least 15 miles up! Too devastating to comprehend!

With hydraulics hooked up, it's time for DAFICS to do their magic. The Air Force was loaded with acronyms, but I always thought DAFICS was the most ingenious—Digitally Automated Flight and Inlet Control System. Think of it as an updated autopilot system with spikes. A DAFICS crew of specialists hooked up their test equipment and ran a computer (preflight) self-test of the entire flight control, autopilot, and spike systems. Basically *every* conceivable movement of the flight control surfaces and the spikes that an aircrew would experience in the air (no matter at what speed) would be operationally checked and simulated for its integrity and airworthiness on the ground.

Both spikes were also measured to make sure they extended and retracted equally. Once extended fully, each spike tip was again measured—they had to be within a *tenth of an inch* of each other. This was very critical. Why? Imagine looking down at an SR-71 as it approaches Mach 1. The shock wave is beginning to form around the airframe, plus the same shock wave is beginning to collect itself on the tip of the spikes. As long as the shock waves form equally, and at the same distance on both spikes, the Blackbird will continue straight and true. However, if one shock wave forms a few inches ahead (or behind) between the two spikes, physics takes over and an unstart, or aerodynamic disturbance (AD), is created.

Remember, the crew was sitting a good 40–45 feet in front of both spikes, so when the main center section of the aircraft responded to an unstart, that force traveled along the centerbody of the aircraft, forward to the cockpits, and the crew took the hit. This could make or break a mission. When you encountered repeated unstarts, there's no way supersonic flight could continue. Mission aborted. So that's what DAFICS did—made sure that not only was every control surface functioning properly, but also aligned. Fred Carmody, in charge of Lockheed at Beale AFB, told me some of the early encounters with unstarts were so violent that pilots returned to base with cracked pressure suit helmets.

With the airframe and DAFICS preflight complete, what next? Since the "gigs" were still hooked up, the crew chief ensured that all four hydraulic systems were filled to capacity. The L and A reservoirs were located in the upper left wheel well; B and R reservoirs in the right. Each reservoir had a quantity sight gauge. Time to disconnect the gigs.

With nobody in the hangar, time for some liquid oxygen (LOX). Yep, same stuff other combat aircraft and the space shuttle use. Remember, the aircrews wore full pressure suits and breathed 100 percent oxygen the entire time, so we had to ensure they always had plenty of LOX. There were three 10-liter LOX converters on board, system 1, system 2, and standby. The standby converter was cross-connected between system 1 and system 2 in case of failure, and "kicked in" to ensure a constant flow of oxygen without any interruption.

Ground Refueling

It took four people to fuel the SR-71. It was accomplished with "power on" and cool "conditioned air" hooked up to the airframe. Anytime power was required for a considerable length of time (over three minutes), conditioned air was utilized to cool internal components. With little black boxes and computers everywhere, they warmed up very quickly. The whole fueling process took about an hour.

The fueling supervisor watched everything on the ground. Ground communications were hooked up so he could talk directly to the mechanic in the cockpit. He also kept an eye on the fueling truck operator, plus the quantity gauges, showing how much fuel was being serviced out of the truck.

The cockpit mechanic controlled the actual fuel distribution. A refueling control box was plugged into the electronics bay and the mechanic could turn each tank on or off with toggle switches. When a tank had the proper amount of fuel, he turned that tank "off" and directed the fuel wherever needed. When all six fuel tanks had the correct amount for the mission, refueling was complete. The fuel quantity indicator in the cockpit had seven settings, allowing the operators to view total fuel load, or the amount in each of the six tanks.

The third mechanic stood by the single-point refueling receptacle with a fire extinguisher, acting as "fire guard." The fourth individual, whom I've already mentioned, is the JP-7 fuel truck driver. Not only did he monitor his truck's operation and outward fuel flow, but observed and took orders from the fueling supervisor.

After fueling, a "fuel sheet" was completed. Think of it as an itemized 1040A tax form. On it is the basic weight of the aircraft, how much fuel was onboard and in each tank, what equipment was uploaded, and what each unit weighed. The weight of the pilot and the RSO was also tabulated.

So take all this data, grab a calculator and a cup of coffee, and in about an hour, you could determine the total weight of the aircraft and the center of gravity (CG). Once the CG was manually computed by the mechanic on the fuel sheet, he put the power on to see what the CG indicator was actually reading in the front cockpit. It's amazing how they always matched up!

About 1-1/2 hours before takeoff, the crew chief rechecked the aircraft forms, mechanics double-checked the airframe, DAFICS had a two-man crew standing by with test equipment to monitor the aircrew's preflight checks—then the liquid nitrogen (LN2) was put on board.

This was normally done by one of the crew chief's assistants. LN2 servicing tanks were wheeled in, adjacent to the nose wheel well. Inside the wheel well were two 104-liter "Dewars," or reservoir containers. Each one was filled to the maximum with liquid nitrogen. There was a "warm-up coil" in each Dewar. When the liquid nitrogen warmed up, it converted to a gas, which expanded six times. The "gaseous" nitrogen was pressure-fed through plumbing, and traveled throughout the entire fuel system of the SR-71.

The limiting factor on how long we could fly the SR-71 on Mach 3 legs became the liquid nitrogen. A third, 50-liter Dewar, was later installed in the left forward side of the fuselage, extending our range.

OK—why did we put gaseous nitrogen in the fuel system? Think of a car's gas tank when it's reading half full. Gasoline occupies the bottom half of the tank, fuel vapors the top half. No big deal, unless your gas tank is moving at 2,000 miles per hour, and the tank heats up to around 300 degrees F. Because those fuel vapors are more volatile than the liquid fuel itself . . . an explosion is imminent! We were purging the fuel vapors and replacing the empty space with inert gaseous nitrogen.

Gaseous nitrogen flowed through all the fuel tanks and had to vent somewhere! A fuel vent check valve was located in the farthest aft section of the fuselage. When the nitrogen pressure within the tanks exceeded 6 psi, the check valve "flapper" cracked open and allowed it to vent overboard.

All servicing was completed, all preflight inspections were done, the aircraft forms were documented, and the "exceptional release" was signed off—ready for engine start. All we needed was an aircrew.

On 17 July 1996, TWA Flight 800, a Boeing 747, exploded 13 minutes after it departed New York. The resulting investigation concluded that highly volatile fumes in its empty center fuel tank ignited, causing the explosion. The debate continues in the commercial world of aviation on using nitrogen to render aircraft fuel tanks inert. When you consider that the SR-71's fuel temperature control valve diverts hot fuel as it reaches 300 degrees F, the need for "inerting" its fuel tanks with nitrogen was paramount.

The refueling steps Steve talks about were for a flight that refueled with the tankers right after takeoff, which was probably 95 percent of the time. However, we had a few sorties that accelerated to Mach 3 immediately after takeoff, and the refueling process for these was a maintenance nightmare. This refueling procedure was called a "yo-yo." In order to *ensure* that an inert atmosphere was present in all six tanks, maintenance had to completely refuel the SR-71 to 80,000 pounds of JP-7. While nitrogen pressure was available, the six tanks were then defueled to the required amount in each tank. This was the only way to have a completely inert atmosphere in the fuel tanks. With a "hot" leg immediately after takeoff, we typically were fueled to 65,000 pounds of gas.

The "Buddy Crew"

An hour before scheduled engine start, the "buddy crew" arrived at the aircraft. First priority for members of the buddy crew was to ensure the aircraft's readiness. They each entered their respective cockpits and set up all the switches for the aircrew and the particular mission. All the information they needed was on the fuel sheet—what bays were loaded with which sensors, how much fuel was in each tank, and where the CG was. They would compare that information against their own CG calculations. With the cockpits complete, the buddy crew waited for the aircrew to arrive. They hung out in the shelter, talking to the crew chief, verifying everything again, and getting a "We're Ready" thumbs-up from the crew chief. While chatting to the many maintenance people they recognized from countless previous launches, the buddy crew continued getting a "thumbs-up" recognition, again and again. They knew the aircraft was ready . . . the "maintainers" let them know through sign language!

Three terms, "buddy crew," "backup crew," and "mobile crew," are used interchangeably. Backup crew, in the event the primary crew cannot fly. Mobile crew, to drive around in a military car, equipped with a variety of radios to stay in contact with the world. Buddy crew stayed in close contact with the mission flyers.

Personally, it was at this point that the trust between the aircrews and maintenance of the SR-71 Blackbird was truly acknowledged and exemplified. This always amazed me! Let me explain. For my first 13 years in aircraft maintenance I worked on single-engine fighters and some trainers. Whether it was an F-100 or F-104 at Luke AFB, Arizona, or an F-4E or F-16 at Hahn AB, Germany, or a T-37 or T-38 at Randolph AFB, Texas, all aircrew members did the same thing. The pilot arrived at the aircraft and asked the crew chief if it was ready to fly. Normal response was, "Yes sir, she's ready!"

The pilot went through the aircraft forms and played "20 questions," then started the deadly "walk-around." The crew chief followed the pilot, normally beginning at the leading edge of the left wing. Everything is touched, thumped, jiggled, and pulled on. At the trailing edge of the wing are the flaps and ailerons. The pilot always pushed up the sagging aileron! Why? What did this prove? Flight controls always sag when no hydraulic pressure is applied! This was later determined as a "test of strength" by us mechanics. Ever watch a movie where the pilot walks up to his air-to-air missiles, or the MK-82, 500-pound bomb rack, and shakes the hell out of the weapon? I always wanted to see a pilot's expression if an AIM-9 heat-seeking missile popped off a wing tip station as he did chin-ups, and he ended up holding it. What a surprise! But seriously, in 23 years I have *never* seen that happen. Most pilots will tell you they are "checking for looseness." Well, in my book, those weapons specialists know their job and do it very well, just like all the maintenance specialists and the crew chiefs.

That's where the "pride" factor came into play with the SR-71. In the eight years I was assigned to the Blackbird, I never saw an aircrew member do a walk-around, or double-check a crew chief, or question any other "maintainer of the airframe!" Everyone knew his job, and I will always miss the bond I shared with the aircrews. Name another airframe in the entire Air Force inventory where the aircrew member does not do a ritualistic walk-around, or where the pilot asks the crew chief if she's ready and, with a "Yes, sir" response, heads directly for the cockpit.

In my early days with the SR-71, I found it very strange that crewmembers did not do a preflight walk-around. I was taught you *always* did one. However, in the case of the SR-71, the trust between maintenance and aircrews was 110 percent.

—Rich Graham

Now don't think the Blackbird was just sitting in this nice, quiet shelter all by itself waiting for the aircrew to show up. Diesel generators just outside the shelter were roaring at a high-pitched scream, providing electrical power to the aircraft. Cooling air was hissing through a 10-inch-diameter duct, stretched from its source, across the shelter floor, and plugged into the nose wheel well receptacle, providing relief to rapidly heating "black boxes." JP-7

One of the biggest myths is leaking fuel. A narrator on the television's Discovery channel says, "The SR-71 leaks fuel so profusely that it *has* to refuel right after takeoff." Nothing could be farther from the truth!

We refueled right after takeoff for several reasons, none of which had to do with leaking fuel. If we lost an engine on takeoff with a full load of gas, our single-engine capability was so marginal, it would be hard to keep the plane in the air. We took off with one of three fuel loads: 45,000, 55,000, or 65,000 pounds. It was the *reduced fuel load* that made it necessary for us to refuel right after takeoff. Besides, we had 35 KC-135Q tankers at our disposal, they needed the practice, and so did we. Another reason was tire and brake heating. Taxiing out with a full load of gas could easily overheat the brakes and tires. However, the Flight Test crews at Palmdale occasionally took off with a full 80,000-pound fuel load.

During ground fueling, maintenance placed shallow drip pans on the floor to collect the dripping JP-7. Once they were removed, JP-7 dripped on the floor . . . *very* slippery to walk on!

—Rich Graham

fuel was leaking everywhere, pooling up on the concrete floor, and gaseous nitrogen was already beginning to vent out the tailcone.

Even when the outside temperature was hotter than 90 degrees, heat must still be applied to the engines, aimed at the oil tank. On the ground, this specially formulated engine oil has the viscosity of STP oil treatment (a thick gel). Applying 100-degree heat kept the oil in a constant liquid form for proper circulation, especially important during the critical engine start phase. Two gas-driven heaters added to the noise we were already encountering.

Finally, hooked up to the "starter" of each engine was what we called a "Buick." A "Buick" is two 400-cubic-inch Buick engines mounted side by side on a four-wheel chassis. Add some hydraulics to operate and extend a "starter coupling" that protruded from the top of the Buick frame. The Buick was positioned directly under the engine, the starter coupling extended until it made contact with the engine starter. From there, one person operated the control panel of the Buick, monitoring engine rpm and ensuring that all lights were in the green.

> We used the Buicks for many years to start the engines, until a pneumatic system was developed in the early 1980s. It was sad to see the Buicks disappear; they were a unique part of our history.
>
> **—Rich Graham**

The black unit to the left is the "Buick" starting cart for the J-58 engine on the right. The "Buick" originally used two Buick large-block V-8 engines, providing over 600 horsepower. With 16 straight pipes, coming directly off the exhaust manifold, it was an awesome sight to see and hear during a night launch. Flames shooting from all 16 pipes, and noise echoing in the hangar could match the commotion of a 3,000-horsepower dragster. *Rich Graham*

Now add the noise of four 400-cubic-inch Buick engines idling at 900 rpm, with straight headers (no mufflers) in our partially enclosed shelter to everything else, and think about holding a normal conversation with the person next to you. It's impossible!

The aircrew arrived at the shelter about 40 minutes before scheduled takeoff and the rest is history. After the pilot started the engines and did preliminary checks before taxiing, the grounds crew pulled the chocks, and the crew chief guided the plane out of the shelter with hand signals.

The Blackbird taxied to the end of the runway, where each engine was run up to full military power, instrumentation was checked, and maintenance did a final "look-see." The buddy crew received clearance from the control tower to access the active runway and made a high-speed run with the mobile car, checking for foreign objects lying on the runway that could damage the tires during takeoff. A truckload of maintenance specialists always followed the Blackbird out, just in case something went wrong. These specialists represented every system on the aircraft, from electrics, to comm/nav, to the crew chief—and they all remained there until the bird broke ground and the "wheels were in the well."

The Det 4 hangar at Edwards AFB. These are the two SR-71s being overhauled for the Air Force to use. This is an excellent shot of the spikes removed from the inlets, with four J-58 engines in the foreground. Notice the blunt section of the SR-71 with the nose removed. In the foreground is tail number 967. In the background is NASA's redesignated tail number 832, given back to the Air Force, and renumbered with its original number 971. *USAF*

So that's about it! You've just preflighted, serviced, and launched your first SR-71 Blackbird.

Everyone has seen pictures or videos of the SR-71 and knows what the capabilities and flight characteristics of this amazing aircraft were. From a maintenance point of view, the end product was watching those twin afterburners blaze flames and "diamonds" down the runway, as she gracefully lifted off and streamlined herself after raising the gear.

The SR-71 Blackbird was the fastest air-breathing aircraft ever developed by man . . . carrying two aviators to the edge of space in defense of a nation. It wasn't all fun and games working on the Blackbird, but the good times definitely outweighed the bad. After eight years I never tired of watching her break ground while feeling the concrete rumble, and seeing those two giant blowtorches push her into the sky.

It's ironic how it was created by man—holds speed and altitude records, had no competition, was never shot down in 28 years defending our country, had constantly upgraded technology—and yet was terminated by man. As in life, some things just don't make any sense.

For three years I was the last production superintendent of the SR-71 flight line for the Air Force at Beale AFB. In January 1990, we had the "official" retirement ceremony, deactivating the squadron, and ending the mission requirements of the SR-71. The 26 of us aircraft maintenance specialists remaining *were not* the only ones who felt the loss. It didn't matter if you were retired, what rank you attained, what your job or duty title was, or when you were on active duty. If you ever "turned a wrench" on an SR-71, scraped a knuckle, or watched her take off one predawn morning as the sun's rays peeked over the horizon, you felt the loss!

The SR-71 Blackbird retired (and still is!) a champion. So are all the people who ever took part in putting her in the sky. That is something no one can ever take away from us.

CHAPTER TWELVE

Colonel (Ret) Frank Stampf

Frank's first operational assignment after graduating from navigator training in April 1972 was flying in the back of the RF-4 as a weapon systems officer (WSO). After logging 1,600 hours in the RF-4 at Bergstrom AFB, Texas, and RAF Alconbury, England, Frank began SR-71 training in August 1979 at Beale AFB. During his tenure in the program, he logged 430 hours and 60 operational missions in the SR-71.

Following graduation from Armed Forces Staff College in 1983, Frank was assigned to the SRC at Offutt AFB. There he served as chief of SR-71 operations until 1986, when he was assigned to be the deputy commander for operations at RAF Mildenhall, Det 4. In 1988 Frank attended the Air War College for a year and was assigned to Air Force Space Command in Colorado Springs, Colorado. He left to command the 12th Missile Warning Group in the summer of 1991, and a year later was finally nabbed for

Frank getting ready to board the KC-135Q tanker after his final tour of duty on Okinawa. Roses and food in one hand, and a basic hook in the other! Habus always greeted each other on arrival and departure, making another reason to have a party back in 318. *Frank Stampf*

a job in the Pentagon, where he was chief of the Space and Combat Integration Requirements Division. Knowing Frank as I do, these were too many staff jobs and not enough flying!

Whenever I went TDY to Okinawa, it seemed as if Frank was there also. We had fun together. We both had an affinity for rock-and-roll music and Bailey's Irish Cream! Frank was once a drummer in a rock-and-roll band, and introduced Habus to the music of Meat Loaf . . . singing many of his songs until the wee hours of the morning.

I asked Frank if he would give the reader some of his thoughts on becoming a Habu and what distinguished Det 1, on Kadena, from Det 4, at RAF Mildenhall. I think you will find his stories enjoyable reading.

The Program—Thoughts of an Aspiring Habu

It might be useful to give an idea of what a typical aspiring SR-71 crewmember experienced—mentally, physically, and emotionally—from the time he first thought about flying such a magnificent machine to the time he was (hopefully) given that privilege. Before I was accepted into the SR-71 program, I spent seven years and eventually accumulated 1,600 hours as a back-seater (weapon systems officer, or WSO) in the RF-4C, the reconnaissance version of the McDonnell Douglas F-4 Phantom II aircraft. Four of those years (1975–1979) were with the First Tactical Reconnaissance Squadron at RAF Alconbury, England. At that time, our squadron was the only night-capable reconnaissance unit supporting NATO's cold war in the northern region. We faced what appeared to be a massive and very respectable Soviet Union and Warsaw Pact military capability. Although a 1960s-vintage airplane, the RF-4C was pretty damn hot to us "recce pukes," who had what we considered the advantage of flying our missions single ship, low level, and at the "speed of heat." We normally flew our missions at 480 knots (570 miles per hour) and 500 feet (lower and faster in selected areas), and relished the sense of "doing it on our own," both in daylight and in the dark of night.

Admittedly, as much as I loved the RF-4, I was fascinated with what little I'd heard and read about the SR-71. I had made up my mind to apply for the program as soon as I'd reached the requisite minimum of 1,500 hours flying time. That was a particularly strange decision, given that I'd never even seen the SR-71 other than in rare photographs or Air Force public relations films. However, as often as I thought about the remote possibility that I might actually be accepted into the SR program, I figured there was still no way I could ever enjoy the SR-71 reconnaissance mission as much as I did that of the RF-4. I was later to discover that that assumption was wrong.

In fact, my interest in trying to get into the SR program led me to request a one-year extension to my initial three-year tour at RAF Alconbury. My express purpose was to build flying time in order to log the minimum required number of hours to apply for the SR-71. I had already prepared my application "package," and the minute I hit the ground from the RF-4 sortie that took me over the 1,500 hour mark, I hoofed it over to the base personnel office and submitted my application through channels, starting the process. I was reluctant to put all of my trust into "the system" to get my application the attention I knew it required for me to be seriously considered. After all, I had just barely met the *minimum* required flight time. I knew I'd be competing against much more experienced folks with great records, for possibly only one shot at a slot. Consequently, I decided to hedge my bet a little by hand-carrying a copy of my application to Beale AFB. I hoped to hand over my application package to anyone who might take an interest in seeing me succeed. In the end, it turned out I made the right decision.

I only know of one other aspiring Habu who took the time, effort, and expense to personally deliver his application across the Atlantic Ocean. I was the 1st SRS commander the day Captain Bob Coats handed me his package. He wanted to ensure when it was time for the wing staff to select another RSO, some voting officers would be able to associate his face and personality with an application. It *does* make a difference when you're looking over a stack of 15 to 20 faceless applications, many with similar credentials, deciding which one should get the nod.

—Rich Graham

Early in 1979, just when I'd reached the minimum 1,500 hours of flying time, I volunteered for a "ferry" mission in which we were transferring some of our older RF-4s from England to an Air National Guard unit in Mississippi. I'd already done several ocean crossings in the RF-4. These were *not* fun. Nine to 12 hours strapped into a cramped ejection seat, wearing a bulky, extremely uncomfortable antiexposure ("poopy") suit to protect against cold water temperatures in case of an ejection over the open ocean. Coupled with a stiff neck from flying formation on the tankers the whole way across (it was routine for back-seaters to alternate stick time with pilots on extended missions like this), the tight confines of an F-4 cockpit made middle-seat coach on an overcrowded airliner seem like first class. However, I thought the pain would be worth the eventual gain.

Within hours of landing in Mississippi, I was on a commercial 727 heading for California (at my own expense). I'd done some checking and found that if I could make it to Sacramento that night, I could rent a car early the next morning, drive to Beale AFB, have about five hours on the base to "deliver" my application to somebody/anybody. If I could then make my way to Travis AFB that night (about 2-1/2 hours' drive from Beale), I had a slim chance of getting

> In Vietnam, it was common for F-4 pilots to train their GIBs (Guy In the Back) to fly, refuel, and land the plane for several reasons. First of all, it was nice to have some relief from flying the airplane after long combat missions, and second, it was comforting to know that he could refuel and land the airplane in case you were ever incapacitated in the front seat. When I flew the F-4 Wild Weasel mission in Vietnam, my back-seater, Colonel (Ret) John O S. Williams, was very capable of flying, refueling, and landing the F-4.
>
> **—Rich Graham**

a seat on a C-141 scheduled to go directly back to England. It would arrive the following day, after a 12-hour flight from California. If all went well, it would add up to about 40 hours of travel time for five hours "time-on-target" at Beale. Seemed like a reasonable trade at the time.

Fortunately, my "Rube Goldberg" travel plan worked like a charm, and the next morning I walked unannounced into the SR-71 squadron building, application in hand and searching for a friendly face. Luck was once again with me when I ran into one of the few SR crewmembers who happened to be in the squadron that day—Captain Chuck Sober. Chuck, an experienced SR-71 RSO, listened to my story, had me sign some "nondisclosure" paperwork (my TDY orders verified my security clearances), and took my application out of my (by then) sweaty palms. He then asked if I'd like to take a ride down to the flight line to take a look at the airplane. I thought that would be appropriate, given that I'd just traveled 5,000 miles, and would soon be starting the long 5,000-mile return trip.

The moment we went through the security checkpoint at the entrance to the flight line that was home to the secretive SR-71 and U-2, my heart rate started to increase. That was the first moment I sensed that I really wanted this whole thing to "work" even more than I had previously realized. My first impression of the black form I saw in the hangar surprised me even further.

As I walked around the SR-71 for the first time, it became immediately obvious to me that it wasn't just a "machine." I had an uncanny sense of something animate, something alive, in the hunk of titanium that seemed to be eyeing me as much as I was staring at it. What came to mind was being up close to another living creature whose intelligence we sense, but don't understand. I paced slowly in front, behind, under, and alongside the black beauty that seemed to absorb even what little sunlight made its way through the open door of the hangar. I was unabashedly mesmerized by the experience. That's when I knew in my heart that I wanted to be part of "The Program"—whatever that meant.

A few hours later, I was on the C-141 heading back to England. During the long flight back, I thought about what I saw and what I felt during that very short time I'd spent at Beale. Now I had actually seen and touched what previously had been only a vague concept of a truly amazing airplane. I was pumped up at the possibility of maybe actually making it into the program, and at the same time, uncomfortably apprehensive about how I'd handle the disappointment if I *didn't* make it.

A favorite watering hole at RAF Mildenhall was the Smoke House Inn, just outside the main gate and within walking distance of our quarters. Left to right are Ron Tabor, Frank Stampf, and Jack Madison in 1987. Being "regulars," they had their own beer mugs waiting for them. *Frank Stampf*

Almost two months later, after experiencing daily bouts of what I could only describe as "aviator's PMS"—the ups and downs of thinking about my chances for acceptance—it happened. I was called out to Beale to "interview" for "The Program," which in a sense meant that I actually had a shot, albeit a long one, at being accepted. During my long trip from England to California, this time for the interview, I thought a lot about expectations. What they would expect from me, as well as what I would expect from "The Program" if I were actually accepted. In all honesty, the very fact that the SR-71 squadron was referred to as "The Program" made me wonder what I was asking for . . . .

I made it through the week of physical exams, simulator evaluations, and personal interviews with the squadron and wing staff, and before I departed, was told I'd hear from them shortly as to the outcome. For the second time, I left Beale to return to my RF-4 unit in England. Incredibly, I was even more impressed than the first time. Impressed with the people, the mission, and not least, with the airplane itself.

The Final Decision—A Close Call

One day in May 1979, an agonizing two months after my interview, the deputy commander for operations (DO) at RAF Alconbury called me into his office and handed me what seemed to me (under the circumstances) to be a rather short, unemotional message from his counterpart, the 9th Strategic Reconnaissance Wing DO at Beale. The short transmission, in typical military language of acronyms and jargon, requested my transfer to Beale AFB in July of that year ". . . for the purpose of beginning SR-71 training . . . blah, blah, blah . . . details to follow through personnel channels."

Needless to say, my squadron mates had a great time at the bar that night on my tab. However, I was to find out later that I came very close to *not* receiving that acceptance message, unceremonious as it was. It seems that shortly after my first trip to Beale (during which I handed my "package" to Chuck Sober) the 9th SRW training folks were screening the many RSO applications to narrow them down to a manageable two or three candidates. These would then be called out to Beale to interview and compete for the one RSO slot for the upcoming year. One of the "old head" lieutenant colonels on the wing training staff took a quick look at my application and immediately threw it in the "no-go" pile because he thought I was too junior in rank and didn't have enough flying experience. To my eternal good fortune, Chuck Sober, who was then still just a captain among a room full of senior officers, happened to be present and objected vociferously enough on my behalf that I at least went back into the "consider" pile. I guess that was what it took. I'll be forever grateful to Chuck for sticking his neck out and taking on a senior officer to support a guy he'd met for only a few hours. Because of him, I made it from the "consider" pile to the "interview" pile, and eventually received the short but sweet acceptance message a few months later.

From New Guy to Operational Habu

Shortly after arriving at Beale in July 1979, I met the pilot who, for better or for worse, would be stuck with me throughout the upcoming year of training. We'd stay together if we managed to make it through "The Program," for as long as we could both hang onto this jewel of an assignment. It was a Friday afternoon, and everyone who was in the squadron and not TDY was at the Officers' Club for "happy hour." This was still traditional for flying squadrons in those days. It took me all of about one minute to size up Gil—all 6 feet, 3 inches of him. I had to crane my neck a bit, given I'm barely 5 feet, 7 inches in my flying boots. Gil Bertelson was a nondrinking, nonsmoking, noncussing, straight-arrow Mormon with a friendly smile, a great sense of humor, and as I and the rest of the squadron would later learn, a flair for planning and executing the best practical jokes ("frags") in the wing. As a snapshot of his wit, here's what I received from him after sending him the first draft of my input to this book:

> "I have a couple of thoughts: In your reference to our first meeting, you never mentioned anything about being impressed by my chiseled-looking, handsomely square-cut jaw, the Chuck Yeager-look-alike steely blue green eyes that were kind but also gave the appearance they could cut through steel if necessary, the Robert Redford-like hair, and the humongous solid gold Rolex watch that I sported on my very athletic looking left wrist. How come you failed to mention any of that stuff ???"

We hit it off immediately. That was a tremendous relief. We were about to spend more of the next three or four years together than we would with our families. It was critically important for Habu crewmembers to "work and play well" with their crewmates. Not only would our lives depend on our relationship—solid and instantaneous crew coordination was absolutely essential to make the SR do what it was intended to do, and do it safely—our long-term sanity depended on it as well. Successful Habu crews, although starting out as two individuals, eventually melded into a single "crew personality." Tough to explain, but true nonetheless.

The Torture Chamber

Gil and I made it through our year of training pretty much intact. At times, however, it was no less than torturous. I remember some mornings as we crested the hill from the base housing area driving toward the SR-71 simulator building. Both of us silently wished we'd see a smoking crater in the place of the SAGE building where the simulator was housed. It was a tough transition for all SR crewmembers, coming from our previous flying units where we had pretty much made it to the top of the ladder. We had all proven ourselves as line crew-dogs, instructors, and evaluators in whatever airplanes we came from—F-4s, F-111s, B-52s, F-15s—we even had a former Thunderbird pilot start training after Gil and I had checked out. None of that mattered. In the SR simulator, the experienced Habu instructors reduced us all to common rubble. Suddenly, we found ourselves at the bottom of the heap, starting out as new guys in an airplane in which very little of our "conventional" flying experience, no matter how extensive, seemed to apply to learning how to fly and manage the SR-71.

The SR-71 simulator was located on the ground floor of a huge windowless "blockhouse." The building was originally built to be part of an integrated United States air defense network called the Semi Automatic Ground Environment (SAGE). When the SAGE concept became obsolete in the 1960s, the building became a multipurpose facility, housing over the years the wing commander's office, personnel center, mission planners, film processing and analysis, and various other services.

Our simulator was located at the south end of the SAGE building. The entrance to the simulator facility was a large vault door. Once you spun the correct combination numbers, the massive door unlocked. Inside the facility, we occupied two rooms–one for the simulator instructor crew to claim as their office, and the other for crews to study in and brief/debrief the simulator missions. Before computer miniaturization, the facility had rows upon rows of computer banks, all over 6 feet tall, just to run the SR-71 simulator. The facility sported two features Habus liked, a quiet place to study and plenty of air conditioning!

New crews in training were assigned an experienced instructor crew who, with few exceptions, took them through their entire checkout from day one to mission-ready status—a process that took the better part of a year, if all went as planned. Gil and I were fortunate (although at the time, we weren't always so sure) to have two of the most experienced and capable instructors on the crew force—Lieutenant Colonel Bob Crowder and Major John Morgan. Bob and John were flight instructors of the "traditional" mold. They had a wealth of knowledge to impart about the mysteries of flying the SR-71, and they expected their students to work hard to internalize every golden morsel of information they metered out. The fact that Gil and I were relatively experienced aviators with considerable time in high-performance aircraft under our belts did not exempt us from our instructors' verbalized wrath if we were not performing up to their expectations. Twenty years after our time as new guys in the torture chamber (the SR simulator), Gil and I still reminisce in vivid detail about one of those sessions.

We had already made it through what we thought was a critical point in the training program as we drove over the crest of the hill that Monday morning. Once again, we were greatly chagrined to see the simulator building standing intact, rather than the remnants of a mushroom cloud over the spot where we were about to endure another five hours of humiliation at the hands of our flight inquisitors. As usual, we had put in quite a few hours over the weekend, both individually and as a crew, studying for this morning's sim mission. The prebriefing went reasonably well, with minimal scowls and rolling eyeballs from our teachers. We climbed into "The Box" and began going through the various checklists, procedures, and scenarios for the briefed mission, seemingly without any glitches. Once again, we were too naïve to realize that when everything seems to be going smoothly during a simulator mission, it probably isn't . . . .

I think it was somewhere during the first cruise leg, about 40 minutes into the mission, with everything *apparently* under control, that Gil and I felt (not heard) Bob Crowder's voice. It was about as aggravated a growl as we'd ever heard come through our headsets, with the words every crew in training dreaded worse than crashing and burning. *"Awright, God Dammit—FREEZE THE SIM!"*

Those words of terror usually meant that such a serious sin of commission or omission had occurred that the perpetrators would likely never see the light of day again, let alone eventually get to wear the coveted Habu patch as an operational crewmember. Gil and I were so traumatized that to this day, we still don't even remember what it was we did or didn't do to warrant such a severe reaction. However, we *do* remember, and recall just about every time we get the chance, the words Bob hit us with after freezing the simulator. After what seemed like an eternity of agonizing silence, we heard his slow, growling drawl over the intercom eke out the words: "*AWRIGHT . . . is it because it's MONDAY, or do you think you have it MADE, or are you INTENTIONALLY trying to PISS ME OFF?*"

Consider one pair of experienced aviators sufficiently humbled.

> At the push of the "freeze" button, the SR-71 simulator stopped instantly. During simulated emergencies it was often necessary to freeze the simulator to let the crew in training see their mistakes by looking over the cockpit instruments and gauges. Freezing the simulator at just the right moment was a valuable instructional tool, particularly at Mach 3 speeds, where many emergencies happened so suddenly that it was difficult for crewmembers to analyze what had happened.
>
> It also meant you were screwing up. Trust me, no one ever froze the simulator to congratulate me on how well I was handling a particular emergency!
>
> **—Rich Graham**

Whatever it was that caused such a vehement reaction, we must have been able to overcome it, because we made it through not only the remainder of that simulator mission, but all the way through the training program, relatively on schedule. By sheer coincidence, Bob and John happened to be the senior crew on the island during our very first operational tour to Det 1 on

Okinawa. I remember seeing their names on the TDY schedule along with ours, and thinking, "Oh no, just when we really *did* think we had it made, we'll be in for six more weeks of relentless scrutiny under the eyes of 'The Mad Monk and his Henchman.' "

As it turned out, I couldn't have been more mistaken. As we stepped off the ladder at Det 1 upon returning from our first operational SR-71 sortie, officially making us "true" Habus, Bob and John were there at the bottom step waiting for us with welcoming "hooks" and great big grins. From that point on, it was as though they were proud parents, and Gil and I—their gifted progeny—could do no wrong. When we got back to our lockers and changed into our "orange bags" that day, we found that Bob and John had already affixed our newly earned and greatly treasured Habu patches to our flight suits. What a GREAT tour! The first of many to come as operational Habus.

TDY

Once Gil and I became operational in mid-1980, the TDYs came fast and furious. The cold war demand for SR-71 coverage in Europe was picking up with a vengeance, and the wing was preparing to establish a permanent operational SR-71 detachment at RAF Mildenhall. With a continuous requirement for three crews at Det 1 in Okinawa and two crews at the newly formed detachment (Det 4) in the U.K., the nine existing crews in the squadron were being stretched pretty thin. As much as every crewmember loved the SR mission, and there wasn't much griping to be heard, it was not a healthy situation.

On 18 January 1980, I made the following entry in the 1st SRS Commander's Policy and Information Book:

"Every crewmember entered the SR program knowing that TDY would be part of his life. Others and myself have always considered going TDY with the SR-71 a privilege. The Kadena TDY schedule will never be adjusted for Mildenhall or any other TDY location. The crews on station at Beale will be selected for those deployments as they come up. Some crews may find themselves arriving at Beale after six weeks at Kadena, home a few days, en route to Mildenhall for 3–4 weeks, home briefly, then to Kadena again. If this type of schedule does not meet with anyone's approval, be sure to let me know–there are others fighting to go.

"If you foresee any eventuality such as baby due, sickness, operations, or any other circumstance that will change the TDY schedule let us know ASAP. I will attempt to man the Kadena Christmas TDY rotation with those who have not been before. Realize this is not always possible."

—Rich Graham

Given that it took 14 to 15 months to screen, interview, select, and train each new crew, it would be awhile before "reinforcements" arrived to reduce the TDY commitments. Although I don't remember hearing anyone complain about it—every Habu understood what would be expected of him before he was accepted into the program—the extensive time away from home took its toll on the families. Gil and I spent more than 200 days TDY during our first operational year. That number was reduced somewhat over our second and third years as new crews became operational, but not significantly. This put a tremendous strain on a number of marriages.

"The" Fire

As Gil and I gained experience, we found that flying the SR-71 was not without its occasional adrenaline rush. The reliability of the airplane, along with the skill and hard work of the maintenance folks, ops planners, KC-135Q tanker crews, and all the mission support people kept the truly "scary" in-flight moments to a minimum. However, all crew dogs have at least one story about the emergency that put them closer to "stepping over the side" than anyone cares to be. On 20 March 1982, Gil and I blasted off from Kadena into the clear blue morning sky, expecting another routine operational sortie. Less than three minutes after takeoff, Gil eased the throttles back to level off at 25,000 feet, preparing to rendezvous with the tanker a short distance away over the South China Sea. Immediately after level off, Gil told me he had a fire warning light illuminate on the left engine. While this was not exactly an everyday occurrence, we weren't particularly worried, either. This was precisely the sort of thing for which Crowder and Morgan had prepared us so well during our "torture time" in the simulator.

Gil instantaneously went through the "Bold Face" (immediate action) steps of the emergency procedure. However, it soon became obvious that the fire light was not going out on its own and the engine would have to be shut down, another serious escalation of the situation, to be sure, but still no cause for undue concern. I declared an emergency, and we started running through the myriad compounded checklists that were called for with a single-engine situation. The fire light remained on as we descended. Most of our fuel had to be dumped in order to bring the aircraft down to a suitable landing weight. We began to position ourselves for an extended straight-in, single-engine approach back at Kadena. It was several minutes after the engine was shut down before the fire light finally went out. Worth mentioning here is that the SR-71 single-engine approach speed is considerably higher than that required for a normal approach. Consequently, the pace of events picked up noticeably as we were screaming toward the runway at about 250 knots. All was going well up to that point. Once again, we should have recognized that "Crowder's Law" was about to kick in. That is: *The smoothness with which an emergency situation seems to be progressing is usually directly proportional to the seriousness of the surprise that probably awaits you just as you "think you have it made."*

So it was to be on this day. The hydraulic system that powers the SR-71's main landing gear system is in turn powered by—you guessed it—the left engine. Since we had to shut the left engine down, we no longer had the luxury of "normal" landing gear extension. Still—no sweat. One of the last of many procedures to execute in this situation was the "emergency landing gear extension" checklist. After I pulled a circuit breaker in the rear cockpit to disable the landing gear's electro-mechanical locks, the last step in this procedure was for Gil to pull the emergency landing gear T-handle in the front cockpit. The T-handle, located on a panel directly between Gil's legs, is connected to a 6-inch cable, leading directly to the mechanical locks holding the gear up. The combination of these events would (supposedly) allow the landing gear to fall and (eventually) lock into place via the force of good old gravity. At least that's how it was *supposed* to work. On this occasion, "Crowder's Law" was waiting in the wings.

Up to this point, we had gone through the many interconnected emergency checklists for this situation like clockwork, using the standard "challenge and response" manner common to all aviators worldwide. For example, I would read a checklist step aloud such as, "Throttle affected engine—IDLE," and Gil would immediately respond with, "Throttle, left engine—IDLE," as he completed the action called for. This assured both of us that the correct procedure had been called for and executed in the correct sequence. We'd then proceed with the next step and the next checklist, until all necessary procedures were accomplished. However, on this day, when we got to the step where I called for, "Emergency landing gear handle—PULL," I didn't get an immediate response from Gil, as I had for all the other steps up to that point. The four or five seconds of silence from the nose turret seemed like an eternity as we careened closer and closer to the runway with no landing gear. I naturally assumed that Gil had his hands full and simply had not heard me.

(This would be a good time to remind the reader that Gil was a "straight-shootin', no drinking, no smokin', no cussing" devout Mormon from whom I had *never* heard a word harsher than "darn." Foul language was simply non-existent in his lexicon.)

Several seconds (seemed like hours) after I repeated the all-important checklist step to Gil, the response I heard from the front cockpit was bone chilling, to say the least: "Well, FART, Frank—it (the T-handle) broke off in my hand! What do I do now??" Unless you've lived, worked, and played for a couple of years with someone who never even *thought* in terms of swear-words, you have no idea what a shock hearing a statement like that can be, particularly at such a delicate moment. It seems the 6-inch cable that connected the T-handle to the landing gear lock simply snapped as Gil pulled it out, fluttering back into its little hole in the instrument panel like a wound-up clothesline. This left Gil with the stick in one hand, the useless T-handle in the other, and neither of us with any landing gear as the ground and the runway rushed closer and closer to our "wheel-less wonder."

(At that point, the thought went through MY meager brain that it would be absolutely wonderful to hear Crowder's growl in our headsets right then saying "Awright, God Dammit—FREEZE the sim . . . !") No such luck.

About that time, Gil realized that we had at least a noticeable amount of hydraulic pressure in the left system. This was due to the lifeless engine's compressor blades "windmilling" because of our relatively high speed as we barreled down final approach. It took about one-zillionth of a second for us to discuss the possibility of trying to make that little bit of "oomph" work for us. Since that was about the only option, we reversed the few previous checklist steps so that when Gil put the normal landing gear handle down, there might be a tiny chance the little hydraulic pressure we had would cause the gear to do what we wanted it to do.

Well, our prayers were answered. Almost. The left main wheel came down almost immediately and locked into place. That was good, but not great. We were still screaming toward the runway in an "unlandable" condition, which prompted us to begin talking about heading out over the South China Sea, tightening up our straps, and preparing to eject. Then the right main gear clunked into place and locked. Better, but still not great. The emergency procedures checklist told us that two main gear and no nose gear was a definite "eject" situation, rather than an attempt to land. Boy, was that runway getting close. I don't remember how close we were to the end of the runway, but I know it felt like about a week later when the nose gear indicator decided to show us a "down and locked" indication. At that moment, it seemed like a good idea to trust the indicators and continue the approach to touchdown, which was only seconds away. Since we were already low on fuel, we decided to land immediately, rather than attempt a low approach, to allow the tower guy to check our landing gear through his binoculars. They probably wouldn't be any more reliable than our cockpit gear indications, anyway.

My guess is I was the only one in the airplane with his eyes closed the second we felt the gear kiss the runway. Gil did an incredible job of keeping it all together, and as we rolled to a stop, it appeared as though the entire base population was lined up alongside the runway, and every vehicle in sight had some kind of warning light flashing. We came to a stop, and the tower confirmed we had no visible flames coming from the aircraft. This is always welcome information. The ground crew put the landing gear locking pins in place, we shut down the right engine, and opened the canopies to climb out and down the maintenance vehicle's ladder. As I put my foot on the runway, I remember seeing our crew chief's face as he looked at the left engine. His eyes were ready to pop! *The fire had been so intense, it had burned an 18-inch-wide hole right through the titanium nacelle.*

During "postmission hooks" back at the BOQ, I figured that if Gil didn't start drinking and cussing after this episode, his place in heaven would be firmly assured. St. Peter, move over . . .

The Road to Det 4

They say all good things must come to an end. Three and a half years from the day I met Gil and started my checkout, my flying assignment to the SR-71 came to an all-too-early end. Due to an unexpected early promotion to major, I found myself heading to Armed Forces Staff College in early 1983. Although I had asked for an operational deferment to delay going to school (based on the continuing shortage of SR crews and still-high TDY rate), my request for a stay of execution was denied by the powers that be, and off I went.

Following school I was assigned to the Strategic Reconnaissance Center at Offutt AFB. After a few months of learning the ins and outs of headquarters staff work, I found myself as chief of the SR-71 branch. Our primary function was to be the intermediary between the Joint Reconnaissance Center (JRC) in Washington, D.C., and the SR-71 wing and operational detachments. All operational tasking for strategic reconnaissance missions worldwide, including the U-2, RC-135, and SR-71, among other platforms, came from the JRC. As experienced crewmembers of those platforms, we at SRC, along with our

Rich Graham's favorite job was visiting each Detachment under the 9th Wing. He is standing in the middle with Nevin Cunningham, Det 4 commander, to his right and Frank Stampf, Det 4 director of operations, to his left. Behind the Det 4 sign is hangar 538, housing all of the operations and intelligence personnel. Inside the hangar were numerous processing vans that took the raw SR-71 data and turned it into meaningful intelligence. *Frank Stampf*

counterparts at JRC, did the best we could to unscramble the often confusing (and sometimes conflicting) orders coming from the senior military and civilian agencies demanding reconnaissance coverage for their particular areas of interest. I know the crews on the line who were directed to fly some of the missions we tasked wondered why the Air Force removed what were once the normally functioning brains of their former crewmates, and reinserted them backward. However, years later, as the saga of the SR-71 program continued to its official end, we all eventually learned that the brain reversals were at a much higher level than we originally thought.

I guess somebody up there believed we were trying, because after three years at SRC, I was selected to be the deputy commander for operations (DO) at Det 4 in England in July 1986. The only assignment that could have been better to me at the time would have been reassignment to the crew force. The assignment to Det 4 was almost too good to be true.

First of all, the opportunity to be *directly* involved with the SR flying operation again was a welcome relief from the suffocating staff work of SAC headquarters. Although I wouldn't actually be flying the airplane, I'd still be around the crew dogs and the airplane again. Second, I'd become quite attached to the country and to the Brits themselves. I had many good friends and special relationships there.

Unlike most flying units, the SR-71 squadron commander and both detachment commanders did not fly the Blackbird. With very limited flying time, and extensive TDY commitment, only the combat-ready "crew dogs" routinely flew the plane.

Det 4 . . . the Same as Det 1, but Different

By the time I arrived at RAF Mildenhall in the summer of 1986, the operation had evolved from the "shoestring" mode of the first temporary deployments during the 1970s, to a permanent and growing detachment. Det 4's two Blackbirds were housed in specially designed "drive-through" hangars adjacent to a new maintenance facility. The operations and administration functions, along with the intelligence personnel and their photo processing and interpretation equipment, were accommodated in the large hangar and associated offices previously occupied by the U-2s. We also had the luxury of being colocated with our KC-135Q tanker operations, which made day-to-day coordination and special operations planning much easier. Better still, it allowed closer personal interaction between the tanker crews and Habus. I believe that went a long way to enhancing morale, making the operation run

Here are Frank Stampf and Tom Veltri dancing to "New York, New York" in one of the crew rooms at RAF Mildenhall. It cost crews a lot of money, but we lived well at both Dets. We furnished our room nicely, had three cars at each Det, had our rooms cleaned and beds made daily, and could have our clothes washed and ironed for an occasional bottle of sherry. Life was good! *Frank Stampf*

smoothly and efficiently, as evidenced by the Det's remarkable 98 percent operational effectiveness rate during the mid-to-late 1980s.

With almost 20 years of experience in overseas SR-71 operations on Okinawa, we had a great model to work with in getting Det 4 up and running. However, while there were many similarities in the way the Dets were to function, there were also significant differences. Most of the similarities occurred in the "social protocol" of Det life. For example, the crews chipped in and quickly formed a "car pool" to allow each crew to have its own vehicle during their six-week TDY tours. Once permanent BOQ rooms were assigned to the crews, the bars in each room were quick to follow. The Det 1 tradition of "postmission hooks" (drinks and snacks hosted by the nonflying crews after each mission) was in immediate effect. Most important, from the "quality of life" perspective, the Habus and support folks soon established a social network of friends and associates, both among the local British population and U.S. military folks stationed in the area. Many long-lasting friendships evolved between the men and women supporting the SR-71 operation and people they met during Det 4's relatively short, but very productive existence in the U.K.

The flying operation, on the other hand, had some considerable differences from those we were used to at Det 1 in the Pacific. Perhaps the most basic difference was the frequent need to fly around, near, or over many different countries in a single mission, as opposed to the primarily "over-water" nature of most Det 1 sorties. This made operational coordination for every sortie much more complex, and also complicated the options for emergency recovery should the crews have a serious problem with the aircraft. We operated in close proximity to some countries that were not as receptive to our presence as others. Consequently, it occasionally became necessary for the State Department to become involved in premission coordination. Government-to-government dialogue was also the norm if an SR made an unexpected recovery into a foreign country due to aircraft problems.

Seldom did the crews need to land away. That was largely due to outstanding maintenance support provided primarily by civilian contractors who formed the majority of Det 4's maintenance force. These men and women were a key part of the unit and were every bit as dedicated to the mission as any of us in uniform. They put in many long, hard hours to keep our aircraft and mission systems in top condition, and deserve much of the credit for the remarkable success the Det enjoyed during its operational existence. As a "blue-suiter," I could never thank these folks enough for their unselfish efforts and frequent ability to make the sometimes seemingly impossible possible.

The Sorties

The combination of geography, international political factors, and European weather made for some very interesting flight plans from Det 4. Our mission planners were kept busy for even the most frequently flown profiles because there *always* seemed to be something "different" to consider for each sortie. On average, missions flown from Det 4 were longer in duration, and therefore required more air refuelings than those from Det 1 in the Pacific. It was not unusual to "hit" a tanker over the North Sea within a few minutes after takeoff, and then fly a supersonic leg to meet a second set of tankers off the coast of Norway. From there, a second acceleration to speed and altitude would take the crew over the Barents Sea and around the Kola Peninsula, where Soviet nuclear submarine facilities and fighter bases were the items of interest. After exiting the "sensitive area" the crew would again descend to rendezvous with a third set of tankers off the coast of Norway. After topping off the tanks, a third acceleration to altitude would precede a "thread the needle" pass either around the Baltic Sea or around the periphery of East Germany and several other eastern European borders to monitor Warsaw Pact force status and movements.

These tracks, in and around the politically constrained landmass of continental Europe, were tricky in that the crew would have to slow down to

Mach 2.8 in order to stay on the preplanned "black line" and avoid unauthorized overflights of not-so-friendly countries. Since the SR-71 was designed to fly at Mach 3.0 or faster, its performance, in terms of fuel efficiency and aircraft handling, was less than optimum at these slower speeds. I can't speak for the impressions of other Habus, but I remember that when Gil and I flew those sorties, the second part of the mission seemed to take *forever* at Mach 2.8! Similar to driving at 70 miles per hour on the freeway and suddenly having to slow down to 50 or 55 due to traffic or construction.

The "black line" Frank refers to was the actual black line drawn on our maps, showing the route of flight. We were not allowed to deviate, even slightly, from the black line, particularly in sensitive areas.

—Rich Graham

Assuming the temperatures at altitude cooperated, and the crew stayed on their planned fuel-consumption curve, they flew back west after completing the third "loop" (supersonic leg), descending over the Channel, to arrive at the English coastline subsonic. This was to avoid regularly upsetting the natives with unnecessary sonic booms. The mission profile just described was typical for Det 4. Sometimes the forecast temperatures at altitude would require yet another air refueling before heading into the second "sensitive area," extending the mission by another 30 or 40 minutes. Before recovering into RAF Mildenhall, the crew would have been airborne a little over 5 hours, conducted at least three aerial refuelings, and covered approximately 5,500 nautical miles.

If climb and cruise outside air temperatures were considerably hotter than standard day temperatures, it would make a *significant* dent in your fuel consumption. Crews had to carefully monitor the remaining fuel at each checkpoint to assess the fuel curve. If you were behind, you had to apply every fuel-saving technique you were taught or had heard about from the "old heads."

Not all of the missions out of Det 4 were "typical," however. We sometimes had the opportunity to fly what were termed "coordinated" missions. The SR-71 would fly a profile designed to "stimulate" hostile forces by making it appear we were possibly going to penetrate or overfly their territory. This would often (as we anticipated) arouse their SAM radars and fighter interceptor forces to a higher state of activity. Not wanting to waste all that potentially valuable technical and operational information, other platforms such as RC-135 electronic intelligence-gathering aircraft, were prepositioned far below, and offset from the SR's track to "collect" the hostile radar signals and other data for postmission analysis. This was one part of a very sophisticated network of intelligence resources that kept U.S. forces at least one step ahead of the Soviets when it came to military technology and tactics.

New Sensor Technology—ASARS-1

While the SR-71 had long been equipped with a suite of sensors giving it exceptional optical, electronic, and all-weather, day/night high-resolution radar capabilities, it was the all-weather, day/night coverage that was most in demand, at least in the European Theater of Operations. In particular, the U.S. Navy had a critical need to monitor the Soviet nuclear submarine installations on the Kola Peninsula of the Barents Sea. Additionally, the U.S. Army needed frequently updated information on Warsaw Pact maneuvers in the Eastern Bloc countries near the Federal Republic of Germany's (FRG) borders. In the extreme northern latitudes of the Soviet Union and over much of Europe, the combination of shortened daylight hours in the winter months, and the frequent occurrence of low clouds covering much of the landmass and coastal areas, severely limited the usefulness of optical photography. Consequently, a means to "see" through clouds and darkness was imperative to maintaining the tenuous cold war "balance of power" between NATO and the Soviet-backed Warsaw Pact forces.

The SR-71's high-resolution radar (HRR) sensor had already provided such a capability for many years. However, by the early- to mid-1980s, the HRR was being outpaced by newly available sensor technology, and a concerted effort was undertaken to upgrade the SR-71's all-weather, day/night effectiveness. That upgrade came in the form of ASARS-1 (the number 1 merely indicated it was for the SR-71; ASARS-2 was for the U-2). After several years of testing, evaluation, and refinement by technical personnel and flight-test crews at Palmdale, the time for initial deployment of the capability to an operational environment had come. The intelligence requirements in the European Theater described earlier made Det 4 the natural choice for the initial bed-down of ASARS-1. After engineers worked through a number of technical and operational concept issues, ASARS-1 became fully operational in 1986, several months ahead of schedule, and performed even better than expected.

What had previously shown up from the old HRR system as uniquely shaped radar "blobs," readable only by a highly trained radar imagery interpreter, now appeared as quite clearly definable aircraft, ships, tanks, and even smaller vehicles that could readily be identified by types and numbers. In fact, ASARS-1 had even demonstrated that under certain conditions, it could "see" aircraft that were actually parked *inside* hangars by virtue of the powerful radar signals "bouncing" into open hangar doors on Soviet and Warsaw Pact flightlines. The users of the SR-71's intelligence were clearly impressed and wanted more and more of it.

Unfortunately—and ironically—it was that increased demand for SR-71 coverage by U.S. military and civilian agencies, *other* than the Air Force, that eventually became a factor in the program's premature termination. It was a point of contention with the Air Force senior leadership that those primary "users" of SR-71 intelligence were not the ones paying the bills. Consequently, that leadership, and in particular SAC, adopted an extremely parochial (and many program supporters still argue shortsighted) position, which in effect stated that since the SR-71 didn't "drop bombs or pass gas" (an allusion to SAC's primary role of strategic bombing and the need to provide air-to-air refueling for the bombers), the Air Force and SAC didn't need or want it.

Leaving "The Program"

Although I didn't like it at the time, another assignment to "school"—this time to Air War College—was about to cut short my tour to Det 4. The author of this book, then my wing commander, made a valiant attempt at my request to have my school assignment "operationally deferred," but it was not to be. It saddened me tremendously to leave Det 4 for many reasons—both personal and professional. Undoubtedly, one key reason for my sadness was the knowledge that in all probability I would not return to the "The Program." The political and funding battles surrounding the SR-71 had already begun in earnest. It became all too clear that no matter how hard proponents of this amazing capability fought to assure its continued availability to serve the national interest, logic and operational effectiveness were not going to win out over political and personal agendas of the Air Force leadership at the time.

While I left Det 4 and England reluctantly, I left with the knowledge that at least for a considerable part of my career—and my life—I had the privilege of being part of something that relatively few others in the world would ever have the chance to experience. For that, I will forever be sincerely grateful to "The Program."

CHAPTER THIRTEEN

Lieutenant Colonel (Ret) Gil Bertelson

When I heard we hired a Mormon to be one of our pilots, my first thought was, "How was he ever going to fit into our small group that loved to party for any excuse?" As it turned out, although Gil was a devout Mormon, he always joined in, even if only drinking a Coke. I recall one late-night party in 318 and we could not find Gil. We went to the door of his room and knocked. No answer. After several minutes we decided (I seem to recall it was actually his RSO, Frank Stampf, who had the idea) that maybe music could lure him out of the room. We used a "boom box" playing at full volume, one of Meat Loaf's songs with the starting words, "Would you offer your throat to the wolf with the red roses?" Within 30 seconds Gil came out laughing and joined in with the rest of us, partying until the wee hours of the morning.

Gil entered the SR-71 program as a captain in 1978 and reluctantly departed in 1983. Before that time, he attended undergraduate

Gil at Korat RTAFB, Thailand, in 1975 with his F-111 behind him. Habus came from many flying backgrounds in the Air Force. Because of the F-111's high-speed flight, air-refueling capability, and its relatively complex aircraft systems, we found it to be an excellent source for future pilots and RSOs. *Gil Bertelson*

pilot training (UPT) at Laredo AFB, Texas, from September 1969 to October 1970. Gil's first assignment following UPT was back to Laredo as a T-37 IP.

After three years of instructor duty at Laredo, Gil was assigned to the F-111F program at Mountain Home AFB, Idaho. He spent about two years at Mt. Home and was then assigned to Korat Royal Thai Air Base, Thailand, for a one-year remote assignment (not accompanied by his family), where he flew the F-111A (there were significant differences between F-111 models, especially in engines and avionics). Following Thailand, Gil returned to Mt. Home for another 1-1/2 years, and then moved (with his family this time) to RAF Lakenheath in England. He spent just short of two years at Lakenheath before his assignment in 1978 to the 9th SRW at Beale AFB to fly the SR-71.

Top Speed

When I first joined the SR-71 program there was one permanent operating location for SR-71s at Kadena AB. The unit at Kadena was known as Detachment 1 (or Det 1) of the 9th SRW. Habus were deployed to Det 1 for six weeks at a time and each crew made the trip four to six times a year. About twice a year, there was a requirement to temporarily activate an additional Det at RAF Mildenhall in England. Although we'd had two SR-71s permanently stationed at RAF Mildenhall since 1981, it wasn't until 5 April 1984 that Prime Minister Thatcher formally announced SR-71s would be permanently based at Mildenhall. This unit was known as Det 4 of the 9th SRW. Dets 2 and 3 of the 9th SRW were U-2 operating locations, at Osan AB, Korea, and RAF Akrotiri, Cyprus, respectively.

There was a significantly different flying environment between the two detachments. The weather was almost at opposite ends of the spectrum. The missions were not quite as "routine" as many of the Okinawa missions.

When we first started regular six-week tours to RAF Mildenhall, some crews were not as thrilled about spending time in England as Gil was. On 18 March 1981, I made the following entry in the Commander's Policy and Information Book:

"Any TDY schedule I make out (or have made out) does not reflect personal convenience for anyone. My prime consideration is always 'what is best for the I SRS.' Other than that, I attempt to make everything equitable for all. I have to develop TDY schedules under certain constraints levied by the DO and wing commander, but beyond those, I couldn't care less who is home for the reunion, where your friends are located, or how much you hate going to Mildenhall. As personnel changes occur, it stands to reason that certain TDY schedules will change also."

—Rich Graham

Because of the more demanding missions at Mildenhall, each new SR-71 crew had to fly its first operational sorties at Kadena. Every SR crew lobbied long and hard to get on the schedule for Mildenhall. And London was not far away!

Frank Stampf, my RSO crewmate on the SR-71, and I were fortunate to get on the schedule for Mildenhall after only two trips to Okinawa. For both of us, it was like going home. Just before entering the SR-71 program, Frank had been stationed at RAF Alconbury for about four years as an RF-4 crew dog. And, as mentioned before, I had been stationed at RAF Lakenheath for a couple of years. As the "crow flies," Alconbury is only 30 miles from Mildenhall and Lakenheath is only 3 miles from Mildenhall. We were both anxious to visit the old flying buddies we had known and worked with in our careers before we became Habus.

On one occasion, I arranged to meet several of my F-111 friends at the Lakenheath Officers' Club for dinner. We met in the bar and had a few drinks (as a real, live, dyed-in-the-wool teetotaler, I assume I was drinking grapefruit juice or 7-Up). We shared numerous laughs while trying to outdo each other with tales of unequalled courage and great feats of airmanship. I'm sure our hands were getting a good workout—pilots gesticulate a lot!

At some point in the evening, the Aardvark (F-111 nickname) guys began to press me, in a good-natured way, for classified information about the SR-71. Probably the most frequently asked Blackbird question is—how high and how fast does it really fly? That question was being actively pursued that night at Lakenheath.

I need to back up about a year and a half to set the stage as to why they seemed intent on pushing that particular question. In most Air Force buildings, at least the flying squadron buildings I used to frequent, there were numerous locations where the base fire marshal had posted information regarding fire classifications and appropriate reactions upon discovering different types of fires. These posters were displayed in the restrooms, in the halls, near the duty desks, in the crew briefing rooms, and next to all of the fire extinguishers. I can't remember all the specifics other than there was one fire classification identified as a category or type 3.

At some point in my application for assignment to the SR-71, I was requested to go to Beale for my "tryout" for the Blackbird program. The whole process from departing Lakenheath until returning back to Lakenheath took about two weeks. During the visit to Beale, I heard and read a number of times that the unclassified speed of the SR-71 was listed as Mach 3-plus. A "3+" patch is displayed on flight suits worn by SR-71 squadron crewmembers.

When I arrived back to Lakenheath, I was really pumped up and excited about the prospects of being selected to fly the SR-71. I didn't want to forget the experiences I had at Beale or to lose sight of my goal. To help me remember, and to keep my attention focused on what I wanted to do, I began adding a black grease pencil + sign to all of the 3s on the fire code posters. There were so many added + signs around the base that the very diligent safety officer in the 493rd Tactical Fighter Squadron actually called the base fire marshal to get information about this "new classification." When he was told there was no such thing as a code 3+, he finally figured it out and started looking for me. I was given a "cease and desist" order and one by one, he began erasing my "unauthorized" + signs.

> I knew instinctively Gil would make a good Habu, for we were always spray-painting black SR-71 silhouettes around the base.
>
> **—Rich Graham**

Now back to the "O" Club a year and a half later. My dinner partners remembered the fuss over the posters and figured now was an appropriate time and place to get the real scoop as to how high and how fast the Blackbird really did fly. They were curious as to what kind of speed that little + sign actually equated to.

I played along for a while, dragging out the inevitable answer of Mach 3-plus, which, when all was said and done, was all I really could tell them anyway. I finally got them leaning in toward me as we sat around the dinner table. I did a pretty good acting job as I began nervously looking around the room to be sure no one else was eavesdropping on what they thought would be a classified conversation.

I have to momentarily divert again. A wonderful aviation poem was written in the early days of powered flight. The author is John Gillespie Magee Jr. The poem is entitled "High Flight." Some of you may remember this poem being recited by Orson Wells late in the evening by TV stations that were about to sign off the air for the night. Yes, there actually was a time when television didn't operate 24 hours a day. As Orson Wells recited this poem with his marvelously deep and resonant voice, the final TV pictures for the day were that of a T-38 dashing in and out of clouds and doing aileron rolls, etc. It was a combination of sight and sound that stirred the blood and emotions of everyone who had the slightest interest in airplanes and the wonders of flight. The poem is as follows:

"Oh, I have slipped the surly bonds of earth,
And danced the skies on laughter, silvered wings;
Sunward I've climbed, and joined the tumbling mirth
Of sun-split clouds—and done a hundred things
You have not dreamed of—wheeled and soared and swung
High in the sunlit silence. Hov'ring there,
I've chased the shouting wind along, and flung

My eager craft through footless halls of air.
Up, up the long, delirious, burning blue
I've topped the windswept heights with easy grace
Where never lark, or eagle flew.
And while with silent, lifting mind I've trod
The high untrespassed sanctity of space,
Put out my hand, and touched the face of God."

Back to the "O" Club again. With the guys leaning in to hang on every word I was about to speak, I said something like, "You've got to promise not to tell a soul what I am going to tell you now. If you do, I'll deny it till the day I die. I'm sure you know I shouldn't be talking about this at all. You know how high the pile will be that they'll stick me in if you tell anyone else." As they gathered closer to make sure they didn't miss anything, I said, "I can't give you specific numbers, but I can give you a point of reference you can use to figure it out. You know the part in 'High Flight'—where it talks about putting out your hand to touch the face of God?" Well," I added, "when we're at speed and altitude in the SR, we have to slow down and descend in order to do that."

So, the word's out. Feel free to share this information with anyone you'd care to tell. You can even use me as the source document. I'm retired now, so who cares?

Fun and Games

Some time later, Frank and I were at Mildenhall again. Requests for SR-71 presence in the Atlantic had been steadily increasing. The airplane routinely proved its capabilities in assisting the commander in chief, Atlantic Command (CINCLANT) accomplish his tasked mission of accounting for all

All dressed up for a dinner party on Okinawa are (left to right) Geno Quist, Gil Bertelson, Frank Stampf, and Nevin Cunningham. Habus often got invites to friend's homes for dinner at both Dets. *Gil Bertelson*

Soviet nuclear missile submarines (the "Boomers") operating in his theater. Det 4 had now become a full-time operation.

Since we were there all the time now, it seemed important, and appropriate, to establish closer ties with British units that, in one way or another, supported SR-71 missions out of the U.K. One of the primary areas of emphasis was that of air traffic control (ATC). On operational missions, we always started engines, taxied, and took off using "radio silent" procedures. We didn't talk to anyone on "open air" radio channels. This was our way of not announcing to the world that we were departing on a mission. It was important to have a good working arrangement with the units that worked to protect our airspace and to just generally watch out for us. This was especially true since they weren't able to routinely communicate with us until we were en route for recovery.

Frank and I were "old heads" at flying in the U.K. from our days at Alconbury and Lakenheath. So, we were asked to be the "unofficial, official"

Whenever the SR-71 was on an operational mission, our flight plan stopped at 60,000 feet. As far as radar controllers were concerned, we dropped off the face of the earth at those geographical coordinates. At 60,000 feet we also had no need to talk to anyone.

When Don and I entered the program in 1974, we were using standard Air Force radio calls on all of our operational missions out of Kadena. Somewhere around 1978, the National Security Agency (NSA) came down from Japan to Det 1 with a briefing. They informed us Soviet fishing "trawlers" just off the coast of Okinawa were easily picking up our radio transmissions and passing the information along to other Communist countries. At that point we changed to total radio-silent procedures.

From the moment we taxied out of the hangar, we never used our radios, until our arrival back at Kadena. Obviously, if we needed to break radio silence in the interest of safety, that was fine. The taxi and takeoff were done with light signals from the tower. The tower officer (a former or current crewmember) knew the needs of the SR-71 intimately, and was in the tower for all takeoffs and recoveries, assisting the controllers with our radio-silent procedures. The same procedures were adopted at RAF Mildenhall.

When I think back on our radio-silent procedures, I am forever amazed that we pulled them off without an incident. Imagine, you could take a Blackbird, fly it halfway around the world, air refuel multiple times, return and land . . . all without talking to anyone. Truly astounding!

—Rich Graham

liaisons with the ATC organization we normally worked with. They were known as Eastern Radar. Their facilities were physically located about an hour's drive north of Mildenhall. We were in their area of control during the critical phases of takeoff, the first refueling, the beginning of the acceleration and climb, final descent, approach, and landing.

We arranged to visit the controllers one Friday night during their end-of-the-week happy hour. Our assignment was to get to know them and to give them a chance to get to know us. There was a possibility we might even talk a little business sometime during the evening. They treated us royally. We weren't allowed to buy a single drink the entire night. Several days before, at their request, Frank and I made a "bubble check" over their station while en route back to Mildenhall. A "bubble check" is the term used to describe a minimum legal altitude flyover. There was a brief interruption in air traffic control in Eastern's sector while all their controllers were outside watching the Blackbird pass by.

As we were preparing to return to Mildenhall that night, the U.S. Air Force officer who served as the "official" liaison and was actually assigned to work at Eastern Radar, pulled us off to the side. He told us it would be well received if we surreptitiously "stole" a prized plaque that was hanging on the wall in the bar area. He said that stealing the plaque was a tradition and he knew they would be pleased, and honored, if we helped carry on this particular tradition.

We obliged by covertly removing the plaque from the wall and slipping out a side door with it in tow. When we got back to our BOQ rooms at Mildenhall, we had our first chance to examine the plaque a little closer. On the front was the official Eastern Radar crest. It was a pheasant being held, as I best recall, in sort of a warrior-looking, steel-like, hand or fist. On the back was a place for everyone who stole the plaque to log the details of their theft. There was a column for the date of the dastardly deed, and another column for the names of the perpetrators of the crime and their unit. And finally, there was a space for any amplifying remarks that seemed appropriate.

As we looked over the log, we saw the plaque had really traveled around. It had previously been in the possession of a number of RAF and USAF units. In the remarks column there were entries that indicated it had been flown on a number of different types of aircraft and missions before being returned to Eastern Radar. We were sure we could do something that would outdistance all of the other entries.

At the time, the most challenging mission we were tasked to fly out of Mildenhall was an early-morning takeoff (well before sunrise) and a trip "way up north" to the Barents Sea. This was an area where, at 1000 hours in the morning, in January, it was still dark—even at 85,000 feet. Was there anything more fitting we could do for the plaque than taking it on a ride to the Barents and back?

The next time we were tasked for a Barents Sea mission, we arranged with the maintenance folks to load the plaque in a sensor bay where it couldn't interfere with anything. The mission was flown uneventfully. The pheasant got to go the Barents at Mach 3-plus in what seemed to us like the middle of the night.

We began making plans for a triumphant return to Eastern Radar. We'd place the plaque back in the hands of its rightful owners—and, there would be a new, grand entry in the "log." It read:

"12 May 1982, Gil Bertelson, Maj. USAF / Frank Stampf, Maj. USAF, Det. 4, 9th SRW. This plaque was flown in an SR-71, #974 at speeds and altitudes in excess of Mach 3 and 80,000 feet over a distance of 7,500 miles. It was flown where 'the sun don't shine.' Its presence contributed greatly to the success of the mission and brought great credit upon itself and the Royal Air Force."

To just walk in and hand it over seemed a little anticlimactic after what it had been through. We decided to schedule another Friday-evening "happy hour" liaison meeting. We contacted the U.S. Air Force officer at Eastern Radar and asked him to get us on the schedule. We alerted him to the fact that we were bringing the plaque back, but we had some bad news. We told him we had put the plaque in one of the mission equipment bays for the flight. We went on to tell him that cooling air to that bay had failed sometime during the mission and the plaque had literally burned up. All we had left to return was a pile of ashes. He knew a little about how hot the airplane actually got in flight, and with our explanation of cooling air failure to the bay, he bought the story hook, line, and sinker. We asked him to not mention the mishandling of the plaque to anyone else. We thought it was best if we explained the problem firsthand.

You needed real faith in the crew chief's placement of valuables aboard the SR-71. Flying a Blackbird from Beale to Okinawa, Don and I gave the crew chief our hang-up bags to stow in a sensor bay. They contained all the clothes we needed for the few days before the tanker arrived with our complete supply of clothes.

My clothes arrived safely, but Don's Air Force hang-up bag had melted! His clothes were singed and everything was ruined from the melted plastic. When he tried to get reimbursed for his loss, it was difficult for the finance office at Beale to understand what happened.

—Rich Graham

I spent a little time writing a poem for the occasion and Frankie made a trip to the Smokehouse Inn (nothing new here) to "borrow" some ashes from the fireplace. We filled a large vodka bottle with the ashes, attached the poem to the bottle with a paper clip chain, and headed out for Eastern Radar. We got there early and hid the plaque behind the bar.

When the "liaison" meeting officially began, we were given some time to talk about "new business." We may have actually had an item or two to discuss, but we soon got to the matter at hand. We acknowledged we had stolen their plaque. We told them we wanted to do something special with it. However, we explained, our plans went awry when we had an aircraft malfunction and the bay temperatures got out of hand. We expressed our regrets that all we had to return to them was this bottle full of ashes. We apologized and hoped they would understand.

We then asked if we could read a poem we hoped would better express our feelings of remorse. (Remember please, this is the one and only poem I've ever written. I suspect the quality of the thing will speak volumes as to why I didn't take up writing poetry for a day job.)

This ash was once a crest so fine,
But all good things must pass with time.
It was once a pheasant and a steel fist,
Now it's just rubble, please don't be miffed.
We borrowed it to give it the ride of its life,
But butchered it badly, as if by a knife.
While on a flight so high and fast;
It smoked, then smoldered, then burned, alas.

At this point we're happy to freely admit,
The story just told is nothing but spit,
Your crest is as good, no, it's better than new,
For the ride we gave it was to say thanks to you.
The service you provide has no parallel,
All who doubt that can just go to hell.
So this bottle of crud and dirty old soot,
It's a trophy of sorts with a purpose to boot.
When flight crews start grumbling and give you some sass,
Tell 'em—radar contact lost, come kiss my ASH.

As I read the last few lines, Frank retrieved the very much "alive and well" plaque out from behind the bar. They whooped, hollered, and loved every minute of it. The bottle of ashes was passed around for everyone to look at. The next thing we knew, the bottle, poem, and attaching chain had been escorted out of the room to be placed in their vault. The reason for putting them in the vault, they explained, was because there were some Dutch controllers visiting at the time. They knew there was nothing the Dutch guys would rather do than "steal" these new gifts the very day they were presented.

The time came for Frank and me to leave and head back to Mildenhall. When we got to our car, we discovered the police-style emergency flasher lights and bar had been removed (i.e., stolen), and they were nowhere to be found. The vehicle was used for "mobile" duty on and around the flight line and the lights actually served a necessary and useful purpose. We finally accepted the fact that "what was good for the goose was good for the gander." The Eastern guys had gotten the last laugh, after all. So, off we headed for home trying to figure out how to explain the missing lights.

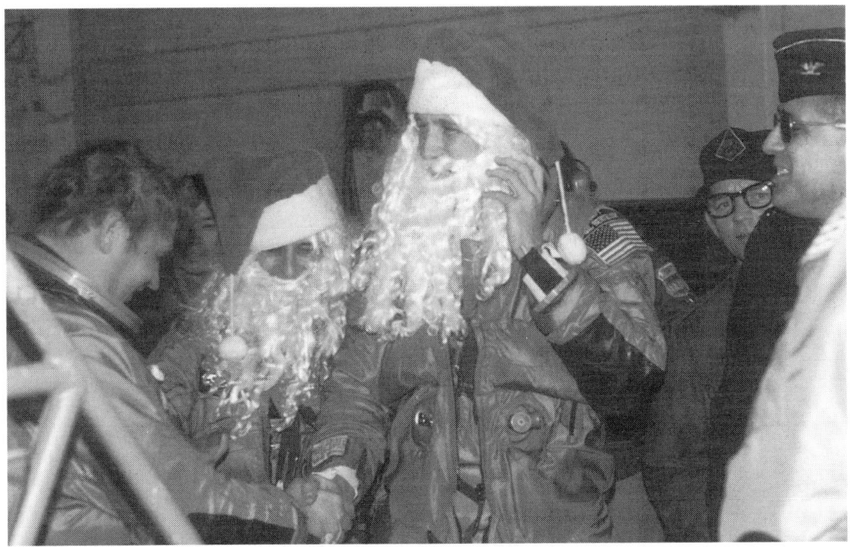

Gil and Frank in Santa Claus suits at Det 1. It was 23 December 1980, and Gil and Frank had just landed from an operational sortie. They put on the beard and hat, came out of the cockpit, and passed out candy. Nevin and Geno were flying their very first training sortie (called a "Debbie") on Okinawa at the same time, so Gil and Frank went over to their plane and greeted them. Geno is shaking hands, and Col. Ray Samay, Det 1 commander, at far right is looking on. *Gil Bertelson*

The next day was Saturday and was the "kickoff" of an annual two-day air show at Mildenhall. The Brits love airplanes and air shows. It was estimated that approximately 500,000 people attended the two-day event. An aviation calendar was being sold that had an SR-71 picture accompanying the month of August. I think the four of us crew dogs, standing duty at the airplane during the show, signed an autograph for each of the 500,000 people. We finally started signing each other's names in an effort to stay awake. When a calendar was thrust in front of us, we had to look for which names were already used up in order to pick a name that was still available to be signed.

The Eastern Radar Wing commander came by during the time we were standing vigil. He thanked Frank and me for participating in the activities of the previous night. He also said he heard about our "emergency lights" dilemma. He told us not to worry because he would see that everything was taken care of. Late that afternoon, when we got back to the car, the lights were all back in place—and they even worked.

I can't verify the accuracy of the following item. I heard it somewhere along the way, but can't recall the source. It seems the plaque continued to travel around quite a bit, which I'm sure is not surprising to anyone. The story I heard was that it was aboard the British ship HMS *Sheffield* when she was sunk during the Falkland Islands war between the British and the Argentines. If the story about the demise of the plaque is true, then bon voyage to an old friend that has once again traveled to a place "where the sun don't shine."

CHAPTER FOURTEEN

Lieutenant Colonel (Ret) D. Curt Osterheld

Curt graduated from the United States Air Force Academy in 1975. Following undergraduate navigator training (UNT) at Mather AFB, California, Curt was assigned to fly RF-4C Phantoms at Shaw AFB.

During his operational flying in the RF-4C, Curt was stationed at RAF Alconbury, England, and flew reconnaissance missions throughout Europe. He served as an instructor weapons system officer and as the 1st Tactical Reconnaissance Squadron's assistant operations officer, finishing with over

Joe Matthews on the left and Curt on the right. Although Curt flew as an RSO, he's a rated pilot in the civilian world and owns a Cessna 172. The bulges in the pressure suit at chest level are "water wings," designed to keep you afloat in water. They inflate automatically when water touches a sensor. Without them, taking water in the pressure suit has proven fatal. *Curt Osterheld*

1,500 hours in the "Photo Phantom." Curt is credited with an aircraft save after his aircraft sustained major damage from birdstrikes while flying a low-level training mission.

Curt was assigned to the USAF's Air Staff Training (ASTRA) program at Randolph AFB, Texas, when he applied for the SR-71 Program. He began training in January of 1983 and had his first operational tour at Det 1 in January 1984. Curt finished his Habu flying with 631 hours and 96 operational sorties.

Assigned to the Pentagon and the U.S. Air Force's Reconnaissance Directorate in 1987, Curt joined Geno Quist during the dark days of the budget battle over the SR-71. After leaving the Air Staff, Curt served as a program manager within the National Reconnaissance Office (NRO). After a brief sabbatical to the Defense Systems Management College, Curt completed his Air Force career on the staff of the Office of the Secretary of Defense (OSD).

I think it's notable to mention that Curt's wife, Lisa, was one of our KC-135Q tanker pilots at Beale AFB and is currently flying with American Airlines. Here are two illuminating stories from Curt.

The Trials and Tribulations of the First Operational Tour

There were many rewards of being a crewmember in the SR-71. After the long, grueling first year of initial training, one of the biggest rewards was to embark on your first operational tour . . . to Kadena Air Base. Your first operational flight would finally entitle you to the highly coveted Habu patch. A Kadena tour meant experiencing the many hallowed traditions of the "Island Paradise."

> One patch on our flight suit had to be earned—the Habu patch. All the other patches could be worn by non-Habus, although few ever did so.

I was privileged to fly with Joe Matthews as my front-seater and accomplice in numerous adventures. Joe was a superb pilot. We'd served together before in the RF-4C Phantom, an aircraft that is deserving of its own book full of flyers' tales. We'd had our share of emergencies during our training at Beale, but that really was to be expected. The simulator and flight training sorties were intended to build not just your knowledge of the jet, but your confidence that you could handle whatever emergencies the airplane had in store for you. It's only fair to reiterate that since each SR-71 was handcrafted, each aircraft had something different up its sleeve for the unwary.

Our first couple of sorties out of Kadena were the perfunctory island orientation training sorties, then a "single loop" operational mission just

Orange bags on Okinawa. Pictured (left to right) Tom Alison, J. T. Vida, Bruce Liebman, and Don Emmons. The Habu patch worn on the left shoulder of the flight suit was only given to those who had flown an operational mission. The patch would show up mysteriously on your flight suit after landing from your first mission. *Lee Shelton*

south of the Korean DMZ. The latter qualified us to wear the long-awaited Habu patch. We could now savor the accomplishment of being fully operational SR-71 crewmembers.

The savoring dissipated slightly during our next operational mission, as we were challenged with a series of malfunctions that left us, for a time, completely mystified. The mission objectives were to perform electronic intelligence (ELINT) gathering over the Yellow Sea, then make a standard photo run through the Korean DMZ. Everything was routine through the first air refueling. Then, during the climb to operating speed and altitude, we began to encounter some moderate clear-air turbulence. From the cockpit, this feels much like sitting on the end of a diving board as it oscillates up and down. At approximately 45,000 feet and Mach 1.4, there was a severe jolt, knocking our helmets against the canopy. After that, the air seemed to smooth out and we continued the climb and acceleration.

At Mach 3 and 79,000 feet, we seemed to be well on our way when, for seemingly no reason at all, the autopilot disengaged. Our center of gravity (CG) was not where it was supposed to be, and fuel readings were erratic. Joe was fighting with the pitch trim, trying to keep the autopilot engaged. I kept using the circular slide rule to "spin" what the CG should be reading, each time not believing the calculations.

In both cockpits was a CG indicator. Inputs from the fuel tank quantity sensors were fed into the CG indicator, providing both crewmembers with a continuous readout of the aircraft's CG. A warning light alerted us when the CG was either too far forward or aft. The pilot had the ability to manually control the CG by moving fuel from the aft tanks to a forward tank if the CG was too far aft, and vice versa, if the CG was too far forward.

The RSO used a circular slide rule in the rear cockpit to manually determine the aircraft's CG. Its purpose was to confirm the automatic CG readout. However, the accuracy of the CG indicator itself, or the RSO's manually "spun" CG, was directly dependent on each fuel tank's reading. If they were incorrect, so was the answer.

Now we were 4,000 pounds down on the "fuel curve," our planned amount of fuel for a specific point in the mission. Then 5,000 pounds. Then 6,000 pounds. Joe was using the periscope to scan behind the aircraft for fuel leaks, but with its very limited field of view, could see nothing abnormal. Again the autopilot kicked off. Now, the nitrogen that served as our inerting atmosphere for the fuel tanks began depleting rapidly.

Our options became very limited. With the remaining fuel, we couldn't continue the mission and had to abort back to Kadena. Truly a disappointing choice to make; we were admitting failure. I made the required abort calls over the HF radio, telling the whole world we were heading home a lot sooner than planned.

The descent was spiced up with a couple of unstarts, but finally we were subsonic and only 80 miles away from Kadena. The mysterious fuel loss had stabilized and it seemed we could now make a normal recovery. There were a few brief moments for Joe and me to discuss "What the hell was all that?" and other topics before talking with Okinawa radar approach control. Both of us were wondering what we had done wrong . . . and what would be the detachment commander's reaction.

Joe made a great landing, followed quickly by an expletive over the intercom and news that the drag 'chute had not deployed. Some judicious use of the SR-71's powerful brakes stopped us. Fortunately, we didn't have to use the emergency arresting barrier—I imagine the effect on the landing gear doors would have been very ugly.

Taxiing in, we ran the appropriate checklists and wondered "what next?" As we pulled into the hangar, a number of the maintenance folks were pointing, wide-eyed, to the back of the aircraft. After shutting down the engines, we had a large contingent of folks swarming over the airplane. Joe and I climbed out, took off the Lockheed ejection-seat "spurs" from our boots and put on protective boot covers. Then we saw the problem. On the right wing, near the fuselage, was a jagged 10-inch gash that looked as if it had been made with a can opener. The drag 'chute that hadn't deployed on landing was missing altogether, as was the right drag 'chute compartment door from the top of the fuselage.

> *Any time* you taxi into the hangar and see all the maintenance troops pointing to some spot on the aircraft, it's not good! One exception in my case was when Don decided to put "Room to Let" and "For Rent" signs on his windows when we pulled into the hangar. However, I knew it was nothing bad (maybe embarrassing), because they were pointing and laughing.
>
> Whenever anyone walked on the surfaces of the SR-71, they had to put protective boot covers over the soles of their shoes.
>
> **—Rich Graham**

We began to piece the mystery together. That jolt of clear-air turbulence we felt at 45,000 feet popped the right drag 'chute compartment door open, and once in the slipstream, punctured the right wing and fuel tank number six as it departed the aircraft. The drag 'chute was then sucked from its shallow container along the top of the fuselage. Note: The genius of Kelly Johnson's engineering was evident here. A ball-and-jaws–type joint connected the large drag 'chute to the aircraft. The jaws only closed around the ball when the pilot pulled the drag 'chute handle on landing. Therefore, if the drag 'chute compartment door opened accidentally, the drag 'chute, still in a bundle and not attached to the jet, could fall freely from the aircraft. One can only imagine the aerodynamic loads placed on the aircraft, even for a brief instant, if the 'chute deployed at supersonic speeds while firmly connected to the middle of the aircraft!

The gash in the wing fuel tank explained the rest. Approximately 6,000 pounds had vented from this hole, along with the nitrogen. In turn, this upset the delicate balance of the CG and caused erratic readings as the fuel transfer system attempted to fix the imbalance. The fuel transfer caused transients in the pitch trim, which in turn, would automatically disengage the autopilot. All very logical when you're standing on the ground looking at the evidence.

This whole experience did have an upside. The instructors in the simulator now had a baffling new scenario with which to humiliate their student crews. Joe and I received little pink bunnies from our senior crew, to provide us with four "lucky" rabbit's feet so something like this wouldn't happen again. We were beginning to feel like experienced Habus, even if it was just our first tour.

Every Pentagon Tour Should Last 45 Minutes

The following thoughts, recollections, and impressions are offered as a complement to those provided by Geno Quist in the next chapter. Just to set the record straight, Geno is one of the great all-time heroes of the SR-71 program. He fought a tremendous battle to sustain the Habu in the face of a determined foe. The result was that the SR-71 flew operationally, protecting our nation's interests, for one year longer than dictated by the "corporate" Air Force. Even today, there are strong grounds for debating the wisdom of the program's early retirement.

Some of the Washington, D.C., Habus getting together at Tom Alison's house. Pictured (left to right) are Tom Alison, Curt Osterheld and daughter Miranda, Joe Kinego, Rich Graham, and Tom Veltri. Whenever Habus come to visit it seems to turn into a mini-reunion of sorts. Many fond memories are relived. *Rich Graham*

In October 1987, I was offered an opportunity to serve on the Air Staff at the Pentagon. In retrospect, one could ask why I wanted to leave operational flying to become a staff weenie in the high-pressure Pentagon environment. It seemed like a good career move at the time, and there were new technologies on the horizon for the SR-71 that would need funding support from Washington.

Specifically, the SR-71 was slated to be fitted with a wideband communications capability that would make it a near real-time platform. Put another way, we would be able to data-relay our radar imagery from ASARS-1 to anywhere in the world for immediate processing and evaluation—a devastating blow to the program's critics, as the SR-71's detractors always whined about having to wait for the film to be processed. Bringing the Habu into the digital age would ensure its viability as a reconnaissance platform for years to come.

Two terms that became buzzwords within the intelligence community during the 1980s were "real-time" and "near real-time." Real-time reconnaissance is exactly what it implies: what you see is happening without *any* delay. Near real-time reconnaissance has a delay of some length, typically from transmission, reception, and processing.

I joined Geno in early November, and he patiently showed me the ropes for working within the five-sided building. Things were beginning to settle into a reasonable routine when, just before Thanksgiving, we were attending a going-away dinner honoring one of our office secretaries. At the restaurant, Geno got a call from Colonel Woody, our boss, tasking us to calculate the costs to shut down the entire SR-71 program. Thus began the worst 18 months of my Air Force career! You can bet that Geno and I spent Thanksgiving in the vault crunching numbers in what seemed to be yet another budget drill. However, like 7 December 1941, this was no drill.

The "vault" Curt refers to was his office in the basement of the Pentagon. It was literally a secure, vaulted office, denying access to those who didn't have the need to know. At Beale we had a similar office we called the vault, where the mission planners worked and many Top Secret documents were stored.

—Rich Graham

The decision to cancel the SR-71 appeared to us to have been made unilaterally by the Air Force chief of staff. While initially we found many general officers who were shocked and surprised by this edict, it didn't take long before all had weather-vaned in line with the chief. The issue soon lost all rational character. It was a witch's brew of emotions, money, egos, distorted facts, careerism, and it seemed to lack focus on what was best for our national defense.

The chief of staff of the Air Force is often referred to as just the "chief." He is the ultimate military boss in the Air Force's chain of command.

On many occasions, I would engage, or try to engage, senior staff officers in a courteous exchange of ideas. When asked what the Air Force was going to use to replace the SR-71, several replied, "I have no clue, but you know how the chief feels, so there's really nothing to discuss."

The numbers game was truly comical. To show the world, and especially Congress, how expensive the SR-71 was to operate and why getting rid of it was a good idea, we were tasked to include costs in our budget for many ancillary items. Among the largest added were for KC-135Q tanker support and maintenance personnel. Did the B-52, F-15, or any other weapons system carry these items on their budgets? Of course not. However, the SR-71 took on a whole host of additional expenses to bump the cost-per-flying-hour to stratospheric levels.

As Geno alludes to in his stories, a good deal of our work was altered farther up the chain of command without a chance for rebuttal. An excellent example of this was our report on the SR-71's vulnerability to the Soviet's SA-5 surface-to-air missile. Without going into details, one can imagine how the SR-71's operational risk escalated at each stop on the way to the chief's desk.

Probably the bitterest memories of this time came from the personalization of this issue by others in the Pentagon. Geno and I were both dedicated officers, but we also felt it our duty to offer a loyal opposition to an action we felt was terribly flawed. The careerists sought to portray us as evil and disloyal (I'm not making this up!) for having an opinion other than the chief's. Some officers within the intelligence community saw this as the next leap forward for satellite reconnaissance dominance (and their own upward mobility) so they jumped on the "kill the SR-71 now" bandwagon. Geno and I were convinced that some took a sadistic delight in the SR-71's struggle for survival. I recall a hall meeting with a colonel (who was not a flying officer) in which he sneered at me and Geno and stated, "It serves you pressure-breathing Prima Donnas right. I hope you all die."

In the summer of 1988 I was tasked to go as the punching bag with an Air Force briefing team to convince the CINCs at various commands to support the Air Force's position on shutting down the SR-71. Again, many commanders expressed concern, but acquiesced to the chief's position. The one exception was the commander-in-chief of Atlantic Command (CINCLANT). Among his many other responsibilities, the admiral was responsible for monitoring and tracking Soviet nuclear ballistic missile submarines. The SR-71 did a superb job of that for the ports along the Kola Peninsula and the Barents Sea. The Air Force proposed using the TR-1s (the same as a U-2) out of England as a gap-filler. The end result was that this issue came to a "tank" session in the Joint Chiefs of Staff arena. In the end, the Air Force chief was coerced into keeping all of the SR-71 detachments active for one more fiscal year to answer CINC requirements. I will leave it to the reader to decide if an adequate replacement capability has ever been fielded.

CHAPTER FIFTEEN

Lieutenant Colonel (Ret) Gene "Geno" Quist

Geno graduated from the U.S. Air Force Academy in 1970. He earned his navigator wings as a distinguished graduate from undergraduate navigation training (UNT) at Mather AFB, California. Geno's first operational aircraft was the RF-4C Phantom flying out of Kadena AB and Udorn RTAFB, Thailand.

During his RF-4 assignments, he flew operational missions along the Korean DMZ under the Peacetime Aerial Reconnaissance Program (PARPRO), accumulating over 245 hours of combat/combat support time in Southeast Asia. Geno was then selected to participate in a two-year Air Force/Navy exchange program. He underwent RA-5C training at Naval Air Station Key West, Florida, and served aboard the USS

Geno Quist in the PSD room at Det 1. Before every flight a PSD technician gave both crewmembers a miniphysical. It consisted of recording your pulse, blood pressure, temperature, weight, clearing your ears, what you ate for dinner, the time you went to bed, and the time you awakened. *Geno Quist*

Kitty Hawk on a seven-month cruise to the Western Pacific. Following his Navy exchange tour, he returned to RF-4Cs at Bergstrom AFB, Texas.

Geno applied for the SR-71 program, was accepted, and reported to Beale AFB in October 1979. He flew the SR-71 until June 1984, amassing 600 hours and 86 operational sorties. With heel marks all the way, Geno was selected to attend the Air Force Institute of Technology, where he earned a Master of Science degree in Industrial and Systems Engineering from the University of Florida. His next assignment was at the Pentagon, starting in the Air Force Manpower directorate, and subsequently moving to the reconnaissance division of the Air Force Operations directorate. He served the next three years as the program manager of the SR-71, enduring continuous scrutiny from Air Force and Congressional staffs as the Air Force dictated the termination of the SR-71 program. Following the Pentagon assignment, Geno finished his Air Force career as the deputy director of operations plans, tactics, and space applications at Headquarters Air Force Space Command, Peterson AFB, Colorado.

I asked Geno, as an insider at the Pentagon during the SR-71's retirement days, to give the reader a feel for all of the turbulence, politics, and Pentagon battles that took place during those highly emotional days of shutting down the program.

The Pentagon Factor

From August 1986 to August 1990, I worked in the Pentagon as part of the Air Staff (HQ U.S. Air Force). It consisted of thousands of Air Force officers, in hundreds of offices, spread throughout the Pentagon. The Air Staff was organized in many different "directorates," each performing certain parts of the entire Air Force staff operations. One of the biggest duties of the Air Staff is the preparation of the Air Force budget. Other duties, especially where I was concerned, included answering Congressional questions. Questions came from the members of Congress themselves, from their staffs, or from their constituency. The Air Staff organizations I was primarily involved with were Programs and Resources (PR), Legislative Liaison (LL), and my own directorate, Plans and Operations (XO).

As the SR-71 program manager, it was my duty to be a proponent for "my" program. All of my papers concerning the SR-71 were truthfully written, to the best of my knowledge, and offered the perspective of a program advocate. Once the decision had been made at the highest levels of the Air Force to cancel the SR-71 program, all of the subservient minions in the chain, being tried and true yes-men and yes-women, steered the chief's course—decision-avoiding, follow the chief regardless of sanity, don't rock the boat, and "dump the SR-71 program" zealots. So any papers, even those seemingly authored and signed by me, produced some depressing, and in many cases false or distorted statements as they were edited and changed on their way up the chain of command and out of the Air Force. Of particular distress, the author's name (mine) remained on these staff summary/coordination documents regardless of the changes made. In other words, because of the system, false and untrue statements could be traced back to an author who never was allowed to participate in the process following the initial authorship.

In one of the papers I was tasked to write, I was responding to a request for information originating somewhere up the chain of command. Of course the pro-SR part was supposed to be weak, so it would better support the party line for canceling the program. I finished the paper and started it up through the coordination process, first stopping at Colonel John Woody, my immediate boss. Colonel Woody is a true gentleman, and a reconnaissance pilot with a long history of being honest and genuine. With his position, he was supposed to be the proponent for *all* Air Force reconnaissance, from RF-4s to C-130s, U-2/TR-1s, RC-135s, and even unmanned aerial vehicles (UAVs). In this case, he read my document, then stormed out of his office, and threw the paper on my desk saying, "We can't say that." What he was referring to was a reference I had cited, stating President Reagan's support for the SR-71 via a letter the president had signed about a year earlier.

Lee Shelton and Bob Coats, my SR-71 predecessors in the office, had gotten the letter to the Office of the President, and he ultimately signed it. Colonel Woody said this was too dated, and that the president hadn't actually written the letter, so it was not valid. I told him I couldn't change the truth, and that many letters and documents signed by high government officials were not self-authored. This seemed to have no effect, and I was again told to change the paper. I said I couldn't do it, because it would not be truthful and would not be telling the whole story. When I was told to change it again, I stated "I quit." I walked out of the office and went to a planned reconnaissance luncheon, thinking I had no job to return to and maybe on my way to a reprimand. I was later told secondhand that Colonel Woody had no idea what to do about an officer who just plain quit! I don't know how that paper left the office, and I don't know who finished it, but I know I didn't!

Air National Guard SR-71s?

One of the options explored for keeping the SR-71 flying was to put it into the Air National Guard. The budget battles were being savagely fought, and the Air Staff felt a lot of pressure from the Hill to maintain the program. An integral part of the budget process is to shift money around and "hide" it for use in pet projects hopefully not discovered by Congress. This proposed move, in my opinion, was an effort by the Air Force to appease Congress by keeping the program, but not having the money taken from the Air Force budget. I believe the Air Force powers were thinking they could put the program into the Air

National Guard (ANG), maybe "give" the ANG a token amount of money (but more than likely not), and therefore be free of a perceived dollar drain on the Air Force, while keeping the actual money for other pet programs (B-2, F-22).

I actually went and briefed the ANG staff at the Pentagon on the proposal. The name of the general officer escapes me, but my reception was not enthusiastic. I'm sure the ANG knew what the Air Force was up to, and they were too smart to play this game. Additionally, there were too many obstacles to overcome. For instance, where would they be based? Who would fly them? How would the crews stay current? How would they be able to be gone for six weeks at a time, for up to 270 days a year? This option was not pursued beyond this meeting and a few further brief discussions.

Jerk, Twit, and Rabbit

We had two colonels working in an office directly above mine, in my direct chain of command. Major (later Lieutenant Colonel) Curt Osterheld, my "sidekick" SR-71 RSO in our office, and I referred to them as Jerk and Twit.

You have to understand that money means *everything* in the Pentagon. Military programs live and die by the dollar. The "package" Geno refers to was a formal Pentagon staff summary, usually concerning Air Force budget issues that needed solving. Since most weapon systems, like the SR-71, cross many organizational turfs, all having a stake, resolution of any budget issues had to be approved by each directorate in the Pentagon.

The program element monitor (PEM) was the sole person responsible for the financial "health" of his program. When a funding issue developed with his program, the PEM initiated putting a package together. It was called a package in Pentagon lingo because of its bulky, packagelike appearance. The cover sheet of the package was the most important feature as far as the PEM was concerned. It listed all the general officer directorates that needed to coordinate (agree) on what effect the issue(s) would have on their programs, as outlined in the package.

As the package percolated its way up the general officer pecking order, significant changes could be made, requiring the PEM to basically start over again. Running a package through all the hurdles was a very time-consuming process, and sometimes dominated a PEM's existence for weeks on end, particularly if it was a sensitive issue, such as the SR-71's retirement. The Pentagon was swamped with PEMs scurrying about its myriad halls and corridors, going from office to office, seeking (a better term would be praying for!) signatures of approval on their packages.

One day, Curt had been running a package in the halls of the Pentagon with the accompanying amount of harassment that came with being associated with the SR-71 program. Curt had been told to make some changes and get it back to the demanding office ASAP. He came back to our office very frustrated and began banging away on the computer keyboard.

Now drop back and picture where this was happening before I continue with the story. We were in an office in the basement of the Pentagon where few normal people could find any office, much less the office of Air Force Reconnaissance. This was a basement with such luxurious accommodations that even the toilets overflowed onto the floor on a routine basis. Virtually all directions to offices in the Pentagon basement referenced turns and passageways leading to or from the infamous purple water fountain, a story in its own right. Many people couldn't find our office even with purple water fountain directions, if they could even find it. In addition to this, we were behind a ciphered, locked door, in a cluster of rooms called a "vault," cleared for use and storage of some of the highest-level classified information in the Pentagon. Only those of us who worked there knew the combination.

On this occasion, as Curt was pounding away at the keys, he had stopped long enough to loosen his tie and collar, and roll up his shirtsleeves, after literally running in the halls and stairs. Just as his train of thought stabilized and he began making the directed changes, the buzzer, used by people who didn't know the cipher combination, rang, requesting access. Mrs. Bowen, our secretary, pushed a button allowing the visitor to enter, where she would check to see if the person was authorized access.

She encountered Jerk, who being our boss' boss, was indeed authorized. After saying a cold "How's it going," Jerk proceeded to order Curt to stand up, at attention—and then unceremoniously verbally reprimanded Curt for being out of uniform and presenting a bad image with his collar loosened and sleeves rolled up. After this fine display of professionalism, he called me into Colonel Woody's office in the next room and showing me the same professional demeanor, reprimanded me as the senior officer present (only Curt, Mrs. Bowen, and I were in the limited-access vault!) for allowing Curt to be in such a state! This was indicative of our support from our superiors, and unfortunately, indicative of many other senior Air Force officers.

Curt and I knew one of General Ron Fogleman's dummies (a major) as Rabbit, because of his facial twitches. Rabbit was always trying to undermine our work, and please the general. Because General Fogleman was intimately involved in the budget process, virtually all papers we produced had to go through his office in the coordination cycle. Rabbit was informally designated as the officer through whom all papers involving the SR-71 should pass on their way to General Fogleman. He was their SR-71 "expert." Though he didn't have the rank or authority to physically change any of our documents, he could read, digest, and subsequently recommend changes for General Fogleman to make. He used this position, and his knowledge of other programs and Air Force efforts, to undermine many of the packages Curt and I generated. He and his cronies proved the adage that for every measure, there is a countermeasure, be it truthful or not. In the end, on Rabbit's departure from the Pentagon, General Fogleman signed his farewell picture with the statement "Thanks for all your help canceling the SR-71 program."

Favorite Missions

As you have probably gathered from all of the stories, some SR-71 missions were just a little bit better than others. The long missions, the most challenging missions, the toughest missions, were dreams come true, because you felt like you had really done something special, and it was just plain fun! Some of these missions were the ones when we were taking an SR-71 to a TDY location to replace another, or bringing one back to Beale so it could go through an extensive maintenance. If your name was at the top of the ladder when one of these came along, near death was the only thing that was going to stop you from climbing into the cockpit!

Nevin Cunningham, the pilot I was crewed with, and I came to the top of that ladder when a Beale SR-71 was programmed to go to Kadena AB. We did all of the mission planning in the days preceding the mission and had gone home to pack, finish our "honey do" lists, and get into crew rest prior to the

Lounging around at the Kadena Officers' Open Mess pool are (left to right) Frank Stampf, Geno Quist, and Nevin Cunningham. North of Kadena, by about a 15-minute drive, was a secluded beach discovered by Habus long ago, given the name of "Secret Beach." A great relaxation spot when not flying. *Gil Bertelson*

premission briefing and launch. I lived on the Beale AFB premises, and had a garden in the backyard. Since this was government property, and hunting was rarely allowed, we had a large deer population on base. These deer knew they were never in danger and took every advantage of it. One of their tricks was to feast on resident gardens, and no amount of "antideer" tactics could foil them of their dinner. I had tried putting up a fence around the garden, and finding that this, too, was no impediment to the deer, I was tasked to get the fence down before leaving for six weeks on Okinawa.

I was dutifully pulling up the metal fence posts when I got to one that just wouldn't budge. Being the ever-resourceful SR-71 RSO, I decided to get the garden hose and saturate the area around the base of the post with water, hopefully making it easier to pull out. Once the ground was wet, I bent over the top of the post, grabbed it with both hands, and gave a mighty yank! It came right out of the ground (at the beginning of that mighty yank) and the top of the post proceeded into my teeth-gritting mouth.

Years before I had broken one of my front teeth in a kid-frolicking tobogganing incident, and the tooth was subsequently capped. This smart fence post didn't find the already fake tooth—it found and knocked out the perfectly good front tooth right next to it! The first words out of my mouth (after spitting out the tooth) were: "It's the good one." The dentist was in church and had to be paged, and I went through a lot of agony getting that tooth capped, but the hardest thing I had to do was have my wife call the commander, and Nevin, and tell them I couldn't take the flight the next day. I don't remember who the replacement crew was, but I do know they didn't turn down the flight! Forgive me, Nevin!

The Defensive (DEF) Systems

Another time, I was on the other end of this scenario—bringing an airplane back to Beale from Kadena. Many times on flights like these, if the maintenance folks had any problematic equipment that they just couldn't seem to fix locally, they would get the equipment operating to the best of their ability, load it on the flight going home, and send word ahead that this particular piece of equipment needed to be torn down and gone through piece by piece. Don't take this wrong: never were we ever asked to fly with anything that was known to be faulty. In this case, I was aware a part of our DEF electronics was suspect, but had tested out good on the ground. Though I never felt the SR-71 was vulnerable to any threats due to its own speed and altitude attributes, the defensive system was an added level of confidence. An operational system was a requirement to fly into the areas of greatest threat.

Our checklist for testing the DEF system did not allow testing until we were airborne, due to cooling and other requirements for system operation. Therefore, after takeoff, we would power up the system, then perform a built-in-test to ensure proper operation. If the system failed this check, we could cycle the power and perform another check, and if this failed, we would have to abort the mission, or at least abort the portion that would take us into hostile airspace. On this particular mission, I had the "gut feel" this system was going to fail its check. Not wanting to admit defeat, and not wanting to chance aborting a mission, I chose to ignore the checks and assume the system would work if we needed it.

We took off, refueled, and flew through the "sensitive" area without incident, and then turned east over the north Pacific. All was going well and we were cruising for our final tanker off the coast of Alaska. Another "no-no" flying the SR-71 was to do something in one cockpit that may affect the airplane without telling the other cockpit what you were up to. In this case, all was going well, and I was going to touch just one little button, so I said nothing. I hit the defensive system self-test button, and suddenly the airplane "bucked," the lights blinked, and the autopilot dropped off line. I heard Nevin make some comment like "what the . . ." and everything stabilized. I finally got the courage to meekly say, "It was me, just checking the DEF—and it's not working." Silence. The rest of the mission went great; however, the radar controllers in California couldn't figure out what object was coming into U.S. airspace at Mach 3 and over 80,000 feet (had nothing to do with DEF!). Some people just never seem to get the word! Needless to say, we kept on coming and safely landed at Beale. Only one maintenance write-up—DEF inoperative!

Another World Record!

Since SR-71 crews didn't get to fly the SR too often, we had what was called companion trainers (T-38s) that we flew on a frequent basis. One of the benefits of T-38s is that they are very reliable and very familiar throughout the military for servicing. This being the case, we were allowed to take them on weekend cross-country flights on a periodic basis. Nevin and I got on the schedule for one of these weekend jaunts, and decided to visit an old Navy friend of mine in San Diego. It worked out that the Friday we were going on the cross-country, we also had an SR-71 flight earlier in the day.

In another twist of fate, our SR-71 sortie was off the coast of California on a mission that we called "Tomcat Chase," playing with the Navy F-14s—letting them practice intercepts on high-altitude, high-speed targets. We were flying in the San Diego area, and I decided I'd give my Navy buddy a call on their squadron radio frequency. We made radio contact, and he, not knowing I had an SR-71 sortie first, thought we were inbound in the T-38. He asked our location and I gave him the old "About 100 miles out, 80,000 feet, and 1725 knots!" No further questions except "Are you going to make it down here for the night?"

Back at Beale we had made prior arrangements with one of our SR-71 crewmates (Rich Judson) to help us set a new "speed record!" (We were always out to set records of some sort.) Rich preflighted and set up our T-38, so all we had to do was strap in and crank the engines. We landed the Blackbird on the first approach, parked immediately, quickly got out of our pressure suits, showered, dressed into our flight suits, went over to maintenance, and debriefed the mission (luckily Code 1—no write-ups), and took off in the T-38 in only 42 minutes, touchdown to takeoff—a world record!

Beale AFB, to the Barents Sea, and Back

On yet another of the highly sought-after flights, on 5 July 1983, we were flying an SR-71 from Mildenhall back to Beale via a mission into the Barents Sea. All went perfect from takeoff, through the first two refuelings, and through the "sensitive area." We were headed back for fuel off the coast of Norway and had begun our descent for the tankers. It was amazing how smooth and quiet the descent was going, almost eerie, when suddenly the aircraft started trembling, and I thought I could hear a thumping noise. A quick check of the instruments showed we had lost our primary supersonic airspeed indications.

As a bit of background, we used regular-indicated airspeed (KIAS, or knots-indicated air speed) while subsonic and transitioned to equivalent airspeed (KEAS, or knots-equivalent air speed) while supersonic. Our KEAS were digitally presented in triple display indicators (TDI) in both cockpits. We started a descent from Mach 3 by pulling back the throttles to minimum afterburner, pausing momentarily, then to full (nonafterburning) military power, and let the speed bleed down to 350 KEAS. We would then descend at a constant 350 KEAS minimum until subsonic.

In this case, our TDIs froze at 350 KEAS without us knowing. We ended up slowing well below 350 KEAS and the engines started compressor-stalling. Nevin immediately transitioned to KIAS (on a conventional airspeed indicator located only in the front cockpit), and I dug out the checklist that gave the descent profile in KIAS. We averted loss of engine(s) and a meeting with the frigid North Atlantic! After we took on a full load of gas, the TDIs began operating. We decided to head for Beale, crossing the North Atlantic. We could always use the KIAS descent checklist if we had to during our final two descents. Shortly after level off at Mach 3, another little gremlin hit.

We discovered our automatic exhaust gas temperature (EGT) system was not operating correctly if we accelerated above Mach 3, and the manual system was also inoperative. Usually, this is not a big problem, but we were already low on fuel after the climb, and we didn't know for a fact our TDIs were going to work descending into the next refueling. We needed to fly across the North Atlantic where there were *no* abort bases once we passed

Iceland. The EGT and speed relationship was our only way to "make up" fuel. We got better mileage in the SR-71 by speeding up, where the plane became more efficient.

The SR-71 had a unique EGT arrangement. Just outboard of the throttles were EGT switches for each engine. In the center position the EGT was automatically controlled. However, if the switch was pushed forward (spring-loaded), the EGT would increase, and if pulled backward, the EGT would decrease. We were manually changing the fuel/air mixture at the fuel control, to modulate the EGT.

In this case, we couldn't speed up because we would have exceeded our EGT limits, doing possible harm to the engines, and we didn't know how we were looking at the other end due to possible low fuel, and we didn't have any other place to go! Needless to say, I watched anxiously out the right window, on this very clear night, as Iceland disappeared behind us. I did many fast calculations to see if we could reach Thule, Greenland, if we needed to, and how soon. I checked the charts for any other habitable location we might be able to reach if necessary. Thank goodness, all went well. We rendezvoused with the tankers off Newfoundland, our TDIs worked throughout the rest of the flight, and we had one more great flight under our belts!!

Engine Flameout!

On a normal operational flight out of Kadena, we got into the airplane, started taxiing out, and did our brake check. The brake check was accomplished as soon as the aircraft moved, by gently tapping the brakes, using each of the two hydraulic systems powering the brakes. In this case, Nevin felt that the brakes on the left hydraulic system were a bit "mushy." As I remember, we had the brakes checked, and decided to go ahead with the flight, since we knew the right system was good. We had an uneventful flight and got back to Kadena with a little extra fuel, so Nevin decided to do a couple of approaches. We needed to do these periodically to maintain our currency requirements.

We made one low approach and were coming back around for another low approach, turning base to final, when I felt a distinct yaw to the inside of the turn (right). I calmly asked Nevin, "What was that?" He calmly replied, "We just lost the right engine." By now, we are moments from being over the runway, no time for any checklist, just maintaining aircraft control. Without giving myself a sanity check, I made the (stupid) statement, "I guess we're going to full stop then?" In other words, here I am in an emergency situation, asking if we are indeed going to land, or are we going to stay up on one engine and play? Nevin calmly (again) ignores the stupidity saying, "Yes."

Now back in touch with reality, I made a radio call declaring an emergency that we had just lost the right engine. This type of call sets *all* kinds of things in motion. The fire trucks start rolling immediately, our mobile crew (the backup crew positioned in a car near the end of the runway) gives whatever assistance they can offer (no time for Les Dyer and Dan Greenwood to do anything in this case), and our detachment operations officer in the tower has to decide if he should arm or dearm the SR-71 arresting barrier on the far end of the runway.

On this occasion we also had our detachment commander, Colonel (Ret) Randy Hertzog, in his car at the end of the runway—word was his newspaper flew all over the car and his pipe nearly got blown out upon hearing the emergency call on the radio! Now, think back for a second—we've lost the right engine, and that also means the right hydraulic system. The only brakes we have remaining are on the left hydraulics, which were suspect at takeoff! We have no clue if we can stop on the runway or not, and we don't really want to take the arresting barrier if we can avoid it. With only one engine working, we didn't have the option of staying airborne to assess the situation further. The moments passed quickly. Fortunately for us, the brakes worked well enough to get stopped on the runway without taking the barrier. We shut the SR down on the runway and let the maintenance tow vehicles finish the job!

What Are You Guys Doing Here?

15 December 1981: Nevin and I were fortunate enough to be at the top of the list when a Giant Reach mission came down from SAC. Giant Reach missions were those tasked to the European Theater of Operations; in this case it was

John Morgan celebrates his 600-hour sortie at Det 1. John eventually achieved 1,000 hours in the SR-71 on 11 April 1985 at Det 4. Joining the festivities are (left to right) Det 1 Commander Ray Samay, Gil Bertelson, John Morgan, Bob Crowder, Geno Quist, Nevin Cunningham, and Frank Stampf. *Gil Bertelson*

a mission into the Barents Sea, north of the Soviet Union. At the time, we didn't have SR-71s permanently stationed in England, so this was a mission to be flown completely round-robin out of Beale. We would take off, refuel in one of our normal refueling areas northeast of Beale, accelerate to Mach 3 to the northeast, entering Canada near the North Dakota border, descend and get another load of fuel near Newfoundland, and then cross the north Atlantic.

The north Atlantic in the wintertime is always a foreboding area, but crossing it at Mach 3 and near 80,000 feet in a comfortable cockpit, cocooned in a pressure suit, was actually a pleasant experience. We didn't have to talk to anybody, and nobody had to talk to us, so all we could hear were the sounds of Mach 3 flight in the SR-71—some gentle "purrs" and "whines" of machinery, and the ever present but subdued (because of the pressure suit) sound of the air passing over and around the cockpit. The entire mission was going like clockwork and the ride was as smooth as it could be. We descended a couple hundred miles off the coast of Norway for a third refueling before a northerly climb around the top of Norway and subsequent entry into the "sensitive" area—the Soviet submarine pens in the Murmansk area.

The loss of the 18,000-ton Russian nuclear submarine *Kursk* on 12 August 2000 brought back memories of just how foreboding and frigid the icy waters looked from 80,000 feet. The Barents Sea, near the Russian city of Murmansk, has to be the most ominous location the SR-71 has ever flown into.

Every time Don and I made the 180-degree turn off the coast of Murmansk to start back, I held my breath. The plane was in a true "coffin corner." If you had any hiccup at all with the engines, inlets, or a number of other systems during that turn, you would quickly be in a dire situation. As I look back on those missions, if we ever had to descend to a subsonic speed and altitude, Soviet MiGs could easily have shot us down, out over the Arctic Ocean, and we would *never* be heard from again. That's how bad it looked outside!

—Rich Graham

In these extreme northern regions of the world, navigation could be a challenge, were it not for our extremely reliable ANS. Without the ANS, we would have to rely on plain old heading, airspeed, and dead reckoning to get us back home again. In the far north, the convergence of lines of longitude made flying constant true headings virtually impossible, and the rapid change of lines of magnetic variation, coupled with the physical location of magnetic north, made flying magnetic headings difficult, at best. Our procedures called for us to switch to what was called "grid navigation" for backup. Some crews used "grid," while the rest of us hoped for the best, and as a backup used an average magnetic heading that would get us out of trouble and back to a tanker if the ANS should go bad.

In this mission, however, all went well through the take area, and continued into the descent to the tanker, again off the coast of Norway, where we were to take on another load of fuel and retrace our flight back across the north Atlantic and return to Beale. Today, however, the ANS gave out during the descent. Had this happened 30 minutes earlier, we would have been sucking a lot of oxygen . . . hoping a directional gyro compass system and dead reckoning navigation (100-knot navigation in an 1,800-knot aircraft!) would get us back to those tankers. We had a lock on the tankers with our radio ranging and direction finding equipment and made the rendezvous without the ANS. During refueling, I tried every trick to get the ANS working again, but to no avail. An airborne alignment to guide us over the north Atlantic and back to Beale was out of the question, so we told the tankers to lead us to good ole RAF Mildenhall, England.

The tankers for this mission were temporarily based at Mildenhall and there was limited SR-71 equipment in place from previous deployments. The U-2s were also stationed there, so we had known assistance available. After what seemed like an eternity—remember we flew back "low and slow"—we landed at Mildenhall 8-1/2 hours after leaving Beale. We had been up since around 0100 hours Beale time and were totally exhausted. However, when we got out of the plane, one of the U-2 crews mentioned that another Habu was in town.

This of course tweaked our interest and brought new life to the now rejuvenated bodies! It turned out our former squadron commander (and coincidentally the author of this book), Rich Graham, was in England on a fact-finding tour for a project he was researching during his tour at the Air Force's Air War College, an advanced education program for senior officers. Being kind, considerate, and respectful lower-ranking Habus, we hatched a plan. We found out from the base billeting office where Rich was staying, and proceeded to his room, pounding on the door yelling, "Security police—open up!"

We didn't know what we would find, it now being afternoon in England, but lo and behold, opening the door was our fellow Habu. Totally bewildered by first expecting the security police for some unknown reason, and now finding some unexpected Habu visitors, the shaving cream–laden ex-squadron commander could only mumble something to the effect, "What the hell are you guys doing here?" He thought he had been safe from Habu distractions and could concentrate on his research, but no!! Let the party begin—the commander is buying!

The staff at Beale were well ahead of the situation and had things in motion even by the time we landed, including getting us back home to be with our families for Christmas. The airplane finally was repaired and another crew later flew it back to Beale. Surprisingly, Nevin and I were back in Mildenhall 20 days later, on 5 January 1982, having manned the spare aircraft on another Giant Reach mission planned to land at Mildenhall.

One More from Pentagon Days

During my Pentagon days, Major Osterheld and I were tasked to give a briefing to General (Ret) Ryan, then commander of Tactical Air Command (now Air Combat Command). We were to give the SR-71 "story," and then the program manager for a classified program (seen as part of the Air Force hierarchy's replacement for the SR-71 puzzle) would give his pitch.

Prior to the brief, General Ryan, then on the TAC staff, "reviewed" the briefings and literally tore ours apart, saying something to the effect (paraphrased): "We can't show this to the commander, it's too patronizing of the SR-71 and that's not the Air Force line." So, in effect, the briefing Major Osterheld was forced to give, totally against our own principles and compromising our personal integrity, did not include all the facts, but a politically correct version thereof. This was just another in the string of episodes exemplifying the Air Force leadership's view of the SR-71 program—"Damn the truth, the chief says cancel the program, and we shall follow."

CHAPTER SIXTEEN

Lieutenant Colonel (Ret) Ed Yeilding

Ed earned his Air Force wings in December 1973. For the next nine years, he flew the RF-4 at Bergstrom AFB, Texas, and on Okinawa, and the F-4E at Moody AFB, Georgia. He applied for the SR-71 program and started his training in July 1983 at Beale AFB. For over six years he flew the SR-71 and became an IP, stan/eval evaluator, and a developmental test pilot at Palmdale, California. During his time at Palmdale, Ed and his RSO, J. T. Vida, flew the final supersonic flight of the SR-71 in its 1990 retirement, and set an aircraft coast-to-coast record of 67 minutes, 54 seconds.

Two happy crewmembers! J. T. (on left) and Ed are answering reporter's questions about their record-breaking flight across the United States. The Air Force did not want the speed record to be set because of the publicity associated with such an event. Some members in Congress and other high places said there *would* be a speed run. *Lockheed Martin Skunk Works*

After flying 785 hours in the SR-71, Ed flew with the 89th Wing in Washington, D.C. There he flew the Gulfstream III aircraft on Special Air Missions (SAM) to Russia, China, Europe, Africa, South America, and the Far East. His passengers included the vice president of the United States, representatives, cabinet members, ambassadors, generals, and the first lady. Ed retired in January 1996 and came aboard with Northwest Airlines, where he currently flies as a first officer on the DC-9.

Among his stories, I asked Ed to tell what it was like flying the last supersonic SR-71 flight (at the time), setting the speed record, and turning the plane over to the National Air and Space Museum at Dulles International Airport in 1990.

Three Sunsets, Three Sunrises, in an Hour

It was fascinating, flying the SR-71 across the "terminator"—the division line between day and night. Because of our high speed, high altitude, and the thin air, the terminator was considerably more distinct than it was down low. When heading from daylight toward the terminator, it often felt as though you were flying into a black wall. Also, when crossing the terminator, you could look toward the sun and see a beautiful sunset or sunrise. Because of our high speed, it was easily possible to fly from east to west and watch the sun rise above the western horizon.

Occasionally our missions carried us across the terminator several times, especially at high latitudes. In late December of 1984, Steve Lee and I had a mission from RAF Mildenhall to the arctic region, where the terminator runs more east-west than north-south during the winter. Our primary sensor was radar, so we were completely unconcerned about whether it would be daylight in the target area. Flying that mission, we were surprised that the supersonic portion of our reconnaissance track crossed the terminator six times. In less than an hour's time, Steve and I had seen three sunsets and three sunrises.

A Real Kick in the Pants!

In 1985 at Mildenhall, I met a medical doctor at one of our Habu parties. She owned a couple of horses and invited me to go riding with her. On the morning of the ride as I dressed, I discovered that my tight-fitting jeans had become a little too tight. To be more comfortable, I decided to wear the jeans with no underwear.

We had a great time riding, talking, and galloping through the beautiful green pastures and along the country roads. After the ride, as we were leading our horses back to the stable, my horse bit her horse on the shoulder. Her horse spun quickly around and tried to kick my horse. It happened so quickly that I barely had time to flinch. The powerful kick caught me on the side on my right thigh. I went sailing through the air and landed about 10 feet away. A professional linebacker could not have hit me harder! I had hoped the doctor thought of me as a cool pilot, but now I wasn't looking so cool, lying on the ground, unable to move my right leg . . . not even a little. Blood was beginning to soak through my jeans.

The doctor and I both assumed that a broken thighbone had punctured the skin. She casually said, "Unbutton your jeans and I'll help you slip them off." I muttered, "Uh . . . uh. How about cutting my jeans along the seam from my ankle to my thigh." She said, "It'd be a lot easier to just slip off your jeans. Listen, I'm a doctor. I see guys in their underwear all the time." It took a couple of minutes to convince her that I definitely would not take off my jeans. I was too embarrassed to tell her why. I'm sure she thought I was an unusually modest pilot.

She did a nice job cutting my jeans along the seam, and decided that the bone was probably not broken. There were no sharp edges on the iron horseshoe, but somehow the force of the kick had caused a nasty cut. She took me to her doctor's office, which was closed for the weekend. She had a key, so she helped me in and did an excellent job putting five stitches in my leg. She lent me a pair of crutches, and took me back to Mildenhall. Her beautiful Arabian horse, Alyf, had previously won a blue ribbon at Ascot, so she kidded me by saying, "Not many people can say they have been kicked by a national champion."

My entire thigh turned black and blue. I spent the next two days on my crutches, exercising my leg as much as I could tolerate. Slowly and reluctantly, my thigh muscles agreed to work again. On the third day after the kick, it was my turn to fly the SR-71. It took all my concentration to walk to and from the mission briefing room table without a noticeable limp. I sure didn't want someone to think I was unfit to fly. I knew I could fly safely, and Steve Lee and I flew that mission without a hitch. I absolutely loved flying the Blackbird and never missed a flight due to sickness.

Two years later at my going-away party, someone read several paragraphs about my years at Beale AFB. One of the sentences read, "Ed discovered that horseback riding in England can be a real kick in the ass!"

One Habu tradition was to give every departing crewmember a "Bat Caver." The Bat Caver was a parchmentlike sheet of paper, encapsulating in words all the humorous, as well as serious, events you became noted for during your brief time in the program. Your peers, who knew you well, wrote them . . . and *nothing* was sacred!

Hurricane Juan

At approximately 0100 hours on 29 October 1985, RSO Steve Lee and I reported for our premission briefing at Beale AFB. Among the briefing personnel was our weather officer, giving us a summary of the weather all along our route. In the middle of his briefing, and without changing his monotone, he casually mentioned that Hurricane Juan was in the Gulf of Mexico, squarely in our planned route of flight. I glanced around the room to see if anyone else seemed concerned about the hurricane. Everyone had the same wee-hour glazed look in their eyes. I felt I was the only one to hear him say that a hurricane was along my route. Partly for my own curiosity, and partly to make sure that our director of operations (DO) had heard him say "hurricane," I asked, "Is turbulence near Hurricane Juan likely to cause us any problems as we fly over it?" I was told, "No." Still, I remained a little concerned. I thought to myself, "What if an engine or inlet malfunction at just the wrong time requires me to descend into the hurricane?" I figured the chances were slim, so I kept quiet and went out to fly the Blackbird.

Later, at Mach 3 and high above it, we approached Hurricane Juan. It didn't seem as large as I had imagined. I could see that, if an emergency caused us to descend, I would be able to turn away from the hurricane. By the time we descended through 50,000 feet, we would be a safe distance away. Then we could easily fly out of the area between the bands of thunderstorms.

Fortunately, the Blackbird flew just fine. We felt no turbulence at 77,000 feet. Over the top of Hurricane Juan, I banked the aircraft and looked directly down into its eye. I was glad I was up here versus down there. Flying over a hurricane was a piece of cake for the Blackbird.

You also have to realize that part of Ed's concern was the fact that the SR-71 has *no* weather radar whatsoever. Coming out of F-4s, with its excellent radar capability, I often felt very naked and uncomfortable blindly dodging thunderstorms at low altitude in the SR-71.

—Rich Graham

"Every Hair . . ."

Approaching the far end of our target area in the Barents Sea, with my RSO, Curt Osterheld, I had been noticing the right engine oil pressure needle fluctuating and getting worse. The fluctuations seemed more real than the false, heat-related fluctuations I had seen in the past. I knew Curt was very busy with his sensors and other duties, but finally decided it would be wise to give him a "heads-up" just in case we were about to have a sudden single-engine emergency. I said, "Curt, the right engine oil pressure has been fluctuating pretty bad and getting worse. I'm not sure it's a false indication from the heat." No response from Curt. I figured he was busy.

There we were at Mach 3, above 77,000 feet, almost 1,000 miles from the nearest friendly base. An engine failure in this area would not be good. It would force us to come down to a subsonic speed near 15,000 feet, with potential hostile interceptors nearby. An engine failure would also be very serious, because a flight control hydraulic failure or a generator failure on the remaining good engine could force an ejection. Here, over the Arctic Ocean, were icebergs all around for hundreds of miles!

After a few minutes of silence, I heard Curt say, "Eddie . . . every hair on my ass is standing on end." Neither of us laughed. We stayed on track and got photo coverage of all our target areas. Fortunately, the fluctuations *were* heat related, the engine ran just fine, and we made it back to Mildenhall with no problem.

Later that evening, at "hooks" with the crews, I related what Curt had said at the far end of our mission. We all got a big laugh. Curt had described, with just a few choice words, just how tense we could sometimes feel during our missions. That next Christmas, I sent Curt a card showing Santa and his reindeer navigating their way through a dark and snowy night. Above the head of the second reindeer, I added the caption, "Rudolph . . . every hair on my ass is standing on end."

Ed confirms what I stated earlier about how inhospitable and foreboding that mission into the Barents Sea could be. Because of this mission, and other missions flown out of Mildenhall, we levied a requirement that new crews had to fly their first operational sorties out of Kadena.

—Rich Graham

Transcontinental Speed Record

Early in 1990, the commander of our Palmdale unit, Colonel Don Emmons, told Lieutenant Colonel Joe "J. T." Vida and me that we would deliver SR-71, #972, to the Smithsonian Institution. We were asked to set a new coast-to-coast aircraft speed record and several city-to-city records during the delivery flight. The ensuing publicity would highlight what a great airplane the SR-71 is, and what an outstanding job it had done for our country since the early 1960s. J. T. and I felt honored and excited about this opportunity, but we also knew that any of the current SR-71 crews had the skill and ability to fly that record flight . . . we were in the right place at the right time. We felt a special obligation to fly that flight and conduct ourselves in a manner that would well represent all of the aircrews, as well as all the hundreds of outstanding people who designed, maintained, and supported the fantastic SR-71. I was especially glad to fly with J. T., a truly outstanding RSO, whom I greatly admired and enjoyed flying with.

Briefing room at Palmdale. The Flight Test facility at Palmdale tested all of the modifications to both the SR-71 and U-2 aircraft before being certified to fly operationally. Ed and J. T. are going over the last-minute details of the record-setting flight on 6 March 1990, before suiting up. *Lockheed Martin Skunk Works*

J. T. and I worked closely with Lieutenant Colonel Bruce Liebman, a former RSO himself, who finalized our precise route, tanker support, and fuel checkpoints across the United States. We also worked with the National Aeronautic Association (NAA), which sets the rules and verification procedures for establishing aviation records. In the Pentagon, Lieutenant Colonel Gene Quist did the bulk of the required coordination work, ensuring the flight went as smoothly as possible. Fuel would be very tight, so our plan was to air refuel over the Pacific Ocean, cross the West Coast near Los Angeles accelerating through Mach 2.5, cruise at our flight manual speed limit of Mach 3.3, and cross the East Coast near Salisbury, Maryland, in a descending left turn for the landing at Dulles International Airport. We planned a short refueling with a KC-135Q tanker just before landing at Dulles, giving us enough fuel to make several passes for the crowd. Shortly before our flight, the Pentagon directed that we make "only one low approach." Once we landed, the Air Force would officially turn our Blackbird over to the Smithsonian's Air and Space Museum in a short ceremony.

Mach 3.17 was the maximum *scheduled* cruise speed recommended for normal operations. The design Mach number of the SR-71 was Mach 3.2. However, when authorized by the commander, speeds up to Mach 3.3 could be flown if the limit CIT of 427 degrees C. was not exceeded.

The Air Force chief of staff was *very* much against any positive publicity regarding the speed run. The Air Force wanted the 1990 retirement of the Blackbirds to happen quickly and quietly . . . no fanfare. The highest-ranking Air Force official that attended the turn-over ceremony at Dulles was Brigadier General (Ret) Buck Adams, a former SR-71 pilot and speed record holder.

With several slight turns in our transcontinental "great circle" route, we also planned three city-to-city records. We were asked to check the feasibility of flying the Los Angeles to Washington, D.C., record in less than one hour, which required flying the 2,300-statute-mile distance at Mach 3.5. We met with Lockheed's SR-71 engineers to determine whether a one-time flight faster than Mach 3.3 was possible. After a brief study, it was determined that going faster than Mach 3.3 would be too dangerous. We were told that with an unstart faster than Mach 3.3, we might not be able to keep the pointed end forward. Our primary goal was to deliver the SR-71 to the Smithsonian safely, putting it on display for the next thousand years or more. We planned a Mach 3.3 cruise. We got an OK from Pratt & Whitney to exceed the 427-degree CIT engine limit for 30 minutes, but that exception was not needed during the flight.

We had what were called tactical limits for the SR-71. If we found the normal operating limits unacceptable because of operations in a hostile area, we were authorized to use the tactical limits *to exit the hostile area by the most expeditious means.* They were to be used only when adherence to the normal restrictions would place the aircraft in a more hazardous situation, because of probable hostile actions. Our margin of safety when using the tactical limits was substantially reduced, and our exposure to the limits had to be as brief as possible.

If you had to use the tactical limits, you were *never* allowed to exceed Mach 3.3, but could increase your speed to a CIT of 450 degrees C. for one hour maximum.

At 0430 on 6 March 1990, J. T. and I took off from Palmdale, California. A crowd had gathered to hear the tremendous power of the SR-71 and watch our afterburners climb steeply and fade away into the night. J. T. and I cruised subsonic to San Francisco at 26,000 feet, then out over the Pacific Ocean, where we rendezvoused with two KC-135Q tankers from Beale AFB. We refueled with each tanker at 27,000 feet, higher than the normal 25,000 feet, to give ourselves a slight fuel advantage for our supersonic climb. It was dark over the Pacific Ocean, no moon, no horizon, requiring more concentration than normal. To our surprise, we were unable to get our fuel total above 74,000 pounds, even after several additional hookups with each tanker. Tank 6 indicated 6,000 pounds short, and the tankers reported 5,000 pounds short of the preplanned off-load. I guessed that we actually had our full 80,000 pounds of fuel, and with a fuel-indicating problem in tank 6, we must have taken off with 5,000 pounds more fuel than planned.

J. T. and I quickly considered several different options and decided to attempt to fly the planned mission. We thanked the tankers for their excellent support and lit the afterburners. With a 200-mile running start, we crossed the California coast near Ventura, accelerating through Mach 2.5 as planned. It was a beautiful sight as we crossed the coast around 0600 hours. In the eastern sky, I could see Venus, Mars, Saturn, and a hint of sunrise. In the early twilight, I could see the white foam of ocean breakers all along the California coastline and the millions of lights below from the Los Angeles area, as well as the lights of San Francisco to the north and San Diego to the south. I knew our sonic boom would serve as a wakeup call to millions of Americans ready to start their day.

While admiring the beauty of the moment, I also noticed that the tank 6 fuel pumps turned off way too early. The tank 6 empty light was on, the center of gravity indication was abnormally far forward, and tank 5 pumps had sequenced on with 1,200 pounds still indicating in tank 6. It appeared that tank 6 *actually was* 6,000 pounds short of fuel and that we might have to abort our transcontinental record attempt. If we had gone back to Palmdale, I'm not sure the generals would have approved another transcontinental record attempt. However, I noticed that the pitch trim position was normal, and guessed that besides a fuel indication problem, tank 6A might actually be full of trapped fuel. Selecting the tank 6 pumps manually did not help, so I deselected them to avoid damaging them in an empty tank. I knew that selecting the tank 5 pumps manually was an override way to provide an open signal to the valves between tank 6A and tank 6B, allowing tank 6A fuel to flow to the tank 6 pumps.

Even though the tank 5 pumps were already on automatically, I manually selected tank 5, hoping the electrical impulse might jar loose the tank 6 valves. Within seconds, I saw the tank 6 pumps come on for a few seconds. I deselected tank 5, then manually reselected tank 5. Again the tank 6 pumps came on for a few seconds. After numerous repetitions, fuel in tank 6A suddenly began freely draining into 6B and to the tank 6 pumps. Fuel shortage was no longer a big problem, and J. T. and I were much happier campers. We were finally able to enjoy our last flight in the Blackbird.

> The six main fuel tanks, numbered one through six, were located along the length of the fuselage. Depending on the fuel distribution throughout those six tanks, the aircraft's CG would vary. Our pitch trim indicator was a good backup check of how well the CG was being maintained, and consequently, how well the fuel burn was going.

About eight minutes after crossing the West Coast, we reached our maximum cruise Mach of 3.3, which we held as we zipped across the good ole USA. I looked down at our great country, made great because of the tremendous dedication and sacrifices of our forefathers. I thought about our brave pioneers taking months to travel territory we were crossing in minutes. I wondered what transportation might be like in another century or two. J. T. and I felt so fortunate to fly the Blackbird and to be a part of such a great program. The Blackbird performed a vital role during the cold war, and everyone took great pride in their individual contributions to the overall SR-71 program. J. T. and I took time to enjoy for one last time our view from the edge of space—the curvature of the Earth, the darkness overhead, the bright band of blue along the horizon, and familiar geographical features sliding by far below. Most of all, we enjoyed flying this fantastic airplane one last time.

> Lieutenant Colonel (Ret) Joseph "J. T." Vida was the first of my SR-71 contemporaries to pass away. After a long, courageous bout with cancer, J. T. died in 1992. He was one of our most highly respected crewmembers and held many top honors among Habu aviators, the most notable being the highest flying time in the SR-71, with 1,392.7 hours. J. T.'s passion and love of flying the Blackbird inspired him to fly it for 16 *continuous* years . . . a feat hard to do with *any* airplane in the Air Force, let alone the SR-71.
>
> **—Rich Graham**

Near Washington, D.C., we terminated the afterburners and began our descent from 83,000 feet. We crossed the East Coast in a descending left-hand turn near Salisbury, establishing a new transcontinental aircraft speed record of 67 minutes, 54 seconds, with an average speed of 2,124 miles per hour. Our city-to-city records were: Los Angeles to Washington, D.C., 64 minutes, 20 seconds, 2,145 miles per hour; Kansas City to Washington, D.C., 25 minutes, 59 seconds, 2,176 miles per hour; St. Louis to Cincinnati, 8 minutes, 32 seconds, 2,190 miles per hour.

We continued our tight left turn and became subsonic at 40,000 feet over Wilmington, Delaware. En route to Dulles airport, we took a little fuel from our tanker. At Dulles, we flew over the field at 800 feet, pitched out, and flew our "low approach" at 200 feet, perpendicular to the runways, giving the crowd a good look at the SR-71. Abeam the crowd, we lit the afterburners to demonstrate the Blackbird's awesome power and show the beautiful "shock diamonds" visible in the bright orange flame. (The *Washington Post* printed a nice picture of the Blackbird with shock diamonds, and as of this writing, there remains another good picture of our flyby on display in the lower Dulles concourse.) We pulled up into a climbing 270-degree turn to downwind and rocked our wings as a final salute from the Blackbird.

We landed and deployed that big, beautiful orange drag 'chute one last time. Lockheed Skunk Works' president, Ben Rich, was there to give us a welcome thumbs-up signal as we deplaned. Senator John Warner and other dignitaries attended the planeside ceremony, as the Blackbird was officially turned over to the Smithsonian Institution. There we hope it will be on display for 1,000 years

Ceremonies at Dulles Airport to turn the SR-71 over to the Smithsonian Air and Space Museum. Former SR-71 pilots (left to right) Col. (Ret. Maj. Gen.) Al Joersz and Brig. Gen. (Ret) Buck Adams on hand for the ceremonies. Buck set the London-to-Los Angeles speed record in September 1974 and Al set the record speed over a straight course in July 1976. Left to right are J. T. Vida and Ed Yeilding. *Lockheed Martin Skunk Works*

or more and serve as an inspiration for future Americans as an example of what ingenious and dedicated men, well ahead of their time, accomplished.

After the ceremony, J. T. and I attended a news conference, and that evening Lockheed sponsored a reception. Two days later, J. T. and I sat separated in the coach section of a United 767 for our flight back to California. While taxiing out at Dulles, we passed close to our SR-71 on the tarmac, and the captain told the passengers that they were seeing the very SR-71 that was in the news that week for setting a new transcontinental speed record. The woman sitting next to me said, "It was worth coming to Washington just to see that plane!" I simply said, "Yes ma'am, it sure was." I didn't tell her that I had been lucky enough to fly it. I felt sad to leave the Blackbird.

About 45 minutes after our takeoff in the 767, a flight attendant came to me and asked, "Sir, were you the pilot of the SR-71 that we saw at Dulles?" I said, "Yes ma'am." She replied, "Well, Captain Aims wants you and Mr. Vida to move up to the First Class section." That was the first time I had ever ridden in a first class passenger section. The service was extra nice, and J. T. and I enjoyed answering questions, signing autographs, and handing out SR-71 pins.

J. T. and I signed a lot more autographs in the coming weeks, but we both knew that we were no more heroic than all those who so conscientiously designed, maintained, supported, and flew the SR-71 throughout the cold war years. The Blackbird had served the United States well. It performed a vital mission in deterring war and aggression, and stood as a beautiful, mysterious symbol of strength for the cause of freedom everywhere.

CHAPTER SEVENTEEN

Major William Michael "Zman" Zimmerman

Better know as Zman in SR-71 circles, he entered the Air Force in 1983 and completed navigator training. From there he was assigned to fly on EC-130H "Compass Call" aircraft at Davis Monthan AFB, Arizona, in 1985. In 1989 disaster hit when Zman was diagnosed with a brain tumor and told he would probably never fly again, but could apply for a flying evaluation after three years. After surgery he was assigned as a program

Zman (take a look at his nametag on the jacket) in the RSO seat of a Det 4 Blackbird. The rear cockpit was considerably roomier than the front, although no more comfortable. Flying from RAF Mildenhall to Beale AFB, Don Emmons once carried a 2-foot-tall, empty *glass* Bell's whiskey bottle in the rear cockpit. If we had to eject, it would not have been a pretty sight! *Mike Zimmerman*

manager to the Compass Call aircraft at Wright Patterson AFB, Ohio, doing research and development.

In 1992, Zman's three-year waiting period was up, and he began the daunting medical evaluation at Brooks AFB. He passed everything on his physical except for the hearing test. He was not regaining his hearing, but in fact, was losing it even further. This led to another surgery. In 1993, Zman became the branch chief for the Compass Call R&D office at Wright Patterson AFB. Through reorganization, Zman ended up in an office called "Big Safari" . . . a unique organization within the Air Force.

Big Safari's purpose has been, and continues to be, to establish and support a limited number of intelligence-gathering assets, both in the air and on the ground, through an approach known as "specialized management." The basic premise of Big Safari uses specialized management to provide an *extremely responsive* acquisition process that is not otherwise possible under normal contracting guidelines in the Air Force. They bypass many channels to expedite results. Zman is often heard saying, "I am looking for problems . . . I have the answers."

In December 1994 he was assigned as the SR-71 reactivation program manager. In 1996 he returned to flying status and left active duty in 1999 as a captain. He joined the Air Force Reserves and was hired by Ball Aerospace as a support contractor. A year later Zman was promoted to major. As a reservist, Zman was assigned to the Big Safari office once again. Due to the events of 11 Sept 2001, he has been recalled to active duty, and is currently a manager for a quick-reaction project for the government of Pakistan doing what Big Safari does best, "stuff to planes."

When Zman was assigned the job of SR-71 reactivation program manager, he had no knowledge of the plane, nor all of the political pitfalls he was about to encounter. He was walking into a minefield. The first time I met Zman, it was obvious he was going to make it work . . . he was experienced, shrewd, and superb at thinking "outside the box!" At our 1997 Blackbird Reunion, he was honored with the Pratt & Whitney Award for his SR-71 reactivation achievements. He has proven himself worthy of being called a Habu, and I would be proud to have him as my RSO anytime!

I asked Zman to give his perspective on the SR-71 reactivation. Here are his stories.

Finding All the Pieces

This was the hardest part . . . and for me, the most daunting. It was during this time that I met Don Emmons and Barry MacKean. I was also amazed at how many others I met were involved in the 1990 shutdown, or were key players in the old SR-71 program. Without Bill Grimes (my boss), Don, and Barry showing me where the multitudes of pieces were stored, my task to reactivate the SR-71s would have been much more difficult. I don't think we could have made the 1 September 1995 Initial Operating Capability (IOC) deadline without them.

Initial operation capability is a military term used to levy an initial operational capability on a unit, by a specific date. It sets the target date by which a program manager strives to meet certain goals.

In this instance, Zman had to have Det 2 ready for operational deployment by 1 September 1995. This was quite a feat, when you consider they didn't even know where they were going to find three former SR-71 crews, or how much training it would take to bring them back up to speed.

Something most aviation experts don't ever consider–it's one thing to bring a highly sophisticated SR-71 out of years of storage and fly it subsonic, but to get that same Blackbird to a *reliable*, *Mach 3 reconnaissance capability* is a completely different story. The searing temperatures at Mach 3 cruise for over an hour, and the harsh environment at 85,000 feet, play havoc on the aircraft's systems and reliability.

One of my many hurdles was being accepted by the SR-71 community. I had served as an EC-130H Compass Call navigator. I hadn't even met an SR-71 crewmember before the Air Staff planning meeting at the Lockheed Skunk Works in November 1994. During this meeting, I heard Lockheed explaining how it was going to bring back the program, and the Air Force saying how it couldn't be done. After hearing both sides, I sensed problems right away! Lockheed had given Congress a $100 million figure and the Defense Aerial Reconnaissance Office (DARO), along with Air Combat Command, was sporting a $107 million figure.

Compass Call is a highly modified C-130 that performs tactical communications jamming. Tactical means that it can jam one frequency, but leave another alone. The job of Compass Call is to listen to the enemy's communications and then selectively jam those frequencies that are important. Deployable worldwide, they saw action in Panama, Desert Storm, and many other locations.

My first task was to determine if the project was achievable within the budget and the schedule that the Air Force was holding me to. I went to Edwards AFB and met with Dave Lutz from NASA Dryden. NASA was the caretaker for three SR-71s, including all of the aircraft parts that the Air Force had loaned them after the Blackbird's retirement in 1990. They also had the simulator and the mission planning computer. During this trip I gathered some very important information about the challenges awaiting me.

First, I had a limited number of usable engines. I couldn't say exactly how many engines were usable because the documentation from the 1990 closure of the program was incomplete, and none of the engines were stored according to Pratt & Whitney specifications. Second, all the sensors and defensive systems were not with NASA, but spread all around the country. No one had a solid idea about what would or could be returned to service. Third, I had a huge supply of tires that were on a limited-use waiver from NASA. Instead of getting 15 takeoffs and landings for each tire, we would be limited to 7 per tire. This was a concern because not only would I go through the tires at a faster than normal rate, but maintenance costs would be higher, due to the increased number of tire changes required. We eventually had the Landing Gear Program Office at Wright Patterson AFB, Ohio, certify the tires to their original specification. This cut our operating costs in the second year.

Last, I learned about this stuff called fuel tank sealant. No one on earth (whom I could find) could tell me if what we had was usable, or how you could even tell. Basically, you mixed up a test batch of the sealant, and if it set up, then it was good to use. If it stayed as it was when it came out of the container, or separated, then it was bad. If all of the tubes of sealant were usable, NASA still only had enough to return one plane to service. If Lockheed couldn't convince the 3M Company to make more sealant, we would be dead in the water. This would also be the end of the NASA program, as they needed tank sealant to maintain the SRs they had. This was my only real show-stopper. The 3M Company agreed to make more of the sealant with an appropriately sized contract, and now NASA probably has a 10-plus-year supply of tank sealant, courtesy of the Air Force.

Politics. "Let's See If They Can Make the Birds Perform."

I was in a no-win position. The Air Force did not want the program, but Congress did (actually the Senate and a minority in the Air Force did). As a program manager, you don't take on a program to fail. You want it to succeed. I was never ordered to not do well, but there were many that did their best to slow me down—withholding funds, delaying funds, asking for data down to a level that no other program had to report on, and to top things off, we had to operate as a normal Air Force flying unit. That's hard enough for an F-16 unit with the manning, aircraft, and funding to meet those requirements.

However, with only two SR-71s, maintaining an 80 percent fully mission-capable rating was extremely hard. Think about it: when one aircraft went down just to change a tire, you were automatically at 50 percent. Therefore, the goal was to have both aircraft ready to go as much as possible so that the average over the month was 80 percent. If I remember right, we only had one or two months when we fell below 80 percent. Many of the "old heads" said the aircraft were the best maintained and had never flown better.

"The SR-71 Is Not Viable Because . . ."

I relied heavily on the folks on the team—they knew more about the airplane and its systems than I did! This allowed me to focus on major areas and problems, such as the airplane in general, tires, tank sealant, sensors, data processing, logistics, defensive systems, and politics. Later, the data link was made a requirement. Once the program was moving along, and we became confident of making the 1 September IOC date, I started working on our detractors.

From the very beginning we were told we were outdated because we were a "stovepipe" system and couldn't operate with anyone in the intelligence arena. Senior Air Force leaders spread the word to the commanders that they didn't have to deal with us because we were an antiquated system. They also indicated that we were too expensive to fly and maintain, and our intelligence products could not be distributed and were outdated. Using these arguments against the program, I ranked them according to which solved the most problems and were the easiest to fix.

A "stovepipe" system is one that the military considers a unique, one-of-a-kind system . . . one that would be incompatible and have little in common with other systems.

I had an opportunity to talk to a high-ranking, well-respected general officer and asked him for suggestions for making the SR-71 more acceptable to those who did not want us. After I briefed him on my upgrades, planned upgrades, and fixes, he suggested the best approach was to get information and our intelligence data out to the war fighters. Once people started using our data and relying on it, then hopefully they would ask questions as to why they couldn't get the same information from other sources if we went away.

At best, this would shake up the system and the war fighters would have access to equal or better intelligence products than before. That statement confirmed my approach. A side note—the upgraded sensors and similar

In military parlance, war fighters are those who will be directly involved in combat operations if hostilities break out. The highest level of war fighters, particularly when you were looking for support for the SR-71, were the theater CINCs. If they found a particular intelligence asset useful, it would most likely be funded.

capability of getting multiple image products of the same target still has not been delivered. A lot of money is being spent looking at ways of combining the information from multiple sensors, but nothing is on the near-term horizon. The SR-71 was capable of doing this, but we were never allowed to deploy and only supported a few exercises in the United States.

"The SR-71 Costs Too Much To Operate."

From day one, the Air Force tried to kill the program. The first try was with the operating cost. The favorite line from those who did not know the facts, or were looking for an easy way to get the support for the program to dwindle, was that the SR-71 cost too much to operate. The word was that the SR-71 cost between $86,000 and $100,000 per hour to fly. I'm not sure where that number came from, but let the games begin!

It started with a phone call from the Pentagon on a Friday around 1630 hours. We had to provide our operating costs first thing Monday morning or we wouldn't get our operating funds released by the time we needed them. I always knew that bad news, or hidden agenda tasking, would come late in the day. I could either stay late, work the weekend, or get proven wrong by giving an answer that was not defendable. Giving the wrong answer was not an option. On Monday morning we had a by-the-book, defendable answer. Of course, whenever you have fixed costs (lump-sum costs that you pay no matter how much you use it) the more you can use the item, the more you can spread out the costs.

Since our SR-71s were 100 percent contractor maintained, I had a work force on contract that gave us coverage 24/7. That was a fixed cost. My variable costs were things such as fuel, lubricants, and other items we used up whenever we flew. Originally, we were given a 200-hour-per-year flying program. That gave me a cost figure of $38,600 per flight hour. Later we realized, with a third SR-71A model (as the original congressional language implied), we could easily achieve 300 flying hours per year and the costs would drop to $27,400 per flight hour. We got the numbers in, and the Pentagon spent the next two weeks reviewing them. As it turns out, I did make a mistake. My numbers were about 2 percent too high.

"So, How Much Does It Take . . . ?"

The cost estimates for the first year required some creative financing. Lockheed's estimate was the number used by Congress—$100 million—although it didn't fully account for government costs. The DARO estimate of $107 million was a sticking point. Since it exceeded the Congressional amount authorized, I had to come up with my own estimate, based on what the Congressional language stated we were to accomplish with the SR-71s. We would not be allowed to proceed if my cost estimate was more than $100 million.

12 January 1995. Greeting NASA pilot Steve Ishmael, right, and flight engineer Marta Bohn-Meyer, is Lockheed SR-71 program manager Jay Murphy. The aircraft was flown subsonic from Edwards AFB to Palmdale for refurbishment and Air Force use. Although we had low-altitude ejection harnesses like the ones they have on, we seldom used them because of the extra protection afforded us by wearing the pressure suit.
Lockheed Martin Skunk Works

To obtain approval to begin the program, I had to produce a credible estimate that was $100 million or less for the first year. My original estimate was $73 million. With that hurdle gone, we were allowed to proceed. About three to four months into the program, Congress amplified its requirements by saying that a data link was required, as it was being tested when the program shut down in 1990. A major issue here was that the work started on the data link for the SR-71 was never completed. In all reality, it was a new capability. Since my original estimate was $73 million, the Air Force returned, and Congress took back $27 million of the original funding. This was one of the many fictitious reports being passed around. We did not cost $100 million in the first year. At least $27 million was taken away. Our first-year costs turned out to be $54 million, with data link included. The remaining funding was rolled over to the second year.

The added data link system accepted digital inputs from the ASARS-1. The imagery was digitally recorded, and when the flight path allowed, it was downloaded in near real-time to a ground station.

Our second-year funding was $35 million total. This included both operating costs and procurement costs. Procurement costs are for such things as spare parts or to repair items. This is an argument for another place and time. You see, instead of providing an amount of funding to be used as needed, Congress provides different *types* of funding. There is procurement funding, modification funding, research and development funding, operation and maintenance funding, military construction funding, and even salaries are a different type of funding. One of the main reasons that government acquisition takes so long and is so complicated is that the services and program managers have to guess ahead of time how much they will need in each category. God help them if they guess wrong, because it literally takes "an act of Congress" to move funds from one account to another. You could easily cut government bureaucracy and the cost of doing business if funds were provided as they are reported on CNN—a lump sum. Our third- and fourth-year costs were going to be $39 million each.

Factors that Reduced Costs

One reason for lower costs and high availability rates was our workforce being fairly senior. Many had started their careers with the SR-71 and were acknowledged as experts in their area of expertise. This level of knowledge and skill meant that fixes took fewer hours than the norm, allowing more hours to be applied to preventive maintenance. It was a wonderful circle to see. The mechanics *wanted* to be there, so they strove to get the jets fixed as fast as possible. Morale was high, with the jets flying better than ever. This allowed the mechanics time to work on preventive maintenance, reducing the amount of time the Blackbirds were down. This increased morale further, which increased the quality of maintenance, allowing the jets to fly with fewer problems. The *only* thing that brought morale down at Det 2 was the lack of Air Force support. The whole team wanted a deployment . . . just one, so we could prove ourselves.

The fact that we never deployed turned out to be one of the main arguments for killing the program. Guess why we never deployed? Surprise! The Air Force never tasked us. Through back-channel friendships in the Air Force, we learned that theater commanders were either being told not to ask for us, or that we were not ready to deploy, or there was not enough money to deploy the SR-71s. All three were blatantly wrong. The fact is, in the fiscal year (FY) 1995 budget I was forced to specifically budget $10 million for an SR-71 deployment. I was denied access to this funding when it became apparent that we wouldn't deploy. I could have used that money for what Congress intended, but the money was given to the Dark Star program and the U-2 program. DARO cited "needs of the Air Force." In FY 1997, Congress reduced each of those programs by $5 million each . . . of our money.

Dark Star was a highly classified Unmanned Aerial Vehicle (UAV), designed to fly for over eight hours on station, at altitudes above 45,000 feet, relaying intelligence back to the war fighters.

Another reason we could keep our costs low was our finding more original parts, material, and documents than originally expected. The other main contributor was that I was a scrounger. Many systems are replaced because something newer or more powerful is available. It doesn't matter if the newer system is overcapable and when used for the same job is overkill. It's newer and therefore used. Think about it. Someone only uses his 286 computer for word processing and maybe e-mail. It works just fine, but because they can get a high-end Pentium with a DVD player, they do—a lot of computer for just basic tasks. If a system was good enough in the 1990s for the SR-71, and it still worked, then we stayed with it. We only upgraded when it made sense or we had to—for example, if we didn't have the spare parts and the vendor was out of business.

The SR-71 was built far ahead of its time, and technology had finally caught up with it. We looked for off-the-shelf solutions when we could. We also evaluated older, available, but supportable solutions. The data link was just one example, but an excellent one. It was listed as excess property by the U-2 program. It wasn't common to other systems in the Air Force inventory and didn't have some of the more desirable functions that the Air Force

The data link antenna added just in front of the nose gear. To the right, you can see some of the black boxes that were located inside an open "chine" bay. The SR-71 has a blended forward wing, called the chine, which extends from the fuselage nose to the wing leading edge, providing a substantial portion of the total lift at Mach 3. All the way back to the start of the wings, both sides of the chine were jammed full with sophisticated sensors and electronic mission equipment. *Lockheed Martin Skunk Works*

wanted for the U-2. We found that by just upgrading one or two of the boxes and replacing some cards, the old L-52M data link was given new life by the SR-71's performance.

We looked at the lowest-common tie-in between our systems and those systems already in the field. If we could make our intelligence data look like a system already in service and tie into their architecture at that point, then everything after the common point (including upgrades) would be taken care of by someone else. As far as the ground stations around the world, and other systems down the intelligence processing chain were concerned, we looked just like any other existing systems in terms of data format and handling requirements. Not only did we not have to create our own architecture, but we also decreased the amount of training required for the analyst. For example, if they knew how to interpret the radar data from the U-2, then they could interpret the radar data from the SR-71. This was the best example of how we leveraged other programs. With this one upgrade, we were no longer "an outdated stovepipe system, unable to integrate its data with the rest of the intelligence systems." We accomplished all of this at a fraction of the cost of buying the newest systems available.

"Enemy Threats Couldn't Kill the Program, but a Point of Order Did."

I found out from people who were with the SR-71 program in 1990 that a point of order in either the Senate or Congress (I can't remember which) prevented the continued funding of the program. That one small step in the bureaucratic process shut down the SR-71 program and removed its worldwide reconnaissance capability.

In fiscal year 1998 (October 1997), President Clinton used the line-item veto to terminate the SR-71 program. Later that year, the U.S. Supreme Court ruled that the line-item veto was unconstitutional. The other two programs that were victims of the line-item veto were reinstated by the Air Force. The SR-71 was not. We never did hear what happened to the $39 million intended for us that year. It was in the budget, so it was available. Senator Byrd was willing to continue the fight for the SR-71, but Senator Stevens was not. So, without the extra muscle in the Senate, the Air Force never asked for the program to be reinstated. Congress stood its ground, saying the funds are available, and questioning the holdup. By bureaucratic stalling, on 1 October 1998 (the start of fiscal year 1999), whatever funding remained had expired and the SR-71 program was not in the FY 1999 budget. It was over. We now began the bitter task of closing the program, this time for good.

"We Can't Use That, It's from the SR-71 Program."

After the shutdown, no one wanted to use our processes or hardware. Fortunately, people from other programs had the integrity and common sense to recognize the tremendous advancements and benefits we made to existing reconnaissance programs. They started incorporating our technology into those programs. Many of our contractors started recommending our work and ideas for use in other areas. It's sad that they had to change the program names and disassociate themselves from the SR-71 program to get approval to implement their ideas. What they did was good for the taxpayers and good for the Air Force.

Our standard Air Force components went to warehouses to be used by the rest of the Air Force. Items that were common to the U-2 went to that program. Overall, very little went to other programs. The SR-71B model trainer, two of the reactivated A models, and all of the spare parts inventory were transferred to NASA, not loaned this time. Unfortunately for the nation, NASA has now terminated its SR-71 program and is in the process of disposing of all its spare parts. The remaining two SR-71s had their wings cut for shipment and were transported to museums. One was given to the Richmond Air Museum in Virginia, and the other was shipped overseas to become part of the Imperial War Museum at Duxford, England.

"We Could Bring It Back."

After the events of 11 September 2001, we were asked if the SR-71 could be brought back. The answer was yes. The quick answer was that we could provide intelligence products within 60 to 90 days for $45 million. This was our estimate for startup and one year of operations. If there were a need for year two, we would probably drop back to around $40 million. The SR-71 could take care of the wide-area mapping needs of the commanders. It could also be a tool to provide a nonlethal show of force around the world. The aircraft carrier is one such tool. Position a carrier in a region and countries take notice. Provide sonic booms, when and where the president decides, and the message would be conveyed that your country or organization is being watched. Whether or not you are introduced to our other pieces of military hardware is up to you.

"I Would Like To Thank Everyone."

Soon there will be a time when using the SR-71 is no longer an option, as each day continues without taking steps to preserve the capability that the SR-71 provides. I have had programs before and after the SR-71, and I can say without reservation or any doubt in my mind, this was the best program ever! Although we didn't have majority support in the Air Force, we had a program that everyone could be proud of. We were efficient, we had esprit de corps, and we had over 40 individual companies working together, rather than competing against one another for a bigger piece of the pie. We had people donating their time and helping in areas outside of their specialties so that the mission would be successful. I doubt there will ever be another program like it. I would like to thank everyone associated with the SR-71 reactivation program for providing me with such fine support and wonderful memories.

Colonel (Ret) Richard H. Graham

I entered pilot training at Craig AFB, Alabama, in 1964 and remained there as a T-37 instructor pilot and flight examiner. In 1970 I began F-4 training and was assigned to the 555th Tactical Fighter Squadron ("Triple Nickel") at Udorn RTAFB, Thailand, and completed 145 combat missions over North Vietnam and Laos in the F-4C/D aircraft.

My next assignment took me to Kadena AB, Okinawa, where I joined the 67th Tactical Fighter Squadron as an F-4C Wild Weasel pilot. In September 1972, until February 1973, I deployed to Korat RTAFB, Thailand, and flew 60 combat missions suppressing SAM sites in North Vietnam. During Christmas 1972, I was fortunate enough to participate in six Linebacker II sorties over Hanoi.

I returned to Okinawa and became spellbound by this mysterious black "spy" plane flying out of Kadena. I applied for the SR-71 program and entered training in 1974 at Beale AFB. After seven years as a crewmember, IP, and chief of stan/eval, I was selected as the SR-71 squadron commander, 1st SRS. My next assignment was a one-year vacation at Air War College in 1981.

In June 1982, I was assigned to the Pentagon as a strategic force programmer. In April 1984, I was selected to work in the Office of the Assistant Secretary of the Air Force, coordinating Air Force budgetary issues with the Office of the Secretary of Defense, the Joint Chiefs of Staff, and the Air Staff.

In June 1986, I returned to Beale AFB as the vice wing commander. I was lucky . . . SAC policy stated that 9th Wing senior staff personnel *had* to fly all of the wing's aircraft, the U-2, T-38, KC-135Q, and SR-71! I soloed in the U-2 and flew all three of the planes on a regular basis (SR only twice). It doesn't get any better than that! In June 1987, good fortune arrived one more time, as I was selected to become the wing commander of the 9th SRW, where I remained until November 1988. I was assigned to the 14th Air Division, Beale AFB, until my retirement in 1989. I ended up with 4,600 flying hours, 760 in the SR-71.

Two months after retirement I joined American Airlines and currently fly as a captain on the MD-80 aircraft, with over 7,500 hours.

The Final Years

The SR-71 program was originally scheduled for closure in 1989. However, with last-ditch efforts from Blackbird supporters in Congress, and the few we had in the Pentagon, it clung to life for another year. After 28 years of flying, the record-setting flight by Ed and J. T. wrote the final chapter for the Blackbirds.

Lee Shelton has often said that at times we were our own worst enemy. He was right. Lee observed from working in the Pentagon that we kept our Blackbird program so covert and secretive from others, when the time came for us to look for supporters and proponents, they were scarce. Few influential people had any inkling of our capabilities. It is extremely difficult to find support in Congress—and in the halls of the Pentagon—if your reconnaissance capabilities are not well known. Over the years, government agencies, such as the CIA and the National Security Agency (NSA), were slowly abandoning their support for the SR-71 program. They loved the intelligence we gathered in the early days, but soon became enamored with overhead satellites.

This was the final group picture of the 1st SRS before the Blackbird's retirement in 1990. The civilian in the center is Fred Carmody, Lockheed Skunk Works boss at Beale AFB for both the SR-71 and U-2 aircraft. To Fred's right was the last squadron commander, Rod Dyckman. *Fred Carmody*

One of the primary reasons the Air Force gave for retiring the SR-71 was that new satellites were able to do the job. Time has proven that wrong. I have no doubts that if SR-71s were utilized during Desert Storm, they would not have retired in 1990. After Desert Storm, General Norman Schwarzkopf and others openly criticized intelligence handling during the Persian Gulf crisis. They complained that the existing satellites, including the newest Lacrosse radar satellites, did not provide enough definition for accurate battle damage assessment. Desert Storm pilots were sent into combat with target photographs over 24 hours old . . . we had better than that in Vietnam!

The synoptic coverage (displaying conditions as they exist simultaneously over a broad area) provided by an SR-71 is far superior to satellite reconnaissance. Broad-area coverage from different approach angles, in a relatively short time span, produces considerably better intelligence than a predictable single satellite pass every 90 minutes. The SR-71 *remains today* the only reconnaissance platform that can penetrate hostile territory, accomplish wide-area synoptic coverage, and still survive. Lee was stationed at SAC Headquarters during the Gulf War and recalls a briefing with the SAC two-star general operations boss (SAC/DO) and the intelligence boss (SAC/IN):

> "At the very beginning of coalition air activities against Iraq (Desert Shield), I was assigned to manage the SAC Battle Staff, supporting SAC's general officers and commanders' significant contributions to the Gulf War. On about the third day of the air campaign, as I presided over a detailed status-of-forces presen- tation to the SAC general staff, the SAC/DO and SAC/IN lamented that they '. . . wished they still had access to the SR-71 for some decent overflight imagery.' I knew their personal history of nonsupport for the Habu and they both knew my background and, following the comment, we three locked eyes for what seemed like forever. Nothing was said . . . and the briefing continued."

Several in Congress also knew the true capabilities of the SR-71. Senator John Glenn summarized the premature retirement of the SR-71 when he spoke before Congress on 7 March 1990. He said:

> "In view of the high costs of other Air Force programs, the costs of this program and its benefits were both affordable and reasonable. The SR-71 provides coverage on demand with little or no warning to the reconnaissance target—it is a highly flexible system. The SR-71 is able to penetrate hostile territory with comparatively little vulnerability to attack, unlike other reconnaissance platforms. While opponents of the SR-71 have argued that national technical means are capable of performing the same mission, these systems are far less flexible and survivable than the SR-71. In retiring the SR-71, the United States has essentially removed itself from the strategic aerial reconnaissance business.

Intelligence systems such as the SR-71 are the eyes and ears for our nation's defense and are therefore true force-multipliers. Mr. President, the termination of the SR-71 was a grave mistake and could place our nation at a serious disadvantage in the event of a future crisis."

When the program was finally closed down in 1990, NASA saw an excellent opportunity. NASA was looking for a high-speed aircraft to use in testing future supersonic and hypersonic engines and aircraft. It borrowed (on loan from the Air Force) two SR-71A models, the SR-71B model trainer and the SR-71 simulator, which they shipped to their facility at Edwards AFB. Even with their small fleet of three Blackbirds, it meant that sole-source vendors, who produce highly specialized items such as oil, hydraulic fluid, and JP-7 fuel, would still be in operation.

Rising from the Ashes

Senators Glenn, Byrd, Stevens, and Nunn, who sat on influential committees in Congress, realized there were shortfalls in the United States' ability to deliver timely intelligence from around the world. In 1995 Congress directed the Air Force to reactivate three SR-71s, and appropriated $100 million to do so. However, during my four years in the Pentagon I learned one rule . . . you do not *direct* the Air Force to do anything, particularly if it comes from Congress! To the Air Force leadership, seeing congressional language in a bill to bring back retired Blackbirds was like having their worst nightmare come true.

As it turned out, the Air Force considered the B-model trainer as one of the three aircraft, so only two SR-71 reconnaissance planes were brought back into service. NASA and Det 2 shared the B-model trainer. Don Emmons, who had the unpleasant job of dismantling the Blackbird fleet in 1990, was hired as a contractor to help put it all back together again. Six former Habus volunteered to leave their current Air Force jobs and returned to fly the SR-71. It was decided that since NASA already had the SR-71 simulator at Edwards, and the basic infrastructure to support its SR-71 operation, Edwards AFB (rather than Beale AFB) would be the location for the Air Force to train and fly its SR-71s.

Using Lockheed maintenance, civilian contractors, and Air Force operations personnel, the unit was soon fully operational, ready for deployment anywhere around the world. Don and others, including former SR-71 pilot Jay Murphy, who was the program manager for the Lockheed Skunk Works, and "Zman," the Air Force SR-71 reactivation program manager, knew instinctively that the two Blackbirds had to be upgraded if they were going to compete with other reconnaissance assets. They modified the two planes with a common data link (CDL), which provided near real-time imagery with a 300-nautical mile line-of-sight. An electrical optical (EO) capability was being integrated into the cameras at the time of the plane's second retirement. Two successful flights had been accomplished at 79,000 feet, giving near real-time EO imagery. Many sophisticated improvements were made to ground equipment, making it portable and compatible with existing military processing capabilities, and permitting immediate worldwide transmission of intelligence.

Believing that the SR-71s were going to stay around for a while, coupled with the fact that it took around nine months to train a crew, the Det needed to select a new crew. Pilot, Major Bert Garrison, only flew 38 hours' training in the SR-71 before the program ended. In the end Bert was given the prized Habu patch to wear on his flight suit. He went on to fly the U-2s at Beale AFB and told me the following story:

> "When they found out I was getting out to fly for the airlines, they removed me from flying status in the U-2. I was put in charge of giving the unit mission briefing (UMB) to visiting dignitaries. One of my last good deeds was to wear the Habu patch given to me by General Halloran. One day I was giving the UMB to a visiting general and numerous other colonels at wing headquarters, when the current 9th Wing Commander interrupted my introduction and asked me what that patch was. I pointed to the wall in the Wing briefing room where all the former 9th Wing Commanders had their pictures hanging, and said, 'Sir, a great man (and I pointed to General Halloran's picture) gave me this patch and I promised him I would never let anyone forget the Blackbird.' He half-grinned and told me to continue. Nobody dared come up to me after the briefing and ask about the Blackbird."

During the reactivation, Det 2 flew 150 training sorties and 365.7 hours with its three SR-71s without incident.

Despite the wishes of Congress, the Air Force had the upper hand on whether the Blackbirds would ever fly operationally or not, and they never did. In 1997, the Air Force finally found a way to get rid of its nightmare when the White House was looking at the Pentagon for items to eliminate from the budget. The SR-71 program was offered up, and in October 1997, President Clinton line-item vetoed the entire SR-71 program. From that day on, all Air Force flights in the Blackbirds ceased. Once again, Don Emmons was put in charge of dismantling the SR-71s. On 9 October 1999, Don was the last man to walk out the door of Det 2.

I personally believe the SR-71 is needed more today than it was 20 years ago. Back then, the United States and the USSR had nuclear-tipped ICBMs pointed toward each other. In spite of the fact that the "Evil Soviet Empire" had its oppressive hand all around the world, there was a global stabilizing effect. With the demise of the USSR, not only has the geography changed dramatically, but many third world countries are now left to their own will and desires. Unfortunately today, third world countries (and terrorists) can buy any military hardware they like, from nuclear materials to front-line MiG fighters. It all goes to the highest bidder.

The SR-71's *expertise* has always been keeping the other guy honest, and like one SR-71 movie states, "It sorts the difference between what a country says and what it does." Right now, SR-71s should be flying reconnaissance sorties over these rogue nations, gathering valuable intelligence on their intentions.

When I asked former SR-71 crewmember Marta Bohn-Meyer, the center chief engineer at NASA's Dryden Flight Research Center, Edwards AFB, what the possibilities were for them flying their Blackbirds in the future, she replied, "As for flying again . . . not even likely." Mike Relja, the NASA Dryden technical assistant for the director of safety and mission assurance, told me that NASA has the last three remaining SR-71s at Edwards AFB. The last time NASA flew a Blackbird was on 19 October 1997 at its annual Base Open House. Mike expects NASA to keep one of the A models (#980) for display purposes, and the other two Blackbirds will most likely be sent to museums (#956 and #971).

This time the Blackbirds will not rise from the ashes. All that remains are memories of the greatest aircraft ever flown. When members of the Blackbird Association meet in Reno for their biennial reunion, stories, tales, and legends of the Blackbird abound. They will survive in our hearts and minds forever . . . *they* can never be retired.

Appendix A

Blackbird Disposition/Current Location

Model	Tail No.	Disposition/Current Location
A-12	924	Blackbird Airpark, Palmdale, CA (AFFTC Museum)
A-12	925	USS *Intrepid* Sea-Air-Space Museum, NYC
A-12	926	Lost
A-12	927	California Museum of Science, Los Angeles, CA
A-12	928	Lost
A-12	929	Lost
A-12	930	Huntsville Space and Rocket Museum, AL
A-12	931	Minnesota ANG Museum, St. Paul, MN
A-12	932	Lost
A-12	933	San Diego Aerospace Museum, CA
YF-12	934	Aft section used to make SR-71C model
YF-12	935	USAF Museum, Dayton, OH
YF-12	936	Lost
A-12	937	Birmingham, AL
A-12	938	USS *Alabama*, Mobile, AL
A-12	939	Lost
A-12	940	Museum of Flight, Seattle, WA
A-12	941	Lost
SR-71A	950	Lost
SR-71A	951	Pima Air and Space Museum, Tucson, AZ
SR-71A	952	Lost
SR-71A	953	Lost

Model	Tail No.	Disposition/Current Location
SR-71A	954	Lost
SR-71A	955	AFFTC Museum, Edwards AFB, CA
SR-71B	956	USAF Museum, Edwards AFB, CA
SR-71B	957	Lost
SR-71A	958	Warner-Robbins AFB Museum, GA
SR-71A	959	Eglin AFB, FL
SR-71A	960	Castle AFB Museum, CA
SR-71A	961	Kansas Cosmosphere & Space Center, Hutchinson, KS
SR-71A	962	Imperial War Museum, Duxford, England
SR-71A	963	Beale AFB, CA
SR-71A	964	SAC Museum, Omaha, NE
SR-71A	965	Lost
SR-71A	966	Lost
SR-71A	967	Barksdale AFB, LA (projected)
SR-71A	968	Richmond Air Museum, VA
SR-71A	969	Lost
SR-71A	970	Lost
SR-71A	971	USAF Museum, Edwards AFB, CA
SR-71A	972	National Air and Space Museum, Washington, D.C.
SR-71A	973	Blackbird Airpark, Palmdale, CA (AFFTC Museum)
SR-71A	974	Lost
SR-71A	975	March AFB Museum, CA
SR-71A	976	USAF Museum, Dayton, OH
SR-71A	977	Lost
SR-71A	978	Lost
SR-71A	979	History and Traditions Museum, Lackland AFB, TX
SR-71A	980	NASA, Edwards AFB, CA (renumbered NASA 844)
SR-71C	981	Hill AFB Museum, UT

Appendix B

SR-71 Key Events Time Line

1950s

1 May 1956	Pratt & Whitney contracts to develop engine J-58 for the Navy
24 Dec 1957	First J-58 engine run
29 Aug 1959	CIA accepts A-12 design
3 Sep 1959	CIA OKs project "OXCART" studies

1960s

30 Jan 1960	CIA approves funding for 12 A-12s
Feb 1960	CIA proposes to Lockheed to begin search for 24 pilots for A-12
Sep 1960	Work begins to lengthen runway at Groom Lake, NV, to accommodate A-12
26 Feb 1962	First A-12 leaves Burbank, CA, for Groom Lake, NV, by truck
26 Apr 1962	First flight of A-12 #924 (J-75 engines), Lockheed Test Pilot, Lou Schalk
4 May 1962	A-12 goes supersonic (Mach 1.1) for first time
5 Oct 1962	A-12 flies with J-75 (left nacelle) and J-58 (right nacelle) engines
28 Dec 1962	Lockheed signs contract to build six SR-71 aircraft
15 Jan 1963	First fully J-58–equipped A-12 flies
24 May 1963	First loss, A-12 #926 crashes near Wendover, UT; Ken Collins OK, pitched up and became inverted during subsonic flight
20 Jul 1963	First Mach 3 A-12 flight
7 Aug 1963	First YF-12 flight; Lockheed Test Pilot, James Eastham

1960s (continued)

29 Feb 1964	President Johnson announces existence of A-11 (actually A-12; showed pictures of YF-12)
Apr 1964	First flight of modified A-12 #940, called the M-21 to carry the drone
9 Jul 1964	Bill Park forced to eject from A-12 #939 on final approach at Groom Lake; stuck outboard aileron servo valve
24 Jul 1964	President Johnson makes public announcement of SR-71
5 Aug 1964	Cuban overflight code name "Skylark" planning starts
7 Dec 1964	Beale AFB, CA, announced as base for SR-71
22 Dec 1964	First flight of the SR-71 at Palmdale, Lockheed Test Pilot, Bob Gilliland First flight M-21/D-21 at Groom Lake; Lockheed Test Pilot, Bill Park (piloted all M-21/D-21 flights)
1 Jan 1965	4200th SRW activated at Beale AFB, CA
22 Mar 1965	Deputy Secretary of Defense Cyrus Vance briefed on Project Black Shield, plan to base A-12s at Kadena AB, Okinawa
3 Jun 1965	Secretary of Defense Robert McNamara inquires USAF practicality of substituting A-12s for U-2s over Vietnam
7 Jul 1965	First T-38 companion trainers arrive at Beale AFB, CA
28 Sep 1965	GAR-9 fired from YF-12A at Mach 3.2 at 75,000 feet, with target at a range of 36 miles, missed target by 6 feet
5 Nov 1965	Project "Skylark" (Cuban overflights) on emergency operational status
7 Jan 1966	SR-71B arrives at Beale AFB, piloted by Ray Haupt and Doug Nelson
25 Jan 1966	First SR-71A crash, #952, near Tucumcari, NM, Lockheed Test Pilot/RSO Bill Weaver ejects at over 3 Mach; Jim Zwayer killed
10 May 1966	First SR-71A arrives at Beale AFB
25 Jun 1966	4200 SRW inactivated, 9th SRW formed
Jul 1966	Fourth D-21, #504, launch from an M-21 #6941, results in the D-21 colliding with the M-21, both crew members eject; Pilot Bill Park survives, but LCO Ray Torrick drowns, ending M-21/D-21 program

<u>1960s (continued)</u>

14 Aug 1966	YF-12A #934 crashes
23 Dec 1966	Decision is made to terminate A-12 operation by 1 June 1968
5 Jan 1967	A-12 #928 lost on training mission from Groom Lake, NV, after running out of fuel due to a faulty fuel gauge; CIA Pilot Walt Ray killed when he fails to separate from ejection seat after ejecting from A-12
10 Jan 1967	SR-71A #950 crashes at Edwards AFB, CA, during maximum gross weight antiskid brake test; Lockheed Test Pilot Art Peterson OK, no RSO on flight
13 Apr 1967	First SR-71, #966, lost by 9 SRW crew, crashes near Las Vegas, NV, as a result of overextended angle of attack and stalled aircraft; USAF Pilot Earle Boone/RSO Richard Sheffield
17 May 1967	First support components for operation Black Shield airlifted to Kadena AB, Okinawa (OL-8)
22 May 1967	First A-12 #937, flown to Kadena AB; civilian pilot, Mel Vojvodich
29 May 1967	Black Shield unit declared operational
31 May 1967	First A-12, #937 mission, over North Vietnam, lasts 3 hours, 39 minutes; CIA Pilot, Mel Vojvodich
25 Oct 1967	SR-71A #965 crashes near Lovelock, NV, after ANS failure; USAF Pilot Roy St. Martin/RSO John Carnochan
30 Oct 1967	Dennis Sullivan flying an A-12 mission over North Vietnam has six missiles launched against him, three detonate; on postflight inspection, small piece of metal from missile is found imbedded in lower wing fillet area
28 Dec 1967	A-12 #929 crashes at Groom Lake, NV, due to cross-wired SAS; CIA Pilot Mel Vojvodich OK
5 Jan 1968	Skunk Works receives official USAF notice closing down YF-12 ops
11 Jan 1968	SR-71B #957 crashes near Beale AFB, CA, due to double generator failure; USAF Pilots Robert Sowers and David Fruehauf OK
26 Jan 1968	First A-12 overflight of North Korea, during Pueblo incident; CIA Pilot, Frank Murray

1960s (continued)

5 Feb 1968	Lockheed receives letter from USAF, instructing it to destroy A-12, YF-12, and SR-71 tooling
8 Mar 1968	First SR-71A #978 arrives at Kadena AB, Okinawa
21 Mar 1968	First SR-71 (SR-71A #976) operational mission flown from Kadena AB over Vietnam; USAF Pilot, Jerry O'Malley/RSO Edward Payne
8 May 1968	Last A-12 mission flown over North Korea; CIA Pilot, Jack Layton
4 Jun 1968	First overseas loss of A-12; #932, crashes for unknown reason (neither A-12 nor pilot ever found) on postmaintenance test hop (FCF); CIA Pilot, Jack Weeks killed
26 Jun 1968	Black Shield pilots Jack Layton, Frank Murray, Ken Collins, Denny Sullivan, Mel Vojvodich, and the widow of Jack Weeks receive CIA Intelligence Star for Valor medal at Groom Lake from the director of the CIA, Vice Admiral Rufus Taylor
26 Jul 1968	SR-71A #974 with USAF Pilot Tony Bevacqua/RSO Jerry Crew positively fired on by SA-2 missile, photographed by SRs cameras
10 Oct 1968	SR-71A #977 crashes at Beale AFB, CA (wheel hub fractures, sending fragments into fuel tanks starting fire on takeoff); USAF Pilot, Abe Kardong/RSO Jim Kogler OK
11 Apr 1969	SR-71A #954 crashes at Edwards AFB, CA (during max weight takeoff test, left tire blows, catching the aircraft on fire); Lockheed Test Pilot William Skliar/RSO Noel Warner OK
18 Dec 1969	SR-71A #953 crashes near Shoshone, CA; USAF Pilot Joe Rogers/RSO Garry Heidelbaugh eject (after loud explosion and loss of power and control difficulties)

1970s

10 May 1970	SR-71A #969 crashes near Korat RTAFB, Thailand; USAF Pilot William Lawson/RSO Gil Martinez
17 Jun 1970	SR-71A #970 crashes near El Paso, TX (after striking KC-135Q during refueling); USAF Pilot Buddy Brown/RSO Mort Jarvis eject and OK, along with tanker and its crew

1970s (continued)

30 Oct 1970	OL-8 (Kadena AB, Okinawa) redesignated OL-RK (Ryukyu, chain of islands southwest of Japan)
23 Mar 1971	T-38 crashes on takeoff; USAF Pilot Jack Thornton (staff) survives, Jim Hudson (SR-71 pilot) killed
1 Apr 1971	99th SRS inactivated as an SR-71 unit
26 Apr 1971	USAF Pilot Thomas Estes/RSO Dewain Vick fly SR-71 #968 15,000 miles in 10 hours, 30 minutes nonstop
24 Jun 1971	NASA YF-12A #936 crashes at Edwards AFB, CA, due to a fire in the right engine, due to fatigued fuel line; NASA Pilot Jack Layton/RSO Bill Curtis
15 Jul 1971	Lockheed receives word of D-21 drone program cancellation
26 Oct 1971	OL-RK redesignated OL-KA (Kadena AB, Okinawa)
20 Jul 1972	SR-71A #978 *Rapid Rabbit* crashes at Kadena AB, due to strong crosswinds; USAF Pilot Denny Bush/RSO Jimmy Fagg OK
20 Sep 1973	President Nixon awards Thomas Estes/ Dewain Vick Harmon International Aviator Award for their record flight on 26 April 1971
12 Oct 1973	Middle East overflights from CONUS during Arab-Israeli Yom Kippur War from Griffiss AFB, NY, and Seymour-Johnson AFB, NC; nine sorties flown: Operation Giant Reach
13 Oct 1973	SR-71A #979 flown in first Giant Reach; USAF Pilot James Shelton/RSO Gary Coleman
9 Aug 1974	Det 1, 9 SRW activated at Kadena AB, replacing OL-KA
1 Sep 1974	First SR-71A visit to U.K., setting world record NY to London: 3,479.41 statute miles in 1 hour, 54 minutes, 56.4 seconds in SR-71A #972; USAF Pilot Jim Sullivan/RSO Noel Widdifield
13 Sep 1974	SR-71A #972 set world record London to LA: 5,446.86 sm. in 3 hours, 47 minutes, 36 seconds. USAF Pilot "Buck" Adams/RSO William Machorek
Jan 1975	Clarence "Kelly" Johnson retires as Head of Skunk Works
Apr 1975	TDY Operations start at RAF Mildenhall, U.K. (Det 4)
Apr 1976	First ops sortie from Det 4 in SR-71A #972; USAF Pilot Maury Rosenberg/RSO Don Bulloch

1970s (continued)

1 May 1976	USAF consolidates SR-71 and U-2 operations at Beale AFB, CA
28 Jul 1976	SR-71A sets world record closed 100-kilometer course; speed: 2,092 miles per hour; USAF Pilot Pat Bledsoe/ RSO John Fuller
28 Jul 1976	SR-71A #962 sets an altitude world record of 85,068.997 feet; USAF Pilot Bob Helt/RSO Larry Elliott
28 Jul 1976	SR-71A #958 sets a world straight 15- and 25-kilometer course record with a speed of 2,193 miles per hour; USAF Pilot Eldon Joersz/ RSO George Morgan
Mar 1979	Det 4 (RAF Mildenhall) activated

1980s

1 Jul 1980	SR-71A #962 flies from Kadena AB to Diego Garcia to test facility, USAF Pilot Bob Crowder/RSO Don Emmons
15 Jan 1982	SR-71B #956 flies 1,000th training sortie
5 Apr 1984	British government officially announces two SR-71s to be based at RAF Mildenhall, U.K. (Det 4)
20 Apr 1985	General Jerry O'Malley and wife Diane and crew of T-39 killed when landing in western Pennsylvania
15 Apr 1986	SR-71A #980 performs postbombing damage assessment flights of Libya in support of Operation Eldorado Canyon; USAF Pilot Jerry Glasser/RSO Ron Tabor
21 Apr 1989	SR-71A #974 crashes off coast of Philippines. Last SR-71 lost; USAF Pilot Dan House/RSO Blair Bozek
1 Oct 1989	USAF SR-71 operations suspended except for minimum-proficiency flights
22 Nov 1989	USAF SR-71 program officially terminated (Thanks Larry Welch)

1990s

21 Jan 1990	Last SR-71 #962 left Kadena AB (Det 1) for Beale AFB, at 0500, Tail art: A tombstone that read, "Det 1 RIP 1968–1990"

1990s (continued)

26 Jan 1990	SR-71 is decommissioned at Beale AFB, CA
6 Mar 1990	Final flight for #972. Sets four world records; USAF Pilot Ed Yeilding/RSO J. T. Vida turn aircraft over to the National Air & Space Museum *U.S. Coast-to-Coast (2,089 nautical miles):* 67 minutes, 54 seconds, for 2,124 miles per hour *Los Angeles to Washington, D.C., (1,998 nautical miles):* 64 minutes, 20 seconds, for 2,145 miles per hour *Kansas City to Washington, D.C., (819 nautical miles):* 25 minutes, 59 seconds, for 2,176 miles per hour *St. Louis to Cincinnati, OH (271 nautical miles):* 8 minutes, 32 seconds, for 2,190 miles per hour
22 Dec 1990	Clarence "Kelly" Johnson dies at the age of 80
28 Sep 1994	Congress votes to allocate $100 million for reactivation of three SR-71s
Mar 1995	ACC selects three crews for the reactivation of the SR-71: Pilots Gil Luloff, Tom McCleary, Don Watkins; and RSOs Blair Bozek, Michael Finan, Jim Greenwood
30 Jun 1995	First USAF crew flies reactivated SR-71, #971
15 Apr 1996	Deputy Defense Secretary John White directs the Air Force to ground the Air Force's SR-71s due to budget interpretations
21 Sep 1996	House and Senate Appropriation committees agree to fund the Air Force's two operational SR-71s for fiscal year 1997
1 Jan 1997	SR-71 and crews are operational at Det 2, Edwards AFB, CA
15 Oct 1997	President Clinton kills SR-71 funding with line-item veto
30 June 1999	Final shutdown of the SR-71 program, Det 2 is shut down, officially ending the USAF SR-71 program
13 Sep 2001	Two days after terrorist attacks in New York City and Washington, D.C., the Pentagon asks if it's possible to bring back SR-71s

Index